New Hampshire
Foundations of Reading
Practice Questions

Mometrix
TEST PREPARATION

Dear Future Exam Success Story

First of all, **THANK YOU** for purchasing Mometrix study materials!

Second, congratulations! You are one of the few determined test-takers who are committed to doing whatever it takes to excel on your exam. **You have come to the right place.** We developed these practice tests with one goal in mind: to deliver you the best possible approximation of the questions you will see on test day.

Standardized testing is one of the biggest obstacles on your road to success, which only increases the importance of doing well in the high-pressure, high-stakes environment of test day. Your results on this test could have a significant impact on your future, and these practice tests will give you the repetitions you need to build your familiarity and confidence with the test content and format to help you achieve your full potential on test day.

Your success is our success

We would love to hear from you! If you would like to share the story of your exam success or if you have any questions or comments in regard to our products, please contact us at **800-673-8175** or **support@mometrix.com**.

Thanks again for your business and we wish you continued success!

Sincerely,
The Mometrix Test Preparation Team

Printed in the United States of America

TABLE OF CONTENTS

Practice Test #1

Multiple Choice Questions

1. Among specific components of reading difficulties, which category is a result of the other two?

a. Difficulties with decoding words
b. Difficulties with comprehending
c. Difficulties with retention of text
d. Difficulties with all are unrelated

2. A third-grade student has difficulties with decoding and struggles to read grade-level texts independently. Which statement is likely to be true based on this information?

a. The student will benefit from additional implicit phonics instruction.
b. The student will also struggle with phonological awareness.
c. The student will also struggle with fluency and comprehension.
d. The student likely has a language processing disorder and requires further evaluation.

3. What is true about speech or language delays and disorders?

a. Delays and disorders both involve abnormal language development sequences.
b. The only difference between delays and disorders is the severity of the problem.
c. Speech or language disorders are more common than speech or language delays.
d. Speech or language delays always involve slower language development rates.

4. What is the best way to utilize picture flashcards to develop children's phonemic awareness?

a. The flashcards that are used should have pictures unfamiliar to the child.
b. The child should be asked to identify a word's first and second phoneme.
c. The child should be asked only to identify the word name of each picture.
d. The flashcards should only be used for children with strong phonics skills.

5. What has research found about systematic, explicit instruction in phonics?

a. Explicit instruction in phonics makes significant improvements in children's reading comprehension.
b. Explicit instruction in phonics makes significant improvements in K-1 word recognition, not spelling.
c. Explicit instruction in phonics makes significant improvements only for children with typical reading development.
d. Explicit instruction in phonics makes significant improvements as a whole language reading program for beginning readers.

6. What is one benefit of implicit phonics instruction?

a. It leads to stronger decoding skills.
b. Its progression from part to whole increases proficiency more quickly.
c. Research suggests it is the most effective approach to phonics instruction.
d. Phonics skills are taught in a meaningful context.

7. A teacher gives students a list of words, including *care*, *home*, and *use*, and asks them to record the definitions. Next, she asks them to add *less* to the ends of the words and record the new definitions. Students are then instructed to write down their observations in their writing journals. What is the primary purpose of this activity?

a. Helping students recognize the meaning of a common suffix
b. Teaching students the *-less* spelling pattern
c. Practicing word analysis skills that will assist with decoding
d. Identifying commonly used prefixes

8. A student can determine how to spell words like *psychology, psychiatrist, psychotic, psychopath, psychoactive,* etc., because they all start with the same Greek-derived prefix. This illustrates which type of spelling strategy?

a. Morphemic spelling strategies
b. Rule-based spelling strategies
c. Phonetic spelling strategies
d. Visual spelling strategies

9. Research shows that developmentally, which of these options is easiest for young children to identify?

a. The medial and final phonemes of words
b. The initial and medial phonemes of words
c. Only the medial phonemes of words
d. The initial and final phonemes of words

10. Regarding speech pre-production learning activities that teachers can use with ELL students to encourage them to speak English, which of the following is accurate?

a. Choral readings afford advantages for beginning ELLs.
b. Echo reading is not spontaneous and thus not useful.
c. Shared reading and writing will not promote speech.
d. Singing is vocal but otherwise irrelevant to speaking.

11. Students in a fifth-grade class are breaking the word *invisible* into its component parts. They identify the prefix *in-*, the root *vis*, and the suffix *-ible*, along with the meanings of each part. What type of activity is being demonstrated?

a. Miscue analysis
b. Structural analysis
c. Syllabification
d. Decoding

12. Which of these best identifies what developing automatic word recognition improves for students?

a. Recall quality and organization, via fluency and comprehension
b. Reading automaticity and speed, irrespective of comprehension
c. Reading comprehension, irrespective of how reading is recalled
d. Recall accuracy, organization, and detail irrespective of fluency

13. A kindergarten teacher notices that one of his students consistently understands and follows directions that are spoken to him. However, when he speaks in any situation, his sentences are often missing key words and don't make sense. The student is demonstrating difficulties with what?

a. Expressive language
b. Receptive language
c. Pragmatic language
d. Articulation

14. A kindergarten teacher pronounces a series of word pairs for her students. The students repeat the pairs. Some of the pairs rhyme (*see/bee)* and some of the pairs share initial sounds but do not rhyme (*sit, sun).* The students help her separate the word pairs into pairs that rhyme and pairs that do not. Once the students are able to distinguish between two words that rhyme and two words that do not, the teacher says a word and asks them to provide a rhyme. When she says *cat* a child responds with *fat.* When she says *sing* a child offers *thing.* How does this strictly oral activity contribute to the children's ability to read?

a. It doesn't. Oral activities must have a written component to be useful to emergent readers.
b. It is helpful in that it demonstrates how different sounds are made with different letters.
c. It actually discourages children from reading. By emphasizing orality over literacy, the teacher is suggesting to the children that reading is not an important skill.
d. Being able to identify rhyme is an important element of phonological awareness.

15. Which of these best reflects recommendations in instructional plans for teaching children the alphabetic principle?

a. Practice opportunities with cumulative review and new relationships
b. Explicitly teaching letter-sound correspondences in words to children
c. Special weekly opportunities to practice letter-sound correspondence
d. Opportunities to apply learning to unfamiliar, correctly spelled words

16. A teacher asks her students to say /ake/. She then tells students to add different consonant sounds to the beginning of /ake/ to see which real and nonsense words they can form. Which component of phonological awareness are students practicing in this activity?

a. Syllabification
b. Onsets and rimes
c. Phoneme isolation
d. Segmentation

17. Which of the following activities best demonstrates a phonics activity?

a. Sorting rhyming words
b. Playing alphabet bingo and covering a letter when the teacher says its name
c. Matching picture cards to the consonant blends they begin with
d. Listening to a fictional story read aloud by the teacher and identifying the setting

18. The most effective strategy for decoding irregular sight words is:

a. Segmenting sight words into syllables. Beginning readers are understandably nervous when encountering a long word that isn't familiar. Blocking off all but a single syllable at a time renders a word manageable and allows the reader a sense of control over the act of reading.
b. Word families. By grouping the sight word with similar words, patterns emerge.
c. A phonemic approach. When students understand the connection between individual words and their sounds, they will be able to sound out any sight word they encounter.
d. None; irregular sight words cannot be decoded. Readers must learn to recognize these as whole words on sight.

19. For students with problems retrieving or naming, which is the best instructional strategy to teach letter-sound associations?

a. Decoding closed-syllable, CVC words should begin after students master all consonant associations.
b. Decoding closed-syllable, CVC words should begin after students master all short vowel associations.
c. Decoding closed-syllable, CVC words should start after students master all consonants and one to two vowels.
d. Decoding closed-syllable, CVC words should begin once students master one to two short vowel sound-letter associations and several high-frequency sound-letter associations.

20. Which of these is true about using music to teach sight words to kindergarten students?

a. Singing words to catchy tunes is a mnemonic device.
b. Singing is fun for children but does not aid memory.
c. Singing helps retain new words but not the spellings.
d. Singing is an activity that young children do not like.

21. Which of these is one of the signs that a student has difficulty with retaining reading?

a. The student's oral reading disregards punctuation.
b. The student's reading omits, or disregards, details.
c. The student's insertion of additional words that are not in the text is frequent.
d. The student's connection of text ideas is deficient.

22. Of the following, which is most correct in regard to children matching voice to print?

a. It is not normal for a second grader to finger-point to words when reading.
b. Giving young children creative, fun pointers is wrong, as these are crutches.
c. Older student finger-pointing shows reading struggles and impedes fluency.
d. Using bookmarks/popsicle sticks sideways has no effect on finger-pointing.

23. Which choice represents a likely progression of phonological awareness skills?

a. Onset and rime manipulation, rhyming, phoneme deletion, syllabification
b. Phoneme deletion, syllabification, onset and rime manipulation, rhyming
c. Rhyming, syllabification, onset and rime manipulation, phoneme deletion
d. Syllabification, phoneme deletion, rhyming, onset and rime manipulation

24. Which statement best describes the relationship between phonological awareness and phonemic awareness?

a. Phonological awareness and phonemic awareness are interchangeable terms.
b. Phonological awareness is one specific component of phonemic awareness.
c. Phonemic awareness is one specific component of phonological awareness.
d. Phonological awareness typically develops after phonemic awareness.

25. Which of the following activities best demonstrates a multisensory approach to teaching letter formation?

a. Locating words containing a certain letter in a book
b. Tracing prewritten letters on paper with a pencil
c. Identifying letters on flashcards
d. Writing letters in shaving cream

26. Maria, a third-grade student, is reading a new chapter book for the first time. Her teacher observes as Maria struggles to decode the word *scapegoat* in the following sentence: "John frowned when he realized he was being made the scapegoat." Which of the following strategies would most likely assist Maria with decoding this word?

a. Using syntactic cues
b. Blending the sounds
c. Using context clues from the sentence
d. Chunking

27. A student is reading a fictional book and has difficulty decoding the word *maple*. Which spelling pattern could the teacher explain to help the student decode this word and similar words in the future?

a. Vowel digraph pairs
b. R-controlled vowels
c. Closed syllables
d. Open syllables

28. Which of the following options best demonstrates a kinesthetic activity to build sight word recognition?

a. Circling sight words found in a magazine article
b. Building sight words with letter tiles
c. Reading books containing numerous sight words
d. Hopping along sight words written in chalk

29. A kindergarten teacher says the words *tap* and *top* aloud. She asks students to identify whether the sound that is different is found in the beginning, middle, or ending of the words. Which skill does this activity practice?

a. Phoneme substitution
b. Phoneme discrimination
c. Phoneme deletion
d. Phoneme insertion

30. Which of the following is most accurate about the benefits of various levels of phonological awareness instruction to the development of reading skills?

a. Instruction in rhyming, onsets, and rimes appears most directly beneficial to reading development.
b. Instruction in simpler phonology skills can aid teaching more complex ones and reading development.
c. Instruction that integrates blending and segmenting appears most beneficial to reading development.
d. Instruction that integrates deleting and substituting appears most beneficial to reading development.

31. A student incorrectly pronounces the word *rattle* with a long vowel *a*. The teacher explains a general rule to the student about splitting doubled consonants. This instructional strategy focuses most on using which of these?

a. Structural analysis
b. Spelling patterns
c. Syllabication
d. Morphemes

32. Which of the following is incorrect about teaching students the distinction between vowels as open sounds and consonants as closed sounds?

a. This should be taught for the first time when teaching letter-sound matching.
b. This should be introduced when initially teaching phonemic awareness.
c. This should be reviewed after teaching some letter shapes and names.
d. This should be reviewed after teaching some letter decoding.

33. In an oddity task to demonstrate student ability to identify words with the same and different initial, medial, and final phonemes in words, which of these asks students to identify words with the same medial consonant sound?

a. Identifying *pan* and *cat* from among *pan, top,* and *cat*
b. Identifying *lesson* and *missing* in *lesson, kitten, missing*
c. Identifying *feet* as different among *late, feet,* and *take*
d. Identifying *ten* and *man* from among *ten, sat,* and *man*

34. Students in a second-grade classroom are exploring and building words that contain *eigh*. Which layer of orthography are they exploring?

a. Alphabet layer
b. Pattern layer
c. Meaning layer
d. Conventional layer

35. Researchers have identified five developmental stages of spelling. Which choice orders these stages in the correct sequence of development?

a. Derivational relations spelling, emergent spelling, letter name-alphabetic spelling, syllables and affixes spelling, within-word pattern spelling
b. Letter name-alphabetic spelling, syllables and affixes spelling, within-word pattern spelling, emergent spelling, derivational relations spelling
c. Emergent spelling, letter name-alphabetic spelling, within-word pattern spelling, syllables and affixes spelling, derivational relations spelling
d. Within-word pattern spelling, emergent spelling, derivational relations spelling, syllables and affixes spelling, letter name-alphabetic spelling

36. According to experts, which of the following is an accurate distinction regarding phonological awareness and phonemic awareness?

a. Phonological awareness distinguishes speech sounds from meanings.
b. There is no real distinction; they are synonyms used interchangeably.
c. Phonological awareness involves sounds, phonemic involves speech.
d. Phonemic awareness is the less sophisticated level between the two.

37. Among the following, which is NOT a common academic standard for kindergarten students in decoding and identifying words?

a. Showing knowledge that letter sequences correspond to phoneme sequences
b. Understanding that word sounds and meanings change along with word letters
c. Decoding monosyllabic words using initial and final consonant and vowel sounds
d. Matching letters to consonant sounds; reading simple, monosyllabic sight words

38. Concerning spelling, what statement is correct about how children learn?

a. Children must be taught spelling patterns as they will not learn them incidentally.
b. Children who know basic spelling rules can deduce spellings for words they hear.
c. Children may be able to spell words, but this does not mean they can read them.
d. Children's reading and writing skills promote spelling, but the reverse is not true.

39. According to research findings, which of these is an example of effective instructional practices to support English language acquisition for ELL students?

a. Encouraging independence by assigning projects only individually
b. Writing problems and directions in shorter and simpler sentences
c. Emphasizing how quickly students finish work, not how accurately
d. Asking only questions they can answer using lower level cognition

40. For supporting language acquisition in ESL/ELL students, what is most accurate about research-based instructional practices?

a. Teachers should only state directions verbally to give ELLs English decoding practice.
b. Teachers should encourage ESL students to respond rapidly to get them up to speed.
c. Teachers should use idioms without explanations to familiarize ELL students to these.
d. Teachers should give ELL students models and examples of what they expect in tasks.

41. Which of the following choices describes the best introduction to a unit on oral traditions from around the world?

a. Introducing games that practice new sight words, encoding words based on phonics rules, and answering short comprehension questions.
b. Setting up video-conferencing with a school in Asia so that students can communicate with children from other countries.
c. Inviting a guest speaker from a nearby Native American group to demonstrate oral storytelling to the class.
d. Creating a slide show presentation about various types of oral cultures and traditions and characteristics of each.

42. Homonyms such as *bare* and *bear* are similar in sound yet have different meanings. What would a teacher suggest a student do to avoid misusing these words?

a. Memorize the definitions of the difficult words.
b. Check a dictionary or thesaurus to verify a word's usage.
c. Avoid encountering difficult words.
d. Ignore being precise in the definition.

43. When a teacher instructs elementary school students in analyzing phonetically-regular words, which of the following would best represent a sequence from simpler to progressively more complex?

a. Long vowels, short vowels, consonant blends, CVC (consonant-vowel-consonant) and other common patterns, individual phonemes, blending phonemes, types of syllables, onsets and rimes
b. Onsets and rimes, short vowels, consonant blends, long vowels, blending phonemes, CVC and other common patterns, types of syllables, individual phonemes
c. Types of syllables, onsets and rimes, CVC and other common patterns, consonant blends, blending phonemes, individual phonemes, long vowels, short vowels
d. Individual phonemes, blending phonemes, onsets and rimes, short vowels, long vowels, consonant blends, CVC and other common patterns, types of syllables

44. A student learning English as a second language (ESL) who has limited comprehension of English and can speak one- to two-word English answers, essential English words, present-tense English verbs, and some familiar English phrases is in which stage of second-language acquisition?

a. Preproduction
b. Early Production
c. Speech Emergence
d. Intermediate Fluency

45. As one approach to gathering student input, what is correct about a K.I.M. chart for learning vocabulary?

a. The K in K.I.M. stands for Know, the I for Identify, and the M for Meaning.
b. Under the K in a K.I.M. chart, the student enters the definitions of the word.
c. Under the K in a K.I.M. chart, the student enters the new vocabulary words.
d. When students make K.I.M. charts, they never include drawings or pictures.

46. Collaborative Strategic Reading (CSR) is a teaching technique that depends on two teaching practices. These practices are:

a. Cooperative learning and reading comprehension
b. Cooperative reading and metacognition
c. Reading comprehension and metacognition
d. Cooperative learning and metacognition

47. A sixth-grade science teacher wants to help his students recognize connections between words containing the same Latin root. Which activity would most likely achieve this goal?

a. Defining words containing the root using a dictionary
b. Creating a semantic map
c. Searching for words containing the root in the science textbook
d. Comparing and contrasting words containing the root using a Venn diagram

48. Educational researchers have found which of the following literary genres most appropriate for improving reading comprehension in public schools?

a. Novels
b. Poems
c. Short stories
d. Drama (plays)

49. What is a valid guideline for teachers to follow in instructional activities that help students practice evaluating information sources?

a. Practicing evaluation during ongoing discussion can engage students more deeply.
b. Practicing evaluation should be reserved until after students have discussed topics.
c. Teachers should provide long, complete passages from different topical resources.
d. Students should evaluate material using unlimited numbers of open-ended questions.

50. Every year, a social studies teacher teaches her students a large variety of vocabulary words that are new to her students. She wants students to not only learn the definitions but also have a deep understanding of the concept of the new words. Which of the following activities would work best to achieve this teacher's goal?

a. When a new vocabulary word is introduced, assist students in creating word maps on the new words.
b. Make sure that each set of desks includes dictionaries so students are always able to look up the meanings of words they are unsure of.
c. Create a list on the wall of new topics so students know they are not expected to have learned them until this year.
d. When speaking in class, use the new vocabulary words as much as possible to ensure a deeper understanding.

51. Which of these teaching/learning strategies associated with indirect instruction most promotes student visualization, organization, and application of ideas they have learned?

a. Reading for meaning
b. Concept mapping
c. Cloze procedures
d. Case studies

52. Which of the following questions requires students to make an inference about a fictional text?

a. Did the author support her points with strong evidence?
b. How do you think the character felt when she said that?
c. What do you think will happen next?
d. Does this character remind you of any characters in other books you have read?

53. Among principles of effective writing instruction, which of these reflects teaching discourse knowledge that enables more effective student writing?

a. Varying levels of explicit instruction, using small groups, and varying amounts of writing instruction time
b. Allowing sufficient time for systematic writing opportunities in both ELA classes and all content subjects
c. Incorporating reasons and methods for explicit writing instruction, including feedback and collaboration
d. Organizing writing effectively for various subjects, plus spelling, vocabulary, syntax, etc., for the subjects

54. When can making a KWL chart help students with reading comprehension?

a. Before, during, and after students read
b. Before and during but not after reading
c. During and after but not before reading
d. Before and after but not during reading

55. The use of analogies is most appropriate for helping students achieve which instructional objective?

a. Analyzing common roots and affixes
b. Defining words
c. Identifying word origins
d. Recognizing the relationships between words

56. Before asking students to read a new fiction book independently, the teacher conducts a picture walk with the class. What is the teacher's primary goal for conducting the picture walk?

a. Encouraging the use of syntactic cues
b. Setting a purpose for reading
c. Activating students' prior knowledge
d. Developing students' metacognitive skills

Refer to the following for question 57:

A third-grade science teacher gives her students one hour to read an article about penguins, take notes on important information, and use the notes to write a three-paragraph expository essay. Before they begin, the teacher writes the words *Spheniscidae*, *plumage*, and *Aptenodytes forsteri* on the board. She explains the meaning of each word. At the end of the hour, one student, Joshua, only has his notes completed. The teacher examines his notes, part of which are shown below.

> Penguins are animals that live in the Southern Hemisphere.
> Many people believe that penguins live in the Arctic, but that is not true.

Penguins in Antarctica huddle together to stay warm. They take turns standing on the outside of the huddle, where it is colder.
Penguins' feathers help protect them from the water and cold air.
Penguins live in groups called colonies.

57. Which strategy would be most helpful for the teacher to focus on with Joshua to prepare him for similar tasks?

a. Grouping the notes into three sections to correspond with the paragraphs of the essay
b. Selecting only a few facts to record before moving on to the essay
c. Using drawings rather than words
d. Recording only key words and phrases rather than sentences

58. Using E. B. White's *Stuart Little* as an example, which response represents evaluative comprehension?

a. "Stuart Little, who is the main character in this story, is a mouse."
b. "Stuart's parents, Mr. and Mrs. Frederick C. Little, are humans."
c. "Stuart's size and doing things a mouse can do help his family."
d. "Stuart likes to be first up in the morning; I like to sleep late."

59. In writing instruction, which of these correctly represents some of the things that teachers should instruct students to consider about the audience for whom they will be writing?

a. They must consider who will read it, but the format (oral presentation, blog, school newspaper, etc.) is irrelevant.
b. They must consider reading level(s), vocabulary, and writing length the audience expects more than the message.
c. They must consider the message they want to convey more than the format in which the audience will receive it.
d. They must consider the type of writing that their intended audience will expect as much as who that audience is.

60. Which of the following options best demonstrates a specific and measurable reading intervention goal for a first grader?

a. The student will increase his score on the DIBELS Nonsense Word Fluency: Whole Words Read assessment from 10 to 15 by May 30 of this year.
b. The student will read at a DRA level 14.
c. The student will increase his oral reading rate on the DIBELS: Oral Reading Fluency assessment by December 15 of this year.
d. The student will meet grade-level benchmarks on the DRA.

61. Which of these is mainly a sign that a student has problems with reading comprehension?

a. The student has trouble recognizing words out of context.
b. The student reads laboriously, reading one word at a time.
c. The student has trouble separating the main idea from details.
d. The student has trouble relating a text to prior knowledge.

62. Practical instructional activities that develop student listening skills include which of the following?

a. Teaching students how to follow rather than give directions
b. Teaching students how to give rather than follow directions
c. Teaching students interpersonal communication skills
d. Teaching students to appreciate conversation, not oral literature

63. Mr. Suarez teaches a preschool class containing students in the preliterate stage of writing. He wants to help his students understand the relationship between spoken and written words using a familiar topic, so he has planned an activity relating to the class's recent field trip to the apple orchard. Mr. Suarez will help the group record memories of their field trip in writing while they contribute ideas, and Mr. Suarez will read the writing back to students repeatedly throughout the week. Which activity would be most appropriate?

a. Shared writing
b. Independent writing
c. Interactive writing
d. Partner writing

64. Students in a sixth-grade classroom are reading a persuasive essay about the importance of recycling. Which question can the teacher ask to help students develop evaluative comprehension skills?

a. Do you agree with the author that recycling is an easy way for everyone to help the environment?
b. Which material takes longer to decompose: plastic or glass?
c. What types of materials can be recycled?
d. Who should you contact in your city if you want to help organize a recycling program?

65. Which instructional strategy is most closely related to and is a key component of schema theory?

a. Summarizing
b. Activating prior knowledge
c. Identifying main idea
d. Recognizing story elements

66. To help students find and use evidence from nonfictional text to support their ideas, which instructional strategy is most applicable?

a. Inquiry Charts (I-Charts)
b. Graphic organizers
c. Journaling
d. RAFT

67. William, a third-grade student, recently wrote, "The cars drives down the street," in his writing journal. His teacher notices that he makes similar errors in other sentences he writes. He also makes these types of errors when reading. For example, he recently said, "The birds flies in the sky," while reading a text. Which grammatical skill should the teacher work on with William?

a. Pronoun-antecedent agreement
b. Consistent verb tenses
c. Subject-verb agreement
d. Complex sentences

68. A teacher wants to introduce the concept of connotative and denotative meanings while reading a novel. He plans to use character traits as a way to introduce this topic. Which set of words to describe a character would best help him introduce and explain connotative and denotative word meanings?

a. Kind and nice
b. Happy and joyful
c. Determined and persistent
d. Frugal and cheap

69. Which instructional strategy would be most appropriate to assist a student with retention difficulties in analyzing the plot of a fictional text?

a. Providing the student with a story map
b. Having the student read the story twice before responding to questions
c. Playing an audio version of the story rather than having the student read a printed version
d. Asking the student to complete a KWL chart before and after reading

70. Among instructional strategies that aid in student comprehension of nonfictional text, which of these is most useful for promoting critical thinking?

a. Answering open-ended questions about texts
b. Skimming the text for features that give signs
c. Establishing connections between text and life
d. Establishing connections between text and self

71. Among reading materials teachers can select to promote student comprehension of nonfiction, most content-area textbooks used in public schools feature which type of writing?

a. Narrative
b. Persuasive
c. Descriptive
d. Informational

72. Of the following, which represents an indirect way in which students receive instruction in and learn vocabulary?

a. Being exposed repeatedly to vocabulary in multiple teaching contexts
b. Being exposed to vocabulary when adults read aloud to them
c. Being pre-taught specific words found in text prior to reading
d. Being taught vocabulary words over extended periods of time

73. Young children are more likely to respond to analogies in stories rather than to metaphors because:

a. They are old enough to understand the abstract thinking and symbolism that analogies express.
b. The ability to understand the kinds of abstraction expressed in metaphors is not developed until later in childhood.
c. They can apply the concepts expressed in analogies to their own daily lives, but metaphors do not compare things that children are familiar with.
d. Metaphors and symbols are usually found only in books that children find boring because of their abstractions.

74. Which of the following is the most effective way for a first-grade teacher to enhance students' reading proficiency?

a. Provide effective phonics instruction
b. Encourage oral storytelling in the classroom
c. Replace basal texts with real literature
d. Have students make daily visits to the school library

75. Teachers must consider student developmental levels when assigning cooperative learning projects and/or discussions. For example, students are bored by topics at younger age levels and lost by topics at older ones. In addition to chronological age, which other developmental level does this example relate to most?

a. Social developmental levels
b. Cognitive developmental levels
c. Emotional developmental levels
d. Behavioral developmental levels

76. To provide accommodations for ELL students, which of these should teachers do in vocabulary and reading instruction?

a. Teach ELL students vocabulary in isolation.
b. Teach ELL students vocabulary in context.
c. Teach ELL students vocabulary in volume.
d. Teach ELL students reading by their speech levels.

77. Which of the following methods would give students the most *objective* feedback to enable them to monitor their own performance and progress in speaking and enacting through giving oral reports and presentations?

a. Having classmates offer peer reviews
b. Having a teacher evaluate their work
c. Comparing their work to classmates' work
d. Viewing videos of their performance

78. In a paired reading strategy for identifying the main idea in informational text, two students silently read a selection. Then, taking two-column notes of main ideas and supporting details, they take turns with the following steps. Which choice sequences these steps in the correct order?

a. The pair develops main idea consensus, a student paraphrases the main idea, a student explains agreement or disagreement, they take turns finding supporting details
b. A student paraphrases the main idea, a student explains agreement or disagreement, the pair develops main idea consensus, they take turns finding supporting details
c. They take turns finding supporting details, a student explains agreement or disagreement, a student paraphrases the main idea, the pair develops main idea consensus
d. A student explains agreement or disagreement, they take turns finding supporting details, the pair develops main idea consensus, a student paraphrases the main idea

79. During a reading assessment, which of the following student behaviors reflects a weakness in strategy?

a. The student tries to read every word, with many errors.
b. The student pays attention to the punctuation in a text.
c. The student understands the main idea, but not details.
d. The student takes a holistic approach to reading words.

80. Sixth-grade students are taking a standardized, criterion-referenced reading test. Part of the test involves answering comprehension questions based on reading passages. Some of the passages contain cultural references that some groups of students do not understand, causing them to miss multiple questions. This is an example of a testing concern in which area?

a. Validity
b. Reliability
c. Bias
d. Consistency

81. Which of the following is important when using performance-based assessments of student literacy?

a. Establishing valid norms for student scoring
b. Establishing clear, equitable scoring criteria
c. Establishing single correct answers for items
d. Establishing standard answer keys for scores

82. In a rubric for scoring oral English language proficiency in English language learners (ELLs), which of these would most reflect a criterion at the highest proficiency level?

a. Being able to repeat English words and phrases
b. Being able to name concrete objects upon sight
c. Being able to participate in classroom discussions
d. Being able to communicate well in social contexts

83. A teacher conducts an informal one-to-one reading assessment of rhyme recognition with a young child. Which of the following should the teacher always do first?

a. Ask the child whether he or she knows what rhyming words are.
b. Ask the child to demonstrate by saying two rhyming words.
c. Give the child an explanation by defining what rhymes are.
d. Give the child an example of a pair of words that rhyme.

84. A sentence in a book states, "They had several chores to do." Which of the following examples demonstrates a visual error, if stated by a student reading the text?

a. They had several jobs to do.
b. They had seven chores to do.
c. They had chores to do.
d. They had many chores to do.

85. Which of the following statements is true regarding screening and diagnostic assessments?

a. Screening assessments provide more thorough information than diagnostic assessments about students' specific strengths and needs.
b. Screening assessments are typically used to confirm diagnostic assessment results.
c. Screening assessments are used to identify students who may be at future risk of academic difficulties and may benefit from interventions.
d. Diagnostic assessments are used to identify students who may be at future risk of academic difficulties and may benefit from interventions.

86. Olivia, a first-grade student, has a reading intervention plan to improve her decoding of CVCe words. In addition to working with the teacher in a small group each day, Olivia's teacher gives her 10 new CVCe words to decode each Friday. The number of words read correctly is recorded on a graph, and the teacher notes any improvement made from the previous weeks. Which type of assessment is the teacher demonstrating?

a. Progress monitoring
b. Screening assessment
c. Summative assessment
d. Norm-referenced assessment

87. A sentence in a book states, "The furry dog chases the stick." Which of the following examples demonstrates a structural error, if stated by a student reading the text?

a. The furry dog chases the branch.
b. The furry dog chases the big stick.
c. The fuzzy dog chases the stick.
d. The furry dog chased the stick.

88. A second-grade teacher is planning a lesson on adjectives and will ask students to locate 10 adjectives in a text. Which modified activity would be the most appropriate way for the teacher to engage advanced students in exploring adjectives?

a. Asking them to locate 20 adjectives in the text
b. Asking students to locate vague adjectives in the text and then replace them with more specific adjectives
c. Pairing the proficient readers with struggling readers to complete the activity
d. Assigning the students an additional practice paper to complete after finding the 10 adjectives

89. Which of the following examples demonstrate students using a combination of digital and print-based media?

a. Students put sentence strips in order to retell the main events of a story they read in their reading textbook.
b. Students watch an animated story on an educational website and complete the accompanying online comprehension questions.
c. Students listen as their teacher reads a big book on plants aloud. Then they create a computer slideshow showing the stages of plant growth.
d. Students use free software to create a digital storyboard. Then they film a movie using the storyboard as a guide.

90. What have research studies found about computer-assisted instruction (CAI) programs for teaching reading and communication skills to students with various disabilities?

a. These programs increase reading skills but decrease interaction.
b. Multimedia software plus scaffolding teach this population less.
c. CAI with the Nonverbal Reading Approach was the most useful.
d. Student differences make individualizing instruction paramount.

Refer to the following for question 91:

> A reading teacher is working with a student who has just moved to Texas from Korea. The child knows very few words in English. The teacher offers her a picture book of Korean folk tales. Using words and gestures, the teacher asks her to "read" one folk tale. The child "reads" the familiar tale in Korean. The teacher then writes key English words on the board and asks the child to find those words in the book. When the child finds the words, they read them together.

91. The strategy used in this situation is:

a. Useful. The child will feel more confident because the story is already familiar. She will also feel that the lesson is a conversation of sorts, and that she is communicating successfully. She will be motivated to learn the English words because they are meaningful and highly charged.
b. Useful. The teacher is learning as much as the child is. The teacher is learning about Korean culture and language, and she can apply this knowledge when teaching future Korean students.
c. Not very useful. The child needs to be exposed to as much American culture as possible. Encouraging her to remember her own culture will make her sad and will limit her curiosity about her new home.
d. Not very useful. The first things the child should learn are the letters of the alphabet and associative sounds. Only then can she begin to decipher an unfamiliar language.

92. A teacher uses a mixture of whole-group and small-group reading instruction. Which of the following activities would be the best choice for a whole-group lesson rather than small-group or individualized instruction?

a. Practice applying specific phonics skills
b. Independent reading of unfamiliar texts
c. Analyzing character development after the teacher reads a novel aloud
d. Spelling patterns

93. In investigating the best instructional strategies and tools for planning and implementing school reading programs, what have researchers found?

a. Explicit phonics instruction enables higher achievement only for at-risk students.
b. Instruction incorporating decodable books has been discredited by researchers.
c. Student use of word identification strategies is unrelated to what text they read.
d. Prior student literacy knowledge helps to develop sound-spelling understanding.

94. Some teachers have integrated smartphones into school curriculum as a way of using available technology to support the learning and practice of student research. What is correct about this trend?

a. Smartphones are projected to become too expensive as teaching tools.
b. Teachers should allow students to use the resources that they have.
c. It is unnecessary for a school to create an acceptable use policy for this.
d. Teachers need to know how to get information from students' phones.

95. Which of these best describes characteristics of K-12 curriculum designs for reading?

a. Designing a K-12 reading curriculum requires following a series of steps in rigid order.
b. Regardless of systematic planning and inventive thinking, compromises are inevitable.
c. Curriculum design decisions made at separate stages are independent of one another.
d. Conceptualizing curriculum design precedes specifications, development, and refinement.

96. Four central components of reading instruction reflect various learning opportunities in comprehensive literacy programs. According to the LEAD21 program, what are these components?

a. Whole-class reading, small-group reading, paired reading, and individual reading done by the students
b. Reading to students, large student group reading, small student group reading, and independent reading by the student
c. Interactive and community reading or read-alouds, differentiated reading, guided reading, and independent reading
d. Heterogeneous group reading, homogeneous group reading, reading partnerships, individual reading

97. In LEAD21 reading instruction, which of these factors are differentiated?

a. Teacher expectations and student tasks
b. Text choices and teacher support levels
c. Teacher expectations and support levels
d. Text choices and student tasks assigned

98. Which of these is more characteristic of a summative assessment?

a. The teacher administers it frequently during instruction.
b. The teacher uses its results to inform teaching changes.
c. The teacher gives it after lessons, units, or school years are complete.
d. The teacher relies on it for individualizing student data.

99. Which of these is true of formative assessments?

a. They are most often criterion-referenced tests.
b. They are most frequently norm-referenced tests.
c. They are most frequently standardized measures.
d. They are most often the most objective measures.

100. Which of the following is true about how teachers should use formal and informal instruments for formative assessment in the classroom?

a. Teachers should use multiple formal and informal assessments as bases for student grouping.
b. Teachers should use only formal test instruments for conducting their formative assessments.
c. Teachers should select one specific formal or informal assessment instrument to use exclusively.
d. Teachers should use formative assessments only for evaluating students, not for teaching them.

Integration of Knowledge and Understanding

101. Using the information from the following exhibits and your pedagogical knowledge related to literacy and English language arts, write a response of approximately 400-600 words in which you:

- Discuss one strength and one area for improvement exhibited by the student related to language and literacy development
- Identify one instructional strategy, approach, or activity that could be applied to support the student's strengths and learning needs
- Explain why the instructional strategy, approach, or activity you identified would be appropriate and effective for this purpose
- Support your reasoning with specific examples from the exhibits and your pedagogical knowledge and skills related to English language arts and literacy development

Be sure to support your response with specific examples from all three exhibits.

Exhibit 1

Teacher Notes

Student: Matthew T. **Age:** 5 **Grade:** Kindergarten

Home Language: English **IEP?:** No

2/7: Students worked in three literacy rotation stations today. The first focused on word building using letter tiles. The second was a flash card matching game focused on sight word recognition, and in the third, students practiced letter formation by finger tracing letters using a digital app. Matthew enjoyed moving the letter tiles around but did not produce any correct words. He did very well in station three, and especially liked the fact that he could change the colors of the letters he traced on the app. Matthew had the most difficulty in station two and was becoming visibly frustrated when he couldn't correctly match the vocabulary words with the pictures.

2/10: Today, I conducted oral reading fluency screenings for winter. Matthew's rate is 8 WCPM, which is two words below the winter 50th percentile benchmark of 10+ WCPM with an accuracy rate of 85%. Matthew used his finger for tracking as he read but paused frequently to sound out words. Matthew frequently seems to guess words he doesn't know and left out a few words as he read. He continues to confuse long and short vowel sounds as well as consonant letter sounds, such as "b" and "d".

2/8: Matthew always enjoys circle time when I read aloud to the class. Today, I read a fictional story about an astronaut as part of a thematic unit on outer space, which Matthew found very interesting. He was engaged throughout the reading. Afterward, students completed an activity in which they were asked to arrange picture cards of events in the story, and Matthew sequenced them in the correct order.

2/10: Students selected their own books from the library today. Matthew wanted to check out a book about outer space that was on a third-grade reading level because he liked the pictures inside. I helped him find a similar book that was on grade-level for him. I noticed him looking at the pictures and flipping pages from back to front and redirected him to start from the beginning of the book. Later in the day, we played tongue twister games as a class. Matthew was very engaged during this activity and easily recited the tongue twisters with the rest of the class.

Exhibit 2

Reading Literature

The teacher administers an oral reading assessment and records their performance to determine their oral reading fluency. After having them read aloud a grade-level passage, the teacher asks corresponding comprehension questions. Matthew's performance record appears below followed by a transcript of the discussion of the text between Matthew and the teacher after reading.

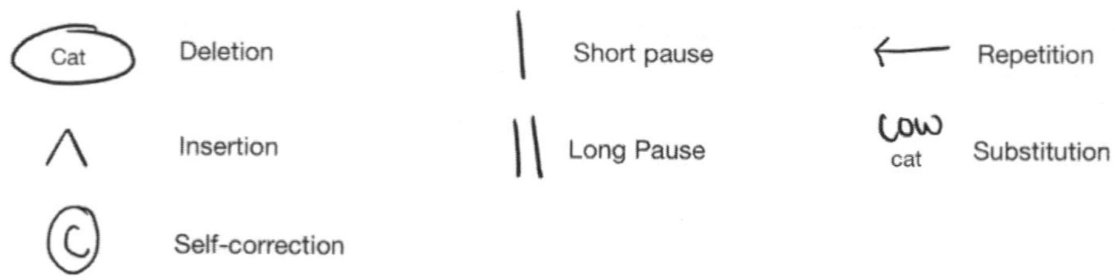

READING PASSAGE:

Have you ever seen a dog in space?

Max the dog is an astronaut.

He is going to the moon. It is far away.

On the way to the moon, Max waves to the stars.

When he gets there, he will walk on the moon.

After Max will go to Mars.

Max rides in a rocket ship. It is blue and very fast.

He wears a space suit. It is big and puffy.

Max says it is fun to go to space.

What a strange job for a dog!

After Matthew reads the passage aloud, the teacher asks some comprehension questions to determine his level of understanding about what he has read. Below is a transcript of their conversation.

Teacher: What do you remember from the story?

Matthew: I think it's about space...or maybe....yes, space!

Teacher: It is about space, that's right! Who goes to space?

Matthew: Somebody's dog I think...

Teacher: Do you remember the dog's name?

Matthew: My dog's name is Jake!

Teacher: What about the dog from the story?

Matthew: I'm trying to remember...

Teacher: That's okay. His name is Max. Do you remember where he is going?

Matthew: Um...to space? On a ship!

Teacher: What is the rocket ship like?

Matthew: I don't know what it said...maybe it's big.

Teacher: What is Max going to do when he gets to space?

Matthew: He's going to go really fast.

Teacher: What does Max think about going to space?

Matthew: Um....that it's good and he can go fast and go to see all the stars from far away!

Exhibit 3

Reading Informational Text

As part of a thematic science unit on the solar system, the teacher gives each student a brief informational passage along with corresponding comprehension questions. The teacher first reads the passage aloud to the class while students follow along and review the comprehension questions. Then, students are asked to reread the text independently and answer the corresponding questions. The reading passage, comprehension questions, and Matthew's responses appear below.

Reading Passage

Look up at the night sky. What do you see? You may see some stars, the moon, and maybe even some planets! This is all part of outer space. Outer space is very big and far away. We need rocket ships that can travel very fast to get there. People who go to outer space are called astronauts. They go to explore and learn. We are always learning more and more about outer space. Maybe one day you can go to outer space!

Comprehension Questions:

1. What can you see in the night sky?
2. What is outer space like?
3. What do we need to get to outer space?
4. What do we call people that go to outer space?

Matthew's Responses:

1. moon and owler spas
2. it is drak and big and has alens
3. roget chip
4. we kal tem astonot

102. Using the information from the following exhibits and your pedagogical knowledge related to literacy and English language arts, write a response of approximately 400-600 words in which you:

- Discuss one strength and one area for improvement exhibited by the student related to language and literacy development
- Identify one instructional strategy, approach, or activity that could be applied to support the student's strengths and learning needs

- Explain why the instructional strategy, approach, or activity you identified would be appropriate and effective for this purpose
- Support your reasoning with specific examples from the exhibits and your pedagogical knowledge and skills related to English language arts and literacy development

Be sure to support your response with specific examples from all three exhibits.

Exhibit 1

Teacher Notes

Student: Madelynn **Age:** 7 **Grade:** 2

Home Language: English **IEP?:** No

10/1: I met Madelynn's mom at open-house last night and she gave me some insight into Madelynn's interests. She said that getting Madelynn to read at home is a struggle because she often becomes frustrated and bored. Her mother did say that Madelynn sometimes enjoys reading nonfiction books, particularly about animals.

10/4: Today I conducted oral reading fluency screenings for fall. Madelynn's rate is 40 WCPM, which is eleven less than the fall 50th percentile benchmark of 51 WCPM with an accuracy rate of 90%. She seemed unfocused and tried to read as quickly as possible without paying much attention to accuracy. Several times, she trailed off and began to mumble as she read, and it became difficult to understand her. She demonstrated significant gaps in overall comprehension and had difficulty pronouncing some multisyllabic words.

10/6: Today students gave oral presentations on self-selected reading books. Madelynn chose a nonfiction book about reptiles and gave a fantastic presentation. She recalled several details about reptiles and explained key facts about them very well. Madelynn was clearly interested in the topic. This presentation went much better than her last one after reading an assigned fictional book.

10/10: To introduce a social studies unit on landforms, students independently read an informational passage and completed corresponding activities. The passage was lengthier than the class was used to, and although Madelynn typically prefers nonfiction, she appeared visibly overwhelmed and frustrated. Several times, I noticed her staring off into the distance and had to redirect her attention. She did not complete the reading assignment in the twenty minutes allotted.

Exhibit 2

Reading Literature

The teacher administers an oral reading assessment and records their performance to determine their oral reading fluency. After having them read aloud a grade-level passage, the teacher asks corresponding comprehension questions. Madelynn's performance record is shown below, followed by a transcript of the conversation between Madelynn and the teacher about the text.

Symbol	Meaning	Symbol	Meaning	Symbol	Meaning
(Cat)	Deletion	|	Short pause	←	Repetition
^	Insertion	||	Long Pause	low / cat	Substitution
Ⓒ	Self-correction				

READING PASSAGE

Title: The Magic Fairy Garden

"I think it just needs a few more sparkly rocks." Amelia thought to herself as she put the finishing touches on her new fairy garden.

"There we go! It's beautiful!" she exclaimed. For days, Amelia had been carefully planning the details and gathering materials to create the most perfect fairy garden that anyone had ever seen. She used cardboard to make benches, built a gate with craft sticks, and decorated it with fresh cut flowers, sticks, leaves, and the most sparkly rocks that she could find in her backyard.

"This is sure to bring out all of the fairies!" Amelia said to herself. "I can't wait to see them all!"

That night, Amelia waited and waited by her bedroom window, hoping to catch a glimpse of a magical fairy, but nothing seemed to be happening. Amelia began to grow tired. Her eyes were heavy and she started to yawn.

"Why don't the fairies want to come and see my beautiful garden? I worked so hard on it!" she said disappointedly. After what seemed like hours of waiting and watching, Amelia finally drifted off to sleep. Suddenly, Amelia was startled awake by a strange, mysterious rustling sound outside. She slowly peeled off her blankets and quietly tiptoed over to her window. When she pulled back the curtain, you would not believe what she saw! A tiny green speck of light was dancing around her fairy garden! Just as soon as it appeared, it flew away into the night.

"Could that have been a fairy?", Amelia wondered.

After Madelynn reads the passage aloud, the teacher asks some comprehension questions to determine her level of understanding about what he has read. Below is a transcript of their conversation.

Teacher: What was the title of this story?

Madelynn: I can't remember the whole thing. The....something about a garden I think.

Teacher: Do you think this story was fiction or nonfiction?

Madelynn: It's probably made-up.

Teacher: Who was the main character of this story?

Madelynn: A little girl named Emily...I mean...Amy. No, Amelia!

Teacher: Good! What was Amelia doing in the story?

Madelynn: Making a garden.

Teacher: Where did the story take place?

Madelynn: Probably outside.

Teacher: What makes you think so?

Madelynn: Because that's where people usually make gardens.

Teacher: Do you remember what kind of garden she was making?

Madelynn: One that she made with a bunch of different stuff.

Teacher: Who did she want to come visit the garden?

Madelynn: Let me think...(*long pause*)...oh yeah! Fairies, right?

Teacher: Yes! Did they visit her?

Madelynn: Yep!

Teacher: What sort of items did Amelia put in her garden?

Madelynn: I can't really remember that. Maybe she planted some seeds. Or a tree. I would probably want to plant seeds in a garden.

Teacher: What was the problem Amelia had in the story?

Madelynn: It took a long time to decorate. And then she fell asleep.

Teacher: Do you remember how the story ended?

Madelynn: I only just remember that she was sleeping.

Exhibit 3

Reading Informational Text

After a slide show presentation on various landforms, the teacher gives each student an informational reading along with a matching activity and corresponding comprehension questions for students to answer in their reader response journals. Students are asked to read the passage independently. The text, matching activity, comprehension questions, and Madelynn's responses appear below.

Reading Passage

What you see when you look outside depends on the geography of where you live. **Geography** is the study of the physical and living things on Earth. This simple definition includes many things, including the landforms that make up the Earth's surface. **Landforms** are the natural physical features that we find when we go outside. Different regions of Earth have different kinds of landforms. Some examples of landforms we might find are deserts, plains, mountains, oceans, lakes, rivers, islands, or peninsulas.

Deserts are very dry, hot, and arid areas of land. Very little rain falls in deserts during the year, and because of that, there is very little water. You will not find a lot of vegetation in deserts, either, and only certain kinds of animals can live there. Even though deserts are quite hot during the day, they get very cold at night.

Plains are large, flat areas of land and can be found on all seven continents. Many plains are grassy, but they can also be deserts or forests. **Mountains** can also be found on every continent. These large landforms stretch high above the ground and can be very steep and rocky. Mountains are usually formed over millions of years by pressure created between tectonic plates.

Areas of land that are surrounded by water on all sides are called **islands**. Islands can be found in almost any large body of water, such as oceans, rivers, or even lakes. Many islands are big enough for people to live on them, and some are even their own countries! Some areas of land are only surrounded by water on three sides. These are called **peninsulas**.

Bodies of water are also landforms. The **ocean** is the largest body of salt water on Earth and makes up 98% of all the water on the planet. All other bodies of water eventually lead to the ocean. We have five names for different regions of the ocean. They are called the Atlantic, Pacific, Indian, Arctic, and Antarctic.

Rivers are bodies of fresh water that flow into other bodies of water, such as the ocean. They can be wide or narrow, shallow or deep, and are constantly moving. Rivers are used by people for many purposes, such as fishing, transporting goods, or even drinking! **Lakes** are another type of freshwater body. These bodies of water are surrounded by land and can either be natural or man-made.

MATCHING ACTIVITY:

Directions: Match each landform with the correct description.

Landform	Student Choices	Answer Choices
River	**a.**	a. Surrounded completely by water
Peninsula	**f.**	b. Hot, dry, arid area of land
Island	**a.**	c. Largest body of salt water on Earth
Mountain	**h.**	d. Body of water surrounded by land
Lake	**e.**	e. Constantly flowing body of fresh water
Ocean	**c.**	f. Large, flat area of land
Plain	**b.**	g. Land surrounded by water on three sides
Desert	**f.**	h. Tall, steep, rocky landform

Comprehension Questions:

1. What is the definition of landforms?
2. What are the two types of freshwater bodies found on Earth?
3. What do we call different regions of the Earth's Ocean?
4. What are some ways that people use rivers?
5. What are two characteristics of deserts?
6. How are mountains usually formed?

Madelynn's Responses:

1. The difnishin of land forms is antyhing we can find on the land
2. Ocens and also rivirs
3. We can call them ether salt water or frish water
4. Mayb for a boat or to ketch fishes
5. Desrts are awlays hot out
6. By mayb wen a vulkano rupts

Answer Key and Explanations for Test #1

Multiple Choice Questions

1. C: Difficulties with decoding words (A) involve problems separating written or printed words into the phonemes their letters represent and hearing and differentiating them. Many experts regard decoding difficulty as the source of most reading problems. Comprehension difficulties (B) result from decoding difficulties (A). Retention difficulties (C) result from difficulties with both comprehension (B) and decoding (A). Thus choice D is incorrect.

2. C: Decoding, fluency, and comprehension are interrelated. The student is likely spending a lot of mental energy trying to decode unknown words, leaving little energy left to focus on comprehension. Additionally, repeatedly stopping to decode words interrupts fluency. This may cause the reader to struggle to make connections between the disjointed words and sentences. Implicit phonics instruction is not the best intervention option, as research has shown that systematic and explicit phonics instruction is most effective. Additionally, there is not enough information available to determine the cause of the student's decoding difficulties. Therefore, it cannot be assumed that it is related to a lack of phonological awareness skills or a language processing disorder.

3. D: Speech or language delays and disorders always involve slower language development rates, but not always in the same ways. Speech or language delays involve a normal *sequence* of language development (A) but at slower rates than normal. Speech or language disorders involve abnormal language development, including development not following the normal sequence. Due to the broken sequence, language development is considered slow as disordered speech prevents children from hitting the appropriate benchmarks on time. Thus, severity is not the only difference (B). Speech or language delays are more common than speech or language disorders, not vice versa (C). In fact, speech or language delays are the most common developmental issue, affecting 5-10 percent of preschoolers.

4. B: When creating picture flashcards to help teach children phonemic awareness, the pictures chosen should be familiar to the child (A) so he or she can name them. The child should be asked not only to name each picture with a word (C), but also, after naming it, to identify the first and second phonemes in the word (B). This helps the child understand that words contain individual sounds. This strategy is particularly helpful for children who do not have strong phonics skills (D), which involve sound-letter correspondences.

5. A: Literacy research funded by the US Department of Education finds that systematic, explicit phonics instruction significantly improves children's reading comprehension, as well as both word recognition and spelling (B), and is especially effective for children having trouble learning to read (C). It does not, however, constitute a whole language reading program (D). Whole Language approaches focus on all aspects of language from a top-down approach, usually targeting whole words and application-based activities before targeting more minute skills, such as phonics. Explicit instruction in phonics is more of a bottom-up approach to language acquisition.

6. D: Implicit phonics instruction uses a whole-to-part approach, with students reading whole texts rather than starting with isolated phonemes. Students learn to recognize whole words by sight. Through analyzing and comparing words, they then discover phonics and spelling patterns. A benefit is that students read authentic texts and learn in a meaningful context rather than practicing skills in isolation. However, research has shown that explicit phonics instruction, which progresses from part to whole, leads to stronger decoding, spelling, and comprehension skills.

7. A: The focus of this activity is on comparing the meanings of the words before and after the suffix *less* is added. Students should recognize that the newly formed words mean *without* (base word) and be able to apply this knowledge to figure out the meanings of other words containing the same suffix. While students may also learn to spell and decode words containing *less* as a result of this activity, the primary focus is on the words' meanings. Choice D is incorrect because *less* is a suffix. Prefixes are letters or groups of letters added to the beginnings of words.

8. A: Morphemic spelling strategies are based on how meaning influences spelling. Students learn these through learning Greek, Latin, and other root and affix derivations, adding affixes to roots, and forming abbreviations and compound words. Rule-based spelling strategies (B) include knowing that multiple spellings can exist for one phoneme, vowel and consonant interactions, and other generalizations. Phonetic spelling strategies (C), which are the easiest and should be taught first, identify a (regular) word's individual phonemes and spell it using the corresponding letters. Visual spelling strategies (D) use visual memory of spelling concepts: correct spellings look right.

9. D: Research (cf. Inverizzi, 2003) shows that in the normal developmental sequence of phonemic awareness abilities, it is much easier for young children to identify initial phonemes (at the beginnings of words) and final phonemes (at the ends of words) than it is for them to identify medial phonemes (in the middles of words). This demonstrates the importance of systematic instruction.

10. A: Teachers can encourage ELLs to speak English through meaningful activities that include choral readings, which are less daunting than solo readings, give a sense of safety and strength in numbers, and provide the least proficient or confident students with multiple models or partners. Echo reading is useful (B) by modeling correct reading that students emulate. Shared reading and writing promote both understanding and use of English language, thus promoting English speech (C). Singing encourages speech (D) by providing an easier way to vocalize in English through the added structure of melody and rhythm and the ability to memorize lyrics beforehand.

11. B: Students are analyzing the structure of the word by identifying the prefix, root, and suffix. Miscue analysis refers to analyzing reading errors to determine patterns in the strategies that students are using. Syllabification refers to breaking words into syllables. Because the suffix *-ible* has two syllables, and students are focusing on the meanings of the word parts, they are not focused on syllabification. Decoding is the process of translating graphemes into phonemes, or letters into sounds. In this example, students are focusing on identifying the word parts and their meanings rather than on simply decoding and reading the word.

12. A: The more words a student can recognize automatically when reading, the more fluently he or she reads, with better comprehension; these in turn dramatically enhance the student's ability to recall the reading more accurately, with greater organization and detail. Fluency without understanding (B), understanding without fluency (C), and improved recall without or regardless of fluency (D) are hence incorrect.

13. A: The student is demonstrating difficulties with expressive language, or ability to use spoken language to communicate as expected. Because he appears to understand and respond appropriately to speech he has heard, he is not displaying any difficulties with receptive language. Pragmatic language involves using language in ways that are appropriate for specific social situations. Because the student's difficulties are occurring in all contexts, they appear to be more related to expressive language than pragmatics. Articulation refers to difficulties making certain sounds. For example, sounds may be added or omitted from individual words. However, the student in this example is omitting entire words.

14. D: Young children use language in a solely oral way. Oral language is composed of separate sounds that are represented in written form by the alphabet. In order to read, a child must first have a sense of the sounds that are used in English (phonological awareness). By helping children hear the difference between rhyming and non-rhyming words, the teacher is preparing them to make the transition to sound–letter association and word families.

15. A: Experts recommend that instructional plans for teaching the alphabetic principle include practice opportunities for both new letter-sound relationships and cumulative reviews of relationships taught earlier; teaching letter-sound correspondences to children explicitly, and in isolation, before applying them to words (B); giving children opportunities to practice these correspondences during daily lessons (C); and giving them opportunities to apply their progressive learning of these correspondences to reading familiar, phonetically spelled words (D).

16. B: When students combine the initial sound in a word with the remainder of the word, they are blending the onset and rime. Syllabification involves breaking a word into syllables. A word may have one or more syllables. Phoneme isolation involves identifying either the beginning, middle, or ending sound in a word. Segmentation involves breaking a word into its individual sounds.

17. C: When students match picture cards with the consonant blends they begin with, they are using their understanding of the relationships between letters and the sounds they make. Therefore, it is a phonics activity. Choice A is a phonological awareness activity because it deals with sounds rather than letter/sound relationships. Choice B is a letter identification activity because students are matching letters to their names without addressing the sounds they make. Choice D is a comprehension activity because students are listening to a story and identifying story elements. They are not decoding the text independently.

18. D: None; irregular sight words cannot generally be decoded. Readers must learn to recognize these as whole words on sight. They either have irregular spelling or do not follow typical phonic patterns, so an attempt at decoding may ultimately mislead the reader. Segmenting them into syllables or using a phonemic approach are ineffective strategies to aid a reader in recognizing a sight word because these approaches depend on rules a sight word doesn't follow. Word families group words that share common patterns of consonants and vowels. The spelling of those words is, therefore, regular because they follow a predictable pattern. Sight words that are irregular, do not follow a predictable pattern, and must be instantaneously recognized for writing fluency. Decoding is not useful.

19. D: It is not necessary for students with retrieving or naming problems to master all consonant letter-sound associations or all short vowel letter-sound associations to begin decoding closed-syllable words with the consonant-vowel-consonant (CVC) pattern. It is also not necessary for them to master all consonants and one to two vowels. Once they have mastered one to two *short* vowel sound-letter associations, like [a] and [i], and several high-frequency consonant sound-letter associations, like [t], [b], [s], [f], and [m], teachers can start this decoding instruction, also gradually adding more letter-sound associations and reviewing often.

20. A: When kindergarten teachers lead children in singing sight words to catchy tunes, the association of words with music is a mnemonic device that is fun and helps them remember (B) both new words and how to spell them (C). Young children generally love singing (D), making this activity entertaining as well as effective for them to learn sight words.

21. D: If a student reads aloud without any vocal changes to identify text punctuation (A), this is a sign of difficulty with decoding words. Students often exhibit difficulties with comprehension by leaving out, glossing over, or minimizing details (B) when reading. When students insert additional words that are not already in the text (C), it is a sign that the student could be rushing through the text too quickly. Having issues with connecting ideas within a text passage (D) is a common sign of difficulty with reading retention.

22. C: Finger-pointing is normal for beginning readers, even into second grade (A); adults should not interfere with pointing. Giving young children "witch fingers," feathers, and other available, recycled, or homemade pointers is fine. These are not crutches (B); they are simply finger substitutes that are creative, fun, and keep book pages clean with younger readers. However, when older students finger-point, it can indicate reading struggles and interfere with reading fluency (C). Having students turn bookmarks or popsicle sticks sideways to mark each line of text helps them transition past finger-pointing (D).

23. C: Phonological awareness skills typically progress in a similar manner. The ability to rhyme often develops first, as it is considered the simplest skill. Later, children develop the ability to break words into syllables, which is usually followed by the ability to manipulate onsets and rimes. Phoneme isolation and other phonemic awareness skills typically develop last, as they are the most complex.

24. C: Phonological awareness and phonemic awareness are distinct terms. Phonological awareness is a broader term that refers to the ability to identify and manipulate sounds in spoken words. Phonemic awareness is one component of phonological awareness involving the ability to identify and manipulate sounds in spoken words at the phoneme level. Because phonemes are the smallest units of speech, phonemic awareness is an advanced component of phonological awareness. It typically develops after simpler skills, like rhyming and blending.

25. D: While all of these options can assist students with learning letter formation, writing letters in shaving cream best represents a multisensory approach. It involves movement, touch, and sight.

26. D: Chunking involves looking for known parts in a word. Because *scapegoat* is a compound word, it is likely that Maria will at least recognize the word *goat*. This leaves a smaller portion of the word to decode. There are many words that would sound right in the sentence, so guessing based on syntax alone is unlikely to result in the correct word. Because the word is multisyllabic and contains multiple spelling patterns, blending may be difficult. Additionally, the sentence provides few context clues to help Maria guess the word correctly.

27. D: The word *maple* begins with an open syllable, spelled *ma*. Open syllables end with a vowel and usually have a long vowel sound. Knowing this will help the student decode this word and other words with open syllables. This word does not contain any vowel digraph pairs, r-controlled vowels, or closed syllables. Vowel digraph pairs consist of two vowels that together make one sound. R-controlled vowels consist of a vowel before the letter *r*. Closed syllables end with a consonant and usually have a short vowel sound.

28. D: When students participate in kinesthetic activities, they are physically engaged in the learning process. These activities involve movement, such as hopping along the sight words written in chalk. While the other activities can also be used to practice sight words and may involve tactile experiences, they involve less movement and physical activity than hopping.

29. B: In this activity, students are identifying the discriminating phoneme in two words. In the example of *tap* and *top*, it is the middle phoneme that is different. To practice phoneme substitution, the teacher would give students a word and then instruct them to change one of the phonemes and identify the newly formed word. In phoneme deletion, the teacher would give students a word and instruct them to remove a phoneme and identify the newly formed word. In phoneme insertion, the teacher would give students a word and instruct them to add a phoneme and identify the newly formed word.

30. C: Researchers have found that instruction in simpler phonological skills like rhyming, onsets, and rimes may not have any direct benefits for reading development (A); however, they find that teaching these simpler skills first nevertheless can make it easier to teach the more complex ones *without* directly benefiting reading development (B). Researchers have also found that the phonological awareness instruction that appears most beneficial to subsequent reading development integrates blending and segmenting (C), not deleting and substituting (D).

31. C: The general rule about splitting doubled consonants pertains most to syllabication, i.e., where to divide words up into their component syllables to inform pronunciation and meaning. Structural analysis (A) pertains to dividing words into component parts like prefixes, roots, and suffixes, which may or may not coincide with syllable divisions. Using common spelling patterns (B) pertains to determining meaning and pronunciation in unfamiliar words by comparing their spelling to the same or similar spellings in familiar words. Using morphemes (D) pertains to identifying the smallest meaningful grammatical units in words, e.g., *-ed* verb endings signify past tense.

32. A: The distinction between vowel and consonant sounds should not be taught for the first time when teaching which letters represent which sounds, but introduced earlier, during instruction in phonemic awareness. This concept should be reviewed after teaching students to decode a small set of letter-sound matches and to recognize and form letter shapes and names.

33. B: Both words identified in this choice have the same medial consonant sound of /s/, whereas *kitten* has the medial consonant /t/. The two words identified in choice A have the same medial *vowel* sound. The one word identified in choice C has a different medial *vowel* sound than the other two. The two words identified in choice D have the same *final* consonant sound; the other word does not.

34. B: The pattern layer of orthography involves looking at groups of letters within words that form patterns. Therefore, exploring and building words that all contain *eigh* involves the pattern layer. The alphabet layer involves letter/sound relationships. The meaning layer involves the relationships between word meanings and their spellings. Conventional spelling refers to spelling words accurately.

35. C: Stage 1, Emergent Spelling: 3 to 5-year-olds begin writing letters without phonemic matches; they learn drawing/writing differentiation, letter formation, writing directionality, and some letter-sound associations. Stage 2, Letter Name-Alphabetic Spelling: 5 to 7-year-olds learn the alphabetic principle, consonant and short vowel sounds, consonant blends, and digraphs. Stage 3, Within-Word Pattern Spelling: 7 to 9-year-olds learn long vowel spelling patterns, r-controlled vowels, more complex consonant patterns, diphthongs, and other less-frequent vowel patterns. Stage 4, Syllables and Affixes Spelling: 9 to 11-year-olds learn inflectional endings and rules, syllabication, and homophones. Stage 5, Derivational Relations Spelling: 11 to 14-year-olds learn consonant and vowel alternations, Greek and Latin roots and affixes, and etymologies.

36. A: According to the National Research Council (Snow, Burns, and Griffin, 1998), phonological awareness is the general ability to distinguish speech sounds from their meanings, whereas phonemic awareness is a more specific ability to distinguish individual speech sounds, i.e., phonemes, within words. Hence phonemic awareness is the most sophisticated level of phonological awareness (D). Therefore, choice B and C are also incorrect.

37. C: Decoding monosyllabic words by referring to the initial and final consonant, short vowel, and long vowel sounds represented by their letters is a common academic standard for 1st-grade students. Typical academic standards for kindergarten students include demonstrating knowledge of letter-sound correspondences; understanding the alphabetic principle; matching letters to their corresponding consonant (and short vowel) sounds; and reading simple, monosyllabic sight words, i.e., high-frequency words.

38. B: Once children have learned the basic rules and principles for spelling in their native language, they can usually figure out how to spell words that are new to them when they hear them spoken. As children accrue experience in communicating with language, they notice basic patterns in letter combinations, syllables, common word roots, prefixes, suffixes, endings, etc., so much of their knowledge of spelling patterns comes through incidental learning (A). Also, children usually can read words that they can spell (C). Therefore, not only do their reading and writing skills support correct spelling, but reciprocally, good spelling skills also support children's reading and writing (D).

39. B: Research findings show that it helps ELL students for teachers to assign them in pairs, particularly for projects (a), experiments, and reports; to write problems and directions for them using shorter, simpler sentences (b); to emphasize student work accuracy much more than student work speed (c); and to ask ELL students many questions that they must use higher level cognitive processes to answer (d).

40. D: Teachers should give students learning English as a second language (ESL) and English language learners (ELLs) clear models and examples of what they expect them to do, how to do it, and how the completed results should look. Stating directions verbally in English alone is insufficient for students learning a foreign language. Teachers must also give ELLs more time to respond because it takes them longer to process the English they hear, mentally translate it into their own language, mentally formulate a response in their own language, translate that mentally into English, and judge whether their translation makes sense before they answer. It typically takes ESLs years before they can "think in English." When using idioms and figures of speech, teachers should explain these to ELLs and add pantomime demonstrations to help them understand. These expressions are not logical and often have no L1 equivalents for ESLs, so they require explicit instruction.

41. C: Oral language is a vital aspect of any language arts instruction. Often, the first concepts of language are transmitted via oral and auditory processes. The first Americans also possessed a rich oral culture in which stories and histories were passed down through generations via storytelling. Inviting a guest speaker who is part of this culture helps students understand more about cultures in their world, as well as the value of oral language and storytelling. This introduction gives students a relevant personal experience with which to connect what they will be learning in class.

42. B: In cases of words that sound alike but have different meanings, checking a dictionary or thesaurus will ensure correct usage of a word.

43. D: To instruct students in word analysis following a sequence progressing from simpler to more complex, teachers would first introduce individual phonemes (speech sounds); then the blending of two or more individual phonemes; then onsets and rimes (i.e., phonograms and word families) such as *-ack*, *-ide*, *-ay*, *-ight*, *-ine*, etc.; then the easier short vowels, followed by the more difficult long vowels; then blends of individual consonants; then CVC (consonant-vowel-consonant) words (e.g., *bag*, *hot*, *red*, *sit*) and other common patterns of consonants and vowels in words; and then the six most common types of syllables (i.e., closed, VCe, open, vowel team, *r*-controlled, and C-*le*).

44. B: Early Production, with the characteristics named, is the second stage of ESL acquisition. Preproduction (A), the first stage, involves no English speech, minimal listening comprehension, and the ability to draw pictures of and/or point at objects represented by some English words. Speech Emergence (C) is the third stage, characterized by good English comprehension; English speech using simple sentences, but still showing pronunciation and grammatical errors; and frequently misunderstanding English-language jokes. Intermediate Fluency (D), the fourth stage, features excellent English listening comprehension and few spoken grammatical errors.

45. C: The acronym *K.I.M.* in a K.I.M. vocabulary chart stands for Key idea, Information, and Memory clue. Under the "K" for Key idea, the student enters a vocabulary word. Under the "I" for Information, the student enters the definition of the word. Under the "M" for Memory clue, students often make a drawing or attach a picture, sometimes including written or printed captions, to remind them of the word's meaning.

46. D: Collaborative Strategic Reading (CSR) is a technique that largely depends on cooperative learning and practice of metacognition. In practice, this look slike putting students into groups and having them self-monitor their own reading comprehension using various reading strategies. One popular reading strategy that can be used includes "click and clunk," which is where students report which parts of the story *click* to them, or which makes sense without much difficulty, and which parts *clunk*, or are not easy to understand. Then the group would collaborate to resolve the clunks and ensure everyone understood the reading assignment. Other strategies can include use of context clues, rereading, or any other reading comprehension strategy, paired with group discussion.

47. B: Semantic maps are used to create visual representations of connections between items. Students can put the root in the middle of the semantic map and display words containing the root on the branches, thus demonstrating what the words have in common. Looking up words in the dictionary or finding them in the textbook does not facilitate making connections unless follow-up discussions or activities occur. While Venn diagrams are used to compare and contrast two or more things, the web-like format of the semantic map better displays the connections between related words.

48. C: Educational researchers (cf. Pardede, 2011) observe that novels can be too long for public school classes to read in limited time (A). Students typically require extensive instruction and time to understand figurative devices and other unfamiliar language in poems (B). Though students can be assigned to read drama, it is often impracticable for crowded classes with limited hours to act out a play (D). In contrast, short stories (C) can be read in one sitting and typically have one plot, fewer characters than novels, and brief, not detailed, setting descriptions, making it easier for students to follow a storyline.

49. A: Researchers find that student engagement can be deeper through integrating their practice with evaluating information sources into ongoing topic discussions; thus (B) is incorrect. Teachers should provide students with *short* passages excerpted from various resources related to the discussion topic (C). They can assign students to individual, paired, or small-group work evaluating material, which they should do using a *few, set* questions, not unlimited, open-ended ones (D), to guide their evaluations.

50. A: Word maps, which are ways to visually organize concepts, are good ways to introduce new vocabulary words and concepts to students in a classroom. Word maps provide a way for students to clearly detail a new vocabulary word and its definition, and also a way to create connections to both the word and the definition. This allows for the students to have a deeper understanding of the new concept, and to ideally form a connection with it so they can build permanent connections in their mind to the vocabulary word. Dictionaries, word walls, and using new vocabulary words regularly can all be helpful in the classroom, but for students to have the best chance to learn new vocabulary, they need to have an opportunity to work with the word and form their own connections to it.

51. B: Concept mapping helps students to visualize, organize, and apply the concepts they have learned. Reading for meaning helps students read actively, including predicting, identifying main ideas/themes, inferring, analysis, comparison, evaluation, etc. Cloze procedures help students develop sequencing awareness and linguistic relationships; search, predict, and reconstruct; and determine meaning from context. Case studies help students apply content knowledge and skills through case analysis and explanation.

52. B: Inferring requires readers to use clues rather than explicit evidence to determine the author's meaning. Choice B requires students to use the character's statements to infer how he or she felt at the time. Choice A requires students to evaluate the writing. Choice C requires students to make a prediction. Choice D requires students to make a text-to-text connection.

53. D: Varying levels of explicit instruction, assigning small groups, and varying amounts of writing instruction time (A) reflects the principle of incorporating differentiated instruction. Allowing enough time for systematic writing opportunities in all content subjects as well as ELA classes (B) reflects the principle of integrating teaching writing across the curriculum. Incorporating reasons and methods for explicit writing instruction (C) reflects the principle of including rationales and methods of explicit writing instruction. Effective organization, spelling, vocabulary, syntax, etc., for different subjects (D) reflect the principle of teaching knowledge that enables more effective writing.

54. A: A KWL chart is a type of graphic organizer that teachers can have students make to assist them with reading comprehension. K stands for *know*: before reading, students record what they already know about the subject of a text. W stands for *want*: before and during reading, students record what they want to know about the subject. L stands for *learned*: after reading, students record what they learned from reading the text.

55. D: Analogies are used to help students recognize the relationships between words. Students are commonly given a pair of words whose relationship they must first identify. They then apply the same type of relationship to complete another word pair. Analogies can be used to help students recognize many different types of relationships, including recognizing synonyms, antonyms, and more. While students may explore word structure, definitions, and origins while completing analogies, the overall objective of analogies is to recognize and apply relationships between sets of words.

56. C: Picture walks are frequently used to activate students' prior knowledge. When readers look at the pictures, they make connections between the content of the new texts and what they already know from other texts or life experiences. These connections can spark interest in the stories and deepen comprehension. Teachers may encourage the use of syntactic cues during guided reading groups, but this is not typically part of a picture walk. Setting a purpose for reading is another beneficial prereading activity, but it is not always a part of a picture walk either. Metacognitive skills, which assist students with self-monitoring during reading, are also beneficial, but they are not typically the focus of a picture walk.

57. D: To allow Joshua more time and energy to focus on his essay, he can record only key words and phrases in his notes rather than writing complete sentences. This will also make it easier for him to locate the key information in his notes when he is ready to add it to his essay. Grouping notes into categories and using visuals can be beneficial, but based on Joshua's notes, recording the key words and phrases is the most pressing need. Recording only a few facts may not provide enough information to complete an entire three-paragraph essay, so it would be more helpful to record additional facts in a more concise manner.

58. D: Literal comprehension is what text states overtly, e.g., story characters, event sequences, stated facts, etc. Choices A and B are examples of literal comprehension responses. Inferential comprehension is deeper or implicit meaning not explicitly stated, which readers must infer by considering text and drawing conclusions, e.g., unstated main ideas, cause-and-effect relationships, generalizations, and predictions. Choice C is an example of an inferential comprehension response. Evaluative comprehension requires readers to form opinions after analyzing text information. Choice D is an example of an evaluative comprehension response.

59. D: For written composition, teachers should instruct students to consider not only who their expected audience is, but also the format in which the audience will read or hear their work (A), which will inform how they write. Who the audience is affects the reading level(s), vocabulary, length, and type of writing the audience expects (D). It also affects what message each student wants to convey (B) just as much as the format does (C). They should not consider any one of these above any other, but consider all equally.

60. A: Choice A includes the current student performance level, the desired student performance level, the assessment used to determine the performance level, and the date the goal is expected to be achieved. Choice B only indicates the desired performance level and the assessment that will be used. Choice C indicates the assessment that will be used and the date the goal is expected to be achieved, but saying that it "will increase his oral reading rate" is too vague. It does not list the current or desired performance levels. Choice D only indicates the expected performance level and the assessment that will be used. It does not indicate the current performance level or the date the goal is expected to be achieved.

61. C: When a student has trouble recognizing words out of context (A), this is mainly a sign that the student has problems with decoding words, as is slow, laborious oral reading (B). Having trouble differentiating main ideas or important information from minor details (C) in text is mainly a sign that the student has problems with reading comprehension. Having trouble relating text to his or her own existing knowledge (D) often reflects difficulty using background knowledge, which can influence comprehension but is conceptually distinct from basic comprehension skills such as identifying main ideas.

62. C: Practical instructional activities that develop student listening skills (cf. Wolvin and Coakley, 1979) include teaching students both to follow and give directions, teaching them interpersonal communication skills, and teaching them to appreciate oral literature.

63. A: In shared writing experiences, students share thoughts during a class discussion, and the teacher records them on paper. Because students are in the preliterate stage of writing, they are not yet using sound/symbol relationships to spell words. Writing at this stage may resemble scribbling or contain strings of pretend letters. If Mr. Suarez records the students' thoughts for this activity, the story can be reread multiple times. If students write independently or with partners, it will be difficult to maintain the message of the story each time it is reread. Similar difficulties would occur with interactive writing because students help write the shared story on paper.

64. A: Evaluative questions require readers to form opinions or judgements based on the text. Asking if readers agree with something the author stated is an evaluative question. The remaining questions ask students to recall information only.

65. B: Schemata are units of existing knowledge used to make sense of newly encountered information. Readers rely on their existing schemata to make sense of information encountered in new texts. Therefore, activating prior knowledge is a key component of schema theory. For example, a child may know that flowers require water to grow. He may use this existing schema to make sense of a new text about the desert, which indicates that few plants grow there. Summarizing, identifying main idea, and recognizing story elements all require finding key information within a text, but they do not necessarily relate this information to what was already known about the topic prior to reading.

66. A: I-Charts or Inquiry Charts guide students to collect evidence from multiple information sources to support their ideas. While I-Charts are one type of graphic organizer, graphic organizers in general (B) organize and depict information more visually and simply; many do not involve finding or organizing information sources as I-Charts do. Journaling (C) helps students develop their own ideas rather than find or use evidence to support them. RAFT (D), i.e., Reader, Audience, Format, Topic, is a reading or writing strategy that helps students understand those four components' roles, comprehend informational text, and think creatively rather than find and use supporting evidence.

67. C: William is making errors in subject-verb agreement. Singular nouns should be paired with singular verbs, and plural nouns should be paired with plural verbs. Pronoun-antecedent agreement refers to ensuring that pronouns agree with their antecedents in number and gender. The sentences in this example do not include pronouns. There are no errors present in verb tense or sentence complexity. Verb consistency refers to ensuring that the verbs within a piece of writing use the same tense. Complex sentences are sentences that contain at least one dependent and independent clause.

68. D: Denotative meanings are the literal meanings of words found when they are looked up in the dictionary. Connotative meanings are the ideas or feelings evoked by the words. Therefore, two words can have the same denotative meaning in the dictionary, yet evoke very different reactions from readers. *Frugal* and *cheap* can both mean costing little, yet *cheap* often carries a negative connotation. For example, people may be insulted if they were called cheap, yet take pride in being referred to as frugal. The remaining pairs of words have similar meanings, and they all evoke positive feelings.

69. A: A story map outlines the main elements of the story, including the characters, setting, conflict, plot, and resolution. Recording these elements will assist the student in remembering and analyzing the story after it has been read. If the student has retention issues, he or she may not recall the story elements even after reading the story twice or listening to an audio version. A KWL chart can be used to activate prior knowledge and help the student reflect on what was learned, but it does not outline the story elements needed to analyze plot.

70. A: Among instructional strategies defined by a master teacher (Robb, 2002), asking students open-ended questions about the texts they read is the most useful for helping students to read critically. Teaching students how to skim text for headings, subheadings, boldface, illustrations, captions, sidebars, the index, and other text features that give signs (B) of pertinent material is most useful for helping students locate information. Guiding students to make connections between text and their own personal experiences (D), everyday life (C), world events, and other texts is most useful for helping students understand the relevance of learning materials.

71. D: Although some history textbooks may use narrative (A) writing to make historical events more interesting by telling a story, these are not in the majority. Persuasive (B) writing seeks to convince readers to agree with the author's position; most content-area textbooks used in public schools present information more objectively. Descriptive (C) writing seeks to convey a vivid impression of something by providing sensory details so readers feel they are experiencing it; most content-area textbooks are more factual. The majority of school content textbooks use informational (D) writing to impart knowledge.

72. B: Indirect ways in which students receive instruction and learn vocabulary include through daily conversations, reading on their own, and being read aloud to by adults. Direct instruction and learning in vocabulary include teachers providing extended instruction exposing students repeatedly to vocabulary words in multiple teaching contexts, teachers pre-teaching specific words found in text prior to students reading it, and teachers instructing students over extended time periods and having them actively work with vocabulary words.

73. B: Analogies are easier for children to understand because they compare known items, whereas metaphors require abstract thinking.

74. A: Phonics instruction in the early grades has proved most beneficial in developing reading proficiency. Storytelling teaches important speaking and listening skills, but these are different from reading skills. While real literature may increase students' interest in reading, basal texts are well-designed to teach the essential skills.

75. B: The topics of cooperative projects and/or discussions and whether they are age-appropriate in difficulty relate most to cognitive developmental levels, i.e., what they can understand. Social developmental levels (A) relate to whether students can interact effectively in peer groups. Emotional developmental levels (C) relate to student emotional intelligence, i.e., emotional self-management plus sensitivity to, understanding of, and appropriate response to others' emotions. Behavioral developmental levels (D) relate to whether students can regulate their behaviors appropriately within peer groups.

76. B: English language learners (ELLs) generally benefit from contextual learning of vocabulary because it helps to solidify the meaning and usage of the newly-learned words. Both vocabulary in isolation (a) and vocabulary in volume (b) typically refer to rote memorization, which does not provide the retention benefits or provide the student with contextual experience. Answer (d) is wrong because speech proficiency levels do not necessarily correspond to a student's reading and vocabulary skills.

77. D: Having classmates offer peer reviews (A), having the teacher evaluate their work (B), and comparing their work to that of their classmates (C) are all valuable sources of feedback for students about their performance and progress in speaking and enacting through oral reports and presentations as they give different perspectives; however, video recordings of student performance (D) are the only type of completely objective feedback among these choices because they provide an exact record of what the student did. This enables students to self-monitor, make changes/improvements, and appreciate their own progress over time.

78. B: In this paired reading strategy, which improves reading comprehension and helps students identify the main idea in informational text, after silently reading a text selection, the pair of students takes turns following these steps: One student paraphrases what he or she thinks the text's main idea is. The other student agrees or disagrees, explaining why. The pair then develops a consensus as to the text's main idea. Then they take turns finding details in the text that support its main idea.

79. D: Making at least the attempt to read every single word, even with many errors (A), is a strategic strength that gives students decoding practice and, even without success every time, enables their potential. Attending to punctuation in text (B) is a strength, since punctuation can significantly affect meaning (e.g., "Let's eat, Grandma" vs. "Let's eat Grandma"). Even without understanding all details, getting the gist of text meaning (C) is also a strength. However, holistic word reading (D) misses plural or verb tense endings and other morphological changes affecting meaning, reflecting a strategic weakness.

80. C: Bias occurs when a test disadvantages a certain group of students. Including questions with cultural references that only a select group of students will understand disadvantages other students who do not understand the references. Students may miss these questions, despite having the reading skills the test is supposed to measure. Validity refers to whether the test measures what it is supposed to measure. Reliability relates to consistency of the test results over time and between participants.

81. B: Performance-based assessments do not involve comparing student performance to norms (A) as standardized tests do. Rather, they evaluate each student's (in this case, literacy) skills based on how that student performs or by products he or she produces. Thus, teachers must establish clear, equitable criteria (B) for evaluating these, because there will not be a single correct answer (C). Student responses will vary widely, so teachers must use these criteria plus their own judgment, not standardized answer keys (D).

82. C: Being able to repeat English words and phrases (A) and name concrete objects on sight (B) are both examples of criteria at the lowest level of an oral ELP scoring rubric. Being able to communicate well in social contexts (D) is an example of a rubric criterion for an intermediate ELP level. At the highest level, the student would communicate *very* well, not only in social but also academic contexts. Being able to participate in classroom discussions (C) is an example of the highest ELP level.

83. A: The *first* thing the teacher should do is always to ask the child if he or she knows what rhyming words are. If the child answers yes, the teacher should ask the child to say two rhyming words (B). If the child gives an incorrect example, or has answered no to the question, the teacher should then explain to the child the definition of rhymes (C). After explaining, the teacher should then give the child an example of two rhyming words (D). The teacher can then offer other word pairs and have the child identify whether they rhyme or not. Once the child masters this, the teacher can ask the child to say two rhyming words again.

84. B: In choice B, the student substituted the word seven for several, and read the rest of the sentence correctly. The words seven and several are visually similar, as the first four letters are the same in each. Choices A and D demonstrate errors related to meaning, as the student substituted words that made sense in the sentences but were not visually similar to the existing words. Choice C contains an omission, as the student did not say several.

85. C: Screening assessments are given to identify students who may be at future risk of academic difficulties and may benefit from interventions. Diagnostic assessments can then be given to confirm or provide additional information about screening results, including identifying students' specific strengths and needs. This information can then be used to guide instruction.

86. A: Progress monitoring is a type of assessment used to track students' progress towards certain goals over time. When students are receiving reading interventions, frequent progress monitoring should be done to assess their progress and determine if the interventions are succeeding. Screening is done initially to determine if students are at risk for academic difficulties, and it is done at greater intervals, such as the start of each school year. Summative assessment occurs at the end of a unit of study or other larger unit of instruction. Norm-referenced tests compare students' performances to the performances of sample groups of similar students, while progress monitoring is done to assess students' progress towards their own personal goals.

87. D: In choice D, the student read the sentence correctly, except for changing *chases* to *chased*. *Chased* still sounds right in the sentence, indicating that the student was using structural, or syntactic, cues to decode the word. In choice A, the student replaced *stick* with *branch*. *Branch* makes sense in the sentence, and it is not visually similar to the existing word. Choice B demonstrates an insertion, as the student added the word *big*. Choice C demonstrates a visual error, as the student replaced *furry* with *fuzzy*. Both words are visually similar.

88. B: Advanced readers and writers should be given opportunities to explore concepts using high-level thinking skills. If they have already mastered identifying adjectives, then evaluating adjective choices in a text and selecting stronger options would be a more challenging activity. Proficient readers and writers should not simply be given additional amounts of unchallenging work, as suggested in options A and D. Pairing students with differing skill levels can have instructional benefits, but the activities should be structured to ensure that both students benefit from the interactions.

89. C: In choice C, students listen and watch as their teacher reads a print-based book aloud, and then they use a digital tool to create a multimedia presentation. This combines both digital and print-based media. Choice A consists of two print-based activities. Choices B and D each contain two digital activities.

90. D: Studies have found some CAI not only increases literacy skills, but also attention and interaction in students with disabilities that include autism, cerebral palsy, Down syndrome, and intellectual disability (A). Using multimedia software (e.g., Delta Messages) plus instructional scaffolding is found effective for students not performing well with conventional instruction (B). Combining CAI with the Nonverbal Reading Approach for students with co-existing severe speech disorders and physical disabilities or autism was found effective, but not necessarily more effective than teacher-only instruction or teacher-plus-CAI (C). Acquisition rates depended on individual students, showing the importance of individualizing instruction (D) for this population.

91. A: The child will feel more confident because the story is already familiar, so this strategy is useful. She will also feel that the lesson is a conversation of sorts, and that she is communicating successfully. She will be motivated to learn the English words because they are meaningful and highly charged. As a newly arrived immigrant, the child feels overwhelmed. Presenting her with a book of folk tales from her country tells her that she needn't lose her culture in order to function in this one. It also comforts her by reminding her that her past and present are linked. Allowing her to speak in Korean helps her express herself without fear of judgment or failure. Presenting her with an English vocabulary that is meaningful ensures that she will eagerly embrace these words, her first words in her new language.

92. C: One of the challenges of large-group instruction is meeting the needs of diverse learners. Reading a novel aloud helps to make the content accessible to all learners. If students were to read it independently, as in choice B, the text would likely not be challenging enough for some readers and too difficult for others. Therefore, basing a comprehension lesson on a book that was read aloud assists all students with participating. While teachers sometimes introduce and practice phonics skills in large groups, students are likely to have differing skill levels in this area. Proficient first-grade readers, for example, may read consonant blends and digraphs with ease, which struggling readers may still be learning the alphabetic principle. Students in a classroom are also likely to have vastly different spelling skills, making the need for differentiation important.

93. D: Researchers have found that explicit instruction in phonics does help students at risk for reading failure particularly, but also promotes higher achievement by all students (A). Research supports the use of decodable books (B) early in first grade. Studies find that the kind of text read by students affects the word identification strategies they use (C), and also that prior student literacy knowledge (indicated by reading readiness assessment), as well as using decodable texts early, contribute to developing understanding of sound-spelling relationships (D).

94. B: This trend has merit in the fact that it allows students to use the resources they already have instead of artificially suppressing the use of technology. Choice A is incorrect because, while not all students have phones, many do. Smartphones are among the most popular, ubiquitous, convenient, and mobile of devices that individuals use. Over time, smartphones have become increasingly prevalent, demonstrating that they are not considered too expensive in general. While it is unreasonable to expect all students to have their own phones, if device usage becomes fully integrated into curriculum, those who do not have access to a phone could be supplied by the school, in a similar fashion to classroom tablets or computers. Choice C is incorrect because device usage plays a big role in instruction, privacy, and safety for students. It is crucial to have acceptable use policies in place for technology. The scenario does not describe the school policy, but teachers who want to integrate technology into instruction must follow district and campus policies to ensure the legality of the practice and safety of the students. Choice D is incorrect as student privacy is inherently tied to the use of personal devices. A teacher should be able to give guidance to students on how to use any appropriate technology, and would ideally have a direct line of communication about classwork, but teachers should not expect to have complete access to students' personal devices.

95. B: Designing a K-12 reading curriculum requires systematic planning, but NOT following a series of steps in rigid order (A). Design pursues optimal functionality, not perfection; despite all efforts to plan systematically and think inventively, compromises among everyone's wishes are inevitable (B). Decisions made at different stages are NOT independent, but interact (C); hence, the design process is often recursive. Though educators may revisit different stages, to make the design process work, they must recognize each stage's challenges and tasks. The first stage is setting design specifications; stages of conceptualizing, developing, and refining the design follow (D).

96. B: LEAD21 (Wright Group, McGraw-Hill) identifies four central components of reading instruction: (1) teachers read to students, (2) teachers read with large student groups, (3) teachers read with small student groups, and (4) individual students read. Choice A represents four sizes of grouping in reading instruction. Choice C represents four types of instructional activities for reading. Choice D represents four types of grouping in reading instruction.

97. B: In LEAD21 (Wright Group, McGraw-Hill) reading instruction, teacher expectations, and student tasks are kept uniform across all students, while the choices of texts and the levels of teacher support (B) are differentiated.

98. C: Summative assessments are administered after instruction and less often than formative assessments, which teachers make more frequently during instruction (A) to inform changes to make their teaching more effective (B). Typical times for summative assessments are after each lesson, unit, and school year is completed (C). Teachers rely on formative, not summative assessments for individual student data (D); they rely on summative assessment results for group data and group comparisons.

99. A: Formative assessments are most often criterion-referenced tests, which measure a student's performance against a predetermined criterion that indicates success or proficiency. They are typically not norm-referenced tests, which measure a student's performance against the average performance (scores) of normative sample student groups, such as standardized tests used as summative assessments. Formative assessments may occasionally be standardized, but most frequently they are informal measures. They are not the most objective—formal tests are—but formative assessments are better for monitoring student progress, evaluating teacher effectiveness, and informing instructional adjustments.

100. A: Teachers should generally use a variety of formal and informal assessment instruments to get a complete picture of student achievement. This is especially applicable for grouping students, which teachers should never do for the long term based on the results of only one assessment instrument. To conduct formative assessments of learning in progress, teachers should use both formal and informal test instruments; and use several different kinds, rather than choosing only one formal instrument to use exclusively. Formative assessment results are valuable not only for evaluating student progress, but moreover for use in the classroom as teaching tools.

Integration of Knowledge and Understanding

101. Scoring Rubric:

Constructed response items will be scored holistically on a scale of 1-4 according to the following performance indicators:

Completion	The degree to which the candidate addresses all parts of the prompt
Organization/Clarity	The degree to which the candidate presents their response and supporting evidence in an organized, coherent manner
Accuracy/Relevancy	The degree to which the candidate demonstrates meaningful and accurate knowledge and skills pertaining to the prompt
Use of supporting evidence	The degree to which the candidate uses specific, appropriate, and relevant examples and reasoning from the exhibits provided

Candidates that receive an overall score of "4" demonstrate excellent pedagogical knowledge and skills related to the prompt.

- All parts of the prompt are addressed with thoroughness and attention to detail
- Information in the response is very well-organized, clear, and accessible to the reader
- The response demonstrates accurate and relevant pedagogical knowledge and skills relative to all items in the prompt
- The response includes ample specific, appropriate, and relevant examples from the exhibits provided with detailed explanations

102. Scoring Rubric:

Constructed response items will be scored holistically on a scale of 1-4 according to the following performance indicators:

Completion	The degree to which the candidate addresses all parts of the prompt
Organization/Clarity	The degree to which the candidate presents their response and supporting evidence in an organized, coherent manner
Accuracy/Relevancy	The degree to which the candidate demonstrates meaningful and accurate knowledge and skills pertaining to the prompt
Use of supporting evidence	The degree to which the candidate uses specific, appropriate, and relevant examples and reasoning from the exhibits provided

Candidates that receive an overall score of "4" demonstrate excellent pedagogical knowledge and skills related to the prompt.

- All parts of the prompt are addressed with thoroughness and attention to detail
- Information in the response is very well-organized, clear, and accessible to the reader
- The response demonstrates accurate and relevant pedagogical knowledge and skills relative to all items in the prompt
- The response includes ample specific, appropriate, and relevant examples from the exhibits provided with detailed explanations

Practice Test #2

Multiple Choice Questions

1. In a fifth-grade classroom, students recently finished reading two informational texts about industrialization in the United States in the 18th and 19th centuries. The teacher plans to assess students' comprehension of the texts, with a focus on understanding the author's point of view. Which of the following activities would be most effective in achieving this goal?

a. Administering a multiple-choice test focused on key ideas in the texts
b. Having students write an expository essay on the topic
c. Grouping students to participate in literature circles to discuss the texts
d. Organizing students into teams to debate the main ideas presented in the texts

2. Utilizing word walls, introducing word families, and incorporating syllable clapping games when introducing high-frequency vocabulary words are all effective strategies for promoting which of the following skills related to the development of automaticity in first-grade students?

a. Expressive language skills
b. Prosody
c. Phonological awareness
d. Orthographic mapping

3. Students in a fifth-grade class have recently finished reading a historical fiction novel as part of an integrated language arts and social studies unit. The teacher is planning to conduct an assessment that measures both students' grasp of the time period and comprehension of the text. Which of the following approaches would be most effective in achieving this goal?

a. Administering a multiple-choice exam that corresponds with the text
b. Prompting students to self-assess their overall understanding and areas for improvement
c. Assigning students to create a diary from the perspective of a character in the text
d. Tasking students with creating a Venn diagram to compare the time period depicted in the text with their own

4. A fifth-grade teacher is planning to introduce compound-complex sentences to her class. Which of the following concepts should the teacher review before introducing this concept to promote student understanding?

a. Parts of speech and conventions of grammar
b. Segmenting and decoding of multisyllabic words
c. Morphological awareness skills
d. Common literary techniques

Refer to the following for questions 5–6:

During a writing activity, a second-grade teacher prompts students to independently write about a favorite memory. Afterward, the teacher reads students' journal entries. Below is an excerpt from one student's journal entry.

My most favorite memory is when I goed to the zoo with my parents. It was a hot sumer day but i still had fun. We seen many animals like: liones bare elefant monkey and zebra. The monkies climb all over their house and one jump off of a tree. The liones and bare was mostly sleeped. I seen all the zebra eat grass and the elefant taked a bath with there trunk. It was a very fun day at the zoo!

5. Based upon the journal entry above, this student likely requires targeted intervention in which of the following areas related to morphemic analysis?

a. Derivational morphemes
b. Prefixes and suffixes
c. Inflectional morphemes
d. Root words

6. Based upon the journal entry above, which of the following targeted interventions would be most effective in developing this student's morphemic analysis skills?

a. Having the student participate in a word-building activity focused on manipulating word endings
b. Implementing peer-editing activities after writing assignments to provide the student with constructive feedback
c. Conducting weekly spelling tests focused on multisyllabic words with prefixes and suffixes
d. Encouraging the student to engage in daily self-selected reading to promote exposure to new vocabulary in a variety of contexts

7. As part of a lesson focusing on the letter *A* and its corresponding sound (/a/), a kindergarten teacher plans to engage students with various activities. Initially, students will be shown images of objects whose names begin with the /a/ sound. Then, students will practice articulating the /a/ sound while identifying additional objects sharing the same initial sound. Students will then have the opportunity to practice writing the letter *A* while vocalizing its associated sound. Considering the importance of reinforcing the alphabetic principle, which additional activity would best complement and solidify understanding of the letter *A* and its corresponding sound?

a. Providing students with a list of words containing the letter *A* and asking them to identify the vowels in each word
b. Playing a game where students match pictures of objects with their corresponding initial letter sounds
c. Having students practice counting syllables in words that start with the letter *A*
d. Asking students to draw pictures of animals that have the letter *A* in their name

8. A fifth-grade teacher is planning a literature unit in which students will read the novel *Charlotte's Web* over the course of several weeks. Prior to beginning the unit, the teacher assigns students to complete the following activity:

Directions: Read through each statement below. Decide whether you agree with each statement (A) or disagree (D). After reading the book, revisit each statement and mark whether your original answers were correct or incorrect.

1. Real friendship can be found despite differences. _____
2. Spending too much time around animals can be a bad thing. _____
3. Farm life is often difficult and unforgiving and is not for everyone. _____
4. Small miracles occur every day if you just look for them. _____
5. Working together helps everyone achieve their goals. _____
6. Change is often difficult and is almost never a positive thing. _____

The above assignment is an example of which pre-reading activity aimed at promoting students' literary analysis skills?

a. An anticipation guide
b. A KWL chart
c. Think-read-share
d. A story map

9. A second-grade teacher is planning a group activity in which students will work to sort short texts according to whether they are intended to explain, inform, or persuade based on the vocabulary used in each passage. This activity is most likely intended to begin developing students' understanding of which of the following concepts?

a. Text structure
b. Graphic organizing
c. Academic language
d. Author's purpose

10. A fourth-grade teacher is planning a reader's theater activity to promote prosodic reading skills and reading fluency among students. Small groups will be assigned by proficiency levels, and students will be assigned to act out a familiar play suited to their abilities. Throughout the week, students will have the opportunity to practice their play and will be encouraged to focus on expression, intonation, tone, and inflection. Which of the following additional strategies could the teacher incorporate to further modify the activity to align with varying reading fluency levels?

a. Instructing students to read the play independently before beginning the reader's theater activity to familiarize them with the text
b. Allowing students to select their preferred roles within the play to enhance engagement and confidence in reading
c. Having students complete self-assessment activities after each practice session to reflect on their progress
d. Implementing guided reading sessions with each group to support struggling readers in mastering their lines and improving overall comprehension and fluency

11. A second-grade student who exhibits difficulty in distinguishing individual sounds within words likely requires additional support in which of the following areas related to early literacy?

a. Understanding concepts of print and sentence structure
b. Recognizing high-frequency sight words
c. Developing fluency in oral reading
d. Enhancing phonological awareness and sound processing skills

12. A second-grade teacher is planning an activity in which students will work with a partner and use syllable cards to create new words. Considering students' abilities in syllabication at this grade level, which of the following sets of syllable cards would be most suitable for this age group?

a. *Cr-unch, st-and, bro-ken, sh-ut*
b. *Ap-ron, dis-like, pre-pare, drum-stick*
c. *Bike, run, jump, sk-ate*
d. *Un-hap-pi-ness, un-break-able, dis-re-spect-ful, mul-ti-play-er*

13. In a first-grade classroom, the teacher conducts weekly word study activities to evaluate students' progress in phonics. For one week, students are assigned to spell words encompassing different phonics elements. The subsequent week, they receive the same list of words to spell again. Upon comparing the students' spellings across both assessments, the teacher observes one student's performance. Based on the information presented in the chart provided, which phonics element does the student still struggle with?

Spelling List	Student Spelling (First Assessment)	Student Spelling (Second Assessment)
frog	frag	frog
chat	cat	chat
sting	stin	sting
grain	--	gran
boat	--	boot
here	her	here

a. Long vowel sounds and vowel patterns
b. Consonant blends
c. Silent consonants
d. Silent *e* rule

14. A third-grade teacher is planning a unit in which the class will read a multi-chapter piece of historical fiction. Throughout the unit, the teacher wants to focus on supporting students' academic vocabulary development. Which of the following strategies would be most effective in achieving this goal?

a. Supplementing the text with a word bank of key vocabulary terms for students to reference as they read
b. Grouping students to participate in literature circles to facilitate discussion about the reading passage
c. Differentiating the complexity of the text to accommodate varying reading proficiency levels
d. Leading class discussions about the historical context of the text and the significance of new vocabulary words as it relates to that context

15. A kindergarten teacher notices that several students in her class struggle with recognizing rhyming words during shared reading activities. Despite repeated exposure to rhyming books and songs, these students often have difficulty identifying words that rhyme. Which of the following instructional strategies would be most effective for addressing this specific challenge and promoting rhyming awareness?

a. Providing explicit instruction on letter-sound correspondences through phonics lessons
b. Engaging students in daily oral language activities to practice identifying beginning sounds
c. Incorporating nursery rhymes and rhyming games into daily literacy instruction
d. Introducing sight words through flashcard drills and repeated exposure exercises

16. Guiding students in locating clue words within a text to determine the meaning of unfamiliar vocabulary is an example of a strategy aimed at developing which of the following skills related to reading comprehension and fluency?

a. Structural analysis
b. Critical analysis
c. Contextual analysis
d. Automaticity

17. Which of the following requires the highest level of proficiency related to morphological awareness?

a. Using knowledge of common affixes, including prefixes and suffixes, to form multisyllabic words when writing
b. Accurately decoding a list of vocabulary terms that share the same base word
c. Identifying the initial, middle, and final sounds of multisyllabic words
d. Recognizing similar structural patterns within a word family

18. A third-grade teacher incorporates weekly word study activities into the literacy curriculum. These activities include exploring word families, analyzing spelling patterns, and applying phonics rules in various contexts. Students are encouraged to create word banks, engage in word sorts, and practice spelling words both in isolation and within sentences. Which of the following aspects of literacy development is most directly targeted by these instructional activities?

a. Developing phonemic awareness skills through sound manipulation exercises
b. Improving spelling proficiency by applying phonics knowledge to spell words accurately
c. Strengthening decoding skills through practice with sight words and high-frequency words
d. Enhancing vocabulary acquisition by exploring word origins and meanings

19. During a phonics lesson for beginning readers, a first-grade teacher introduces the silent *e* rule. The teacher explains that when a word ends with a vowel-consonant-silent *e* pattern, the vowel usually says its long sound. Which of the following instructional strategies would be most effective for reinforcing this phonics rule?

a. Providing students with flashcards of high-frequency words
b. Having students practice segmenting CVCe words into individual phonemes
c. Encouraging students to memorize common sight words
d. Asking students to read sentences aloud with expression

20. In a second-grade classroom, a teacher wants to promote students' understanding during an upcoming unit about goods and services by calling upon their prior knowledge. The class includes several English Language Learners of varying proficiency levels. Which of the following strategies would be most effective in achieving the teacher's goal?

a. Pairing ELL students with native English-speaking classmates that can provide scaffolding and assistance
b. Providing pictures of familiar goods and services and prompting students to categorize them
c. Incorporating gestures and specific body language during direct instruction to help with clarification
d. Displaying an anchor chart in the classroom that includes new vocabulary from the unit

21. In a prekindergarten classroom, the teacher conducts daily read-aloud sessions with the class. While doing so, she brings students' attention to the book's title, author, and illustrator, as well as uses her finger to guide students as she reads aloud from the text. Which of the following best describes how these practices contribute to developing students' foundational reading fluency?

a. By exposing students to the elements of print and book features
b. By encouraging students to focus primarily on the overall meaning of the text rather than individual words
c. By ensuring students remain engaged and focused throughout the read-aloud session
d. By prompting students to ask open-ended questions about the text

22. A kindergarten teacher uses magnet tiles to spell a word and prompts students to read it aloud. Then, the teacher swaps one letter tile for a different one and asks students to recognize the new word. For instance, the teacher might spell out *can* and then switch the *c* for a *p* to form *pan* and asks the students to read the new word. Which of the following skills is the teacher most likely trying to develop in students through this strategy?

a. Alliteration
b. Phoneme substitution
c. Decoding and encoding
d. Alphabetic principle

23. Which of the following actions by a first-grade student best exemplifies proficiency in phonological awareness?

a. Listening to the word *blink*, segmenting its phonemes, and then substituting one phoneme to create a new word
b. Identifying the initial phoneme in the word *giraffe*, isolating it from the rest of the word, and articulating it orally
c. Clapping syllables in the word *elephant*, counting them accurately, and then blending the syllables back together to articulate the word
d. Recognizing that the words *plum* and *glum* share the same final phoneme, explaining how changing the phoneme affects the meaning of the words, and providing another example of a pair of words that share the same final phoneme

24. A third-grade teacher is planning a structural analysis activity in which students will use magnetic tiles to construct words from a list that is read aloud. Considering the structural analysis abilities of third-grade students, which of the following sets of words would be most appropriate for students of this age group?

a. Stretch, peach, bounce, climb
b. Jump, fall, soak, beach
c. Preheated, disliking, unkindness, pre-reading
d. Salty, walking, heavy, apples

25. A second-grade teacher is planning literacy instruction with the intention of developing students' prosodic reading skills. Which of the following activities would be most effective in achieving this goal?

a. Conducting a whole-class echo reading of a poem
b. Having students work in pairs to collaboratively read a text aloud
c. Implementing individual read-aloud sessions with students to gauge prosodic reading skills
d. Having students take turns reading aloud from a work of nonfiction

26. A third-grade teacher is planning a unit in which students will work in small, guided reading groups to explore a work of fictional literature. The class consists of students with varying levels of reading comprehension, and the teacher organizes groups based on student ability. Which of the following additional measures should the teacher consider to further support reading comprehension development for all students?

a. Allow students to choose their own reading based on personal preference
b. Differentiate the complexity of the text according to skill level
c. Incorporate pre- and post-reading activities to encourage active reading
d. Assign students to record their thoughts, opinions, and questions about the text in a reader's response journal

Refer to the following for question 27:

During a language arts lesson, a fourth-grade teacher assigns students to read from a fictional text. While reading, one student encounters the sentence, "As she walked silently through the mystical ancient forest, she couldn't help but wonder how she would ever return to the hustle and bustle of her modern life." Unsure of the words *ancient* and *modern*, the student skips them and continues reading with the hope of grasping the main idea of the text despite their lack of understanding of these unfamiliar terms.

27. Based on the information in the above scenario, this student would likely benefit from a targeted review of which of the following concepts related to contextual analysis?

a. Decoding and encoding
b. Synonyms and antonyms
c. Homophones and sight words
d. Morphology and sentence structure

28. While reading a fictional text, a fifth-grade student encounters the word *aesthetic* and asks for clarification. Which of the following responses by the teacher would most effectively prompt the student to use context clues for deciphering the meaning of the word?

a. "Look at the illustrations. Do you see any clues that might tell you what the word means?"
b. "Does the word have any prefixes or suffixes that could tell us the meaning?"
c. "Can you make an educated guess about what the word means?"
d. "Have you seen any words similar to this one before?"

29. A kindergarten teacher is implementing a phonics-based reading program to build foundational literacy skills. The teacher has noticed that some students in the class are struggling to understand letter-sound correspondence. In keeping with developmentally appropriate practices, which of the following strategies would be most effective in addressing this issue and promoting the development of early reading skills?

a. Providing these students with small-group instruction focused on letter sounds
b. Introducing new letters and letter sounds one or a few at a time
c. Implementing activities to reinforce understanding of the alphabetic principle
d. Conducting daily read-alouds to continuously review letter sounds in context

30. A first-grade teacher is planning her literacy instruction for the upcoming week. She wants to ensure her students develop strong phonics skills to support their reading development. As she considers different instructional approaches, she reflects on the evidence-based practices she learned about in her professional development sessions. Which of the following approaches would be most effective for the teacher to incorporate into her instruction to achieve this goal?

a. Implementing a whole language approach to reading instruction
b. Encouraging students to memorize high-frequency words through repetitive exposure
c. Employing spelling bees and word games to reinforce phonemic awareness
d. Providing explicit phonics instruction using systematic, sequential phonics programs

31. A group of students in a fourth-grade classroom is consistently falling below benchmarks for reading fluency development when compared to their grade-level peers. These students meet twice a week for focused fluency instruction with a reading specialist. This is an example of which type of intervention related to language and literacy development?

a. Tier I response to intervention (RTI)
b. Tier II response to intervention (RTI)
c. Tier III response to intervention (RTI)
d. Individualized education program (IEP)

32. During a literacy lesson, a first-grade teacher introduces a list of high-frequency words for students to learn. Which of the following instructional strategies would be most effective in helping students develop automatic recognition of these words?

a. Providing students with lists of words to sound out phonetically
b. Having students practice writing the words in cursive
c. Encouraging students to read the words in context within sentences
d. Asking students to create flashcards with definitions of each word

33. To enhance decoding skills in first-grade students, a teacher uses a method where students clap out each syllable of multisyllabic words. Which of the following additional strategies would be most effective in promoting the development of this skill for children in this age group?

a. Having students build multisyllabic words using letter tiles
b. Asking students to identify the beginning and ending sounds in multisyllabic words
c. Having students segment multisyllabic words into individual phonemes
d. Creating a vocabulary word wall centered on multisyllabic words

Refer to the following for questions 34–35:

As part of a new literacy unit, a kindergarten teacher displays the following chart on the class word wall:

-all Family	
Ball	Hall
Call	Fall
Small	Wall
All	Tall

34. Based on the information in the chart above, this strategy is likely intended to develop which of the following skills related to reading fluency?

a. Blending and segmenting
b. Automaticity
c. Onset and rime
d. Accuracy and rate

35. Which of the following additional instructional strategies could the teacher implement to reinforce the concepts introduced by the displayed chart and further develop students' reading fluency skills?

a. Including the words displayed on the chart into a weekly spelling list
b. Implementing a word-building activity using magnetic tiles based on the chart
c. Leading a choral reading activity in which the class reads aloud together from the chart
d. Having students practice tracing each word on dotted-line paper before writing them independently

36. During a phonics lesson for second-grade students, a teacher notices that one student is struggling with identifying words containing consonant blends. To provide targeted support, which instructional strategy would be most effective for helping this student develop proficiency with this concept?

a. Implementing a word sorting activity focused on sorting words with and without consonant blends
b. Providing the student with flashcards of high-frequency words for memorization
c. Having the student repeatedly practice writing words with consonant blends
d. Implementing a sentence dictation exercise that includes words with consonant blends

37. Following a successful unit on inflectional morphemes, a fourth-grade teacher conducts a word family exploration to introduce the concept of derivational morphemes to demonstrate how these linguistic units change the meaning and part of speech of root words. Which of the following subsequent activities would be most effective in reinforcing understanding of this concept?

a. Guiding students in clapping out the syllables of multimorphemic words
b. Having students create word matrices in which they attach prefixes and suffixes to root words
c. Incorporating new vocabulary words with derivational morphemes in a weekly spelling test list
d. Having students circle the root word from a list of multisyllabic and multimorphemic words

38. Which of the following scenarios best exemplifies an effective strategy for developing students' understanding of the author's viewpoint in informational texts?

a. Providing students with an outline template to record the main idea and supporting details in the text
b. Supplementing the text with visual aids to help with clarification, such as diagrams and illustrations
c. Assigning students to respond to a series of reflective prompts in their reader's response journals
d. Tasking students to complete a Venn diagram as they read two articles on the same topic

39. A first-grade teacher is planning a lesson centered on retelling major events from a fictional text. Which of the following scaffolds should the teacher consider implementing to promote student success most effectively during this lesson?

a. Instructing students to summarize the text in their own words
b. Assigning students to roles from the story to act out in a reader's theatre
c. Providing students with graphic organizers, such as a story map, to complete while reading
d. Having students complete an anticipation guide as a pre-reading strategy

40. During a literacy assessment for kindergarten students, the teacher observes that many children can identify individual letters and their corresponding sounds. Which of the following additional skills demonstrated by these children would best indicate readiness to begin instruction in decoding multisyllabic words?

a. Recognizing and naming common high-frequency words, such as *the* and *and* in context during shared reading activities
b. Segmenting spoken words into individual phonemes and blending them back together to form the word
c. Demonstrating morphological awareness through the recognition of prefixes, suffixes, and root words
d. Demonstrating knowledge of syllable division patterns and using this knowledge to decode unfamiliar multisyllabic words

41. In the early elementary classroom, reading instruction should focus largely on developing which of the following foundational skills?

a. Sight word recognition
b. Prosodic reading
c. Letter-sound correspondence
d. Oral language proficiency

42. After reading a fictional story aloud to the class, a kindergarten teacher organizes students into small groups and asks them to sort a set of picture cards to correspond with events from the story. This strategy is likely intended to promote which of the following skills related to reading comprehension?

a. Rote memorization
b. Sequencing
c. High-frequency sight word recognition
d. Automaticity

43. A fifth-grade teacher is planning a social studies unit on European colonization between 1400 and 1800 that will incorporate multiple informational texts. During the unit, the teacher aims to focus on developing students' ability to formulate connections between these texts. Which of the following styles of graphic organizer would be most effective in supporting students' achievement of this goal?

a. A timeline
b. A KWL chart
c. A Venn diagram
d. An outline

44. According to Scarborough's reading rope model, which of the following statements is true about reading fluency development?

a. The rate of reading fluency development is largely determined by oral language skills prior to beginning school.
b. Reading fluency occurs when the phonological processor, the context processor, the meaning processor, and the orthographic processor work together to decode words in a text.
c. Reading fluency is developed through a combination of factors related to language comprehension and word recognition.
d. Systematic and sequential phonics instruction is essential to establishing a foundation for reading fluency development.

45. A second-grade teacher plans to evaluate students' decoding skills by assessing them as they read aloud from a list of high-frequency sight words. In addition to these words, which of the following should this teacher also consider including to ensure a thorough and comprehensive assessment of students' decoding abilities?

a. Blended syllables
b. Multisyllabic words
c. Nonsense words
d. Academic vocabulary

46. A fifth-grade teacher assigns students to independently read a passage from a work of fictional literature and complete various annotations as they do so. Below is an example of one student's work.

> **Directions**: As you read, highlight any unfamiliar vocabulary words. Underline any key details or information. Add questions throughout the text as you go along.
>
> "Before I was two years old a circumstance happened which I have never forgotten. It was early in the spring; there had been a little frost in the night, and a light mist still hung over the woods and meadows. I and the other colts were feeding at the lower part of the field when we heard, quite in the distance, what sounded like the cry of dogs. The oldest of the colts raised his head, pricked his ears, and said, "There are the hounds!" and immediately cantered off, followed by the rest of us to the upper part of the field, where we could look over the hedge and see several fields beyond.
>
> (Were they afraid of the dogs?)
>
> My mother and an old riding horse of our master's were also standing near, and seemed to know all about it. (What did they know about?)
>
> "They have found a hare." said my mother, "and if they come this way we shall see the hunt."
>
> And soon the dogs were all tearing down the field of young wheat next to ours. I never heard such a noise as they made. They did not bark, nor howl, nor whine, but kept on a "yo! Yo, o, o! Yo! Yo, o, o!" at the top of their voices. After them came a number of men on horseback, some of them in green coats, all galloping as fast as they could. (Where did the men come from? What were they going to do?)
>
> The old horse snorted and looked eagerly after them, and we young colts wanted to be galloping with them, but they were soon away into the fields lower down; here it seemed as if they had come to a stand; the dogs left off barking, and ran about every way with their noses to the ground.
>
> Sewell, Anna. *Black Beauty* . Jarrold & Sons , 1877. Pp. 12-13

Based on the information in the example above, the teacher is most likely implementing which of the following instructional strategies to promote reading comprehension and critical analysis skills?

a. Guided reading
b. Close reading
c. Chunking
d. Read-pair-share

47. A fourth-grade teacher is preparing a lesson in which students will read an informational text about agricultural practices. During the lesson, the teacher aims to promote comprehension and analysis by calling upon students' prior knowledge and promoting active engagement with the text. Which of the following pre-reading strategies would be most effective in achieving this goal?

a. Leading a whole-class discussion about agricultural methods used throughout different regions
b. Having students complete a KWL chart about agricultural practices
c. Providing direct instruction on key information related to the text
d. Assigning students to complete a Venn diagram to compare and contrast ancient and modern agricultural practices

48. In a second-grade classroom, a student is struggling with mastering high-frequency words. Despite numerous practice sessions and interventions, the student continues to face difficulty in recognizing these common words. The teacher is seeking the most effective intervention to support the student's development in this area. Which of the following interventions would be most effective in addressing this difficulty?

a. Providing additional phonics instruction focusing on letter-sound correspondences
b. Encouraging the student to practice handwriting skills with high-frequency words using various fonts and styles
c. Creating mnemonic devices or visual aids to assist the student in memorizing high-frequency words
d. Integrating high-frequency words into meaningful context through guided reading sessions

49. A fifth-grade teacher is working to build students' evaluative reading comprehension skills. The teacher plans to have students read an informational text, and then respond to a series of prompts in their reader's response journals. Which of the following questions would be most suitable for developing students' ability to read evaluatively?

a. "Do you agree or disagree with the author's point of view? Why?"
b. "How did the author's language impact the overall tone of the text?"
c. "What is one new thing you learned from reading the text? What is one thing you still do not understand?"
d. "Identify the central idea of the text. What are some key details that support the central idea?"

50. Which of the following scenarios best illustrates a foundational understanding of concepts of print?

a. A kindergarten teacher reads a story aloud to her students, pointing to each word as she reads.
b. A first-grade student demonstrates an understanding of left-to-right progression while reading a book independently.
c. A preschooler identifies the cover, title, and author of a book during a shared reading activity.
d. A second-grade student recognizes that the word *dog* starts with the letter *d* during a phonics lesson.

51. A fourth-grade teacher wants to encourage students to incorporate academic language into their writing. Which of the following initial strategies would be most effective in achieving this goal?

a. Providing students with a list of sentence starters to use as a reference
b. Displaying academic vocabulary words on a class word wall
c. Conducting sentence dictation exercises that include academic vocabulary words
d. Providing students with sentence frames to guide students in their writing

Refer to the following for question 52:

Prior to beginning a social studies unit focused on the United States Constitution, a fourth-grade teacher implements an introductory activity that includes several vocabulary words related to the unit, their definitions, and examples of their usage in sentences.

52. Which of the following best describes how this approach contributes to promoting students' grasp of academic language?

a. Prompting students to identify these vocabulary words as they progress through the unit
b. Providing direct instruction about key terms related to the upcoming unit
c. Contextualizing new vocabulary to promote understanding and retention of academic language
d. Encouraging rote memorization of new vocabulary terms to facilitate easy recall

53. A fourth-grade teacher is planning instruction focused on developing students' ability to summarize informational texts. One student in the class is identified as an intermediate level English language learner. To scaffold the lesson, the teacher plans to simplify the complexity of the assigned text. Which of the following additional supports should the teacher consider implementing to support this student's linguistic needs?

a. Providing the student with an outline of the text that highlights main ideas and key points
b. Having the student complete a Venn diagram to compare and contrast different perspectives in the text
c. Providing the student with summary frames to complete after reading
d. Allowing the student option to orally summarize the text

54. A third grade teacher is planning literacy instruction with the intention of developing students' inferential reading skills. As part of one lesson, students will independently read from a work of fictional literature. Which of the following supplemental activities would be most effective in scaffolding this lesson to support the development of inferential reading skills?

a. Assigning students to complete an anticipation guide as a pre-reading activity
b. Pairing struggling students with others that can provide assistance
c. Organizing students into small groups and differentiating the complexity of the text
d. Having students complete a story map as they read the fictional passage

55. After having the class read a fictional short story, a second-grade teacher plans to reinforce students' comprehension through four activity stations that each focus on a specific aspect of understanding. At the first station, students will sequence picture cards to correspond with events from the story. At the second station, students will be tasked with matching word cards with their definitions from key vocabulary from the story. In the third station, students will participate in a short reader's theatre to reenact key events of the story. Finally, the fourth station will consist of a scavenger hunt in which students will look for key objects related to the story throughout the classroom. In addition to differentiating learning, which of the following best describes how this approach promotes the development of reading comprehension skills?

a. Allowing opportunities for student choice in learning activities
b. Scaffolding learning activities to align with varying reading comprehension skill levels
c. Providing students with kinesthetic learning opportunities
d. Facilitating discussion through collaborative learning activities

56. A third-grade teacher has a goal of improving students' reading comprehension skills by promoting active engagement with texts. As part of this effort, the teacher plans to implement reader response journals during an upcoming unit in which students will read from a short fictional novel. Which of the following prompts would be most effective to include in this activity to achieve the teacher's goal?

a. "Describe the setting in which the story takes place."
b. "Do you agree with how the main character solved their problem?"
c. "If you were the main character, what would you have done differently? How would this have changed the story?"
d. "Were there any vocabulary words that you did not understand in the story? How can you find their meanings?"

57. According to the four-part processing model, which of the following should reading instruction incorporate to promote reading comprehension and fluency skill development most effectively?

a. Phonological, orthographic, context, and meaning processors
b. Visual, auditory, interpersonal, and kinesthetic learning opportunities
c. Direct instruction, collaborative learning, student choice, and self-reflection opportunities
d. Visual aids, differentiated instruction, scaffolded learning activities, and formative assessments

58. A teacher is planning a phonemic awareness activity to assess students' ability to segment phonemes orally. Which of the following words would pose the greatest challenge in segmenting individual phonemes?

a. Trunk
b. Spoon
c. Globe
d. Crunch

Refer to the following for questions 59–60:

A third-grade teacher has students read from the following passage about the life cycle of plants and answer corresponding comprehension questions. The passage and an example of one student's work appear below.

Directions: Read the passage about the plant life cycle. Then, answer the comprehension questions below.

Just like humans and animals, plants are alive and experience many changes throughout their lifetime. During the plant life cycle, plants pass through many stages, beginning from a tiny seed to a fully grown plant that can make new seeds. Knowing about the plant life cycle is important for everyone from botanists to gardeners because it helps us understand how plants grow, how to take care of them, and what they need to thrive.

The first stage of the plant life cycle is called the seed stage. The inside of seeds has everything that a plant needs to start growing. Once seeds are planted in soil, they need water and sunlight to sprout.

The second stage in the plant life cycle is called the germination stage. During this stage, the root pushes out of the seed and begins to grow down into the soil. Above ground, you will begin to see a small young plant beginning to grow upward.

After the germination stage, plants begin the seedling stage, where they start to form leaves and grow taller. During this stage, plants must receive lots of sun, water, and nutrients from the soil so that it can grow tall and strong.

The fourth stage of the plant life cycle is called the maturity stage. During this stage, plants grow much taller and stronger, and can begin producing their own flowers and seeds.

During the fifth and last stage of the plant life cycle, the plant's seeds are dispersed and land in a new location. The plant life cycle begins again when the new seeds are planted and find a new place to grow.

Understanding the plant life cycle helps us understand the world around us, why plants are important, and what they need to survive.

Comprehension questions:

a. What is the central idea of the passage?

The life cycle of plants

b. What are the four stages of the plant life cycle?

Seed, germination, seedling, maturity, and seed spreading

c. Describe what happens in each phase of the plant life cycle.

First seeds are planted. Then they need water. They can grow both up and down. Finally they can make new seeds.

d. Why is it important to know about the life cycle of plants?

So we can grow our own food

59. Based on the information presented above, this student likely requires additional support related to which of the following areas related to comprehending and analyzing informational texts?

a. Recalling the main idea
b. Summarizing the text
c. Comparing and contrasting differing viewpoints
d. Recalling key details

60. Based on the information presented, which of the following strategies would likely be most effective in supporting this student's development of reading comprehension and analysis skills of informational texts?

a. Guiding the student through annotating the text as they read
b. Providing the student with a story map to record important information from the text
c. Simplifying the text to align with the student's current reading comprehension and analysis skill level
d. Prompting the student to reflect on their reading in a reader's response journal

61. A fifth-grade teacher is planning a lesson in which students will read from the following passage:

> "The bird put his tiny head on one side and looked up at him with his soft bright eye which was like a black dewdrop. He seemed quite familiar and not the least afraid. He hopped about and pecked the earth briskly, looking for seeds and insects. It actually gave Mary a queer feeling in her heart, because he was so pretty and cheerful and seemed so like a person. He had a tiny plump body and a delicate beak, and slender delicate legs.
>
> "Will he always come when you call him?" she asked almost in a whisper.
>
> "Aye, that he will. I've knowed him ever since he was a fledgling. He come out of th' nest in th' other garden an' when first he flew over th' wall he was too weak to fly back for a few days an' we got friendly. When he went over th' wall again th' rest of th' brood was gone an' he was lonely an' he come back to me."
>
> "What kind of a bird is he?" Mary asked.
>
> "Doesn't tha' know? He's a robin redbreast an' they're th' friendliest, curiousest birds alive. They're almost as friendly as dogs—if you know how to get on with 'em. Watch him peckin' about there an' lookin' round at us now an' again. He knows we're talkin' about him.""
>
> Burnett, Frances H. *The Secret Garden*. Phillips Publishing Company, 1911. Pp. 48-49.

Based on the passage above, which of the following concepts should the teacher review prior to beginning the lesson to promote students' comprehension?

a. Figurative language
b. Point of view
c. Imagery and symbolism
d. Alliteration

62. During a whole-class activity, a first-grade teacher has students take turns reading aloud from a piece of children's fictional literature. Throughout the activity, the teacher noticed that a few students faced challenges with reading fluently, as they were hesitant and appeared to lack confidence. When reading, the students spoke softly, read at a slower pace than their peers, and had difficulty decoding unfamiliar words. Which of the following alternative approaches would be most effective in supporting the development of reading fluency for these students?

a. Providing the students with a copy of the text prior to beginning the activity
b. Engaging the whole class in a choral reading of the text
c. Allowing the students to choose which parts of the text they feel confident reading aloud
d. Providing the students with a simplified version of the text to align with their current reading fluency abilities

63. A kindergarten teacher is planning literacy instruction with the intention of incorporating evidence-based practices to support beginning reading skills. As part of this initiative, the teacher has students participate in a spelling activity using a list of high-frequency sight words that are read aloud. The teacher then analyzes students' performance by categorizing the results of the activity based on the following criteria:

a. Accurate recognition of high-frequency words
b. Incorrect spelling of high-frequency words due to orthographic processing difficulties
c. Incorrect spelling of high-frequency words due to phonemic awareness difficulties
d. Incorrect spelling of high-frequency words due to code-based difficulties (e.g., phonics knowledge)

According to the data collected, which student's response is categorized correctly in the following table?

Student	High-Frequency Word	Student's Response	Category
1	the	the	B
2	said	sed	C
3	here	her	A
4	come	kum	D

a. Student 1
b. Student 2
c. Student 3
d. Student 4

64. A fourth-grade teacher has students individually read aloud from the following passage:

> During the confusion and bewilderment of the second day Mary hid herself in the nursery and was forgotten by everyone. Nobody thought of her, nobody wanted her, and strange things happened of which she knew nothing. Mary alternately cried and slept through the hours. She only knew that people were ill and that she heard mysterious and frightening sounds. Once she crept into the dining-room and found it empty, though a partly finished meal was on the table and chairs and plates looked as if they had been hastily pushed back when the diners rose suddenly for some reason.
>
> Burnett, Frances H. *The Secret Garden*. The Phillips Publishing Company, 1911.

As each student reads aloud, the teacher records students' progress. Below is an example of data collected from one student's reading of the passage:

Total Words in Passage: 100
Time allotted: One minute
Total Words Read: 100
Errors: 11
Words Correct Per Minute (WCPM): 89

Based on the information above, the teacher is most likely assessing which of the following skills related to reading fluency?

a. Prosody
b. Decoding skills
c. Orthographic processing
d. Automaticity

65. A second-grade teacher is preparing an end-of-unit summative assessment in English Language Arts. Which of the following steps should the teacher take to ensure that the assessment is both valid and effective?

a. Ensure that the assessment as well as instruction, learning activities, and formative assessments align with state and district academic standards
b. Implement appropriate accommodations and supports to align with individual student needs
c. Differentiate assessment formats to allow for student choice in demonstration of learning
d. Utilize a norm-referenced assessment approach to measure student mastery in relation to other grade-level peers

66. A first-grade teacher has been crafting activities focused on blending individual sounds to decode words. This approach is most beneficial in developing which of the following foundational reading skills?

a. Phonemic awareness
b. Phonological processing
c. Orthographic processing
d. Sight word recognition

67. Which of the following scenarios best demonstrates strong orthographic processing skills?

a. A second-grade student correctly identifying misspelled words from a spelling list
b. A kindergarten student utilizing inventive spelling to sound out unknown vocabulary words
c. A pre-school student identifying the beginning sound of each picture in a set of flash cards
d. A second-grade student accurately attaching prefixes and suffixes to form multisyllabic words

Refer to the following for questions 68–69:

A sixth-grade teacher is preparing a science lesson in which students will read from the following passage:

> Rocks are all around us, from our backyards and playgrounds to mountaintops and even the ocean floor. Rocks are an important part of forming landscapes, supporting ecosystems, and providing resources for many human activities. Rocks can be categorized as igneous, sedimentary, or metamorphic, and each can be recognized by its distinct features.
>
> Igneous rocks are created when lava cools off and becomes solid. When this occurs underground, it forms intrusive igneous rocks. Lava that reaches the Earth's surface, such as after a volcanic eruption, cools quickly and forms extrusive igneous rocks. These rocks usually have a glass-like appearance and can contain minerals such as quartz, feldspar, and biotite.
>
> Sedimentary rocks form from sediments, which include pieces of other rocks and the remains of plants and animals. Over a very long period of time, these sediments compress together to form sedimentary rocks, such as limestone, sandstone, and shale. You can often find fossils and layers in these rocks that can tell us a lot about Earth's history.
>
> Metamorphic rocks are created when rocks are exposed to high heat and pressure within the Earth's crust. This causes the rocks to go through physical and chemical changes that form them into metamorphic rocks. Some examples include marble, slate, and quartzite. Metamorphic rocks typically appear layered and can contain minerals such as garnet, kyanite, and corundum.
>
> Knowing the characteristics of different kinds of rocks and how they are formed helps us learn about the Earth's history. Each type of rock provides valuable information about how our planet was shaped over many millions of years.

68. Considering the nature of the passage above, which of the following styles of graphic organizer would be most effective for promoting students' reading comprehension?

a. A Venn diagram
b. A KWL chart
c. A timeline
d. An outline

69. Which of the following additional supplemental supports should this teacher consider implementing to further strengthen students' comprehension of the text?

a. Creating multiple versions of the text that vary in complexity to align with different levels of reading comprehension skills
b. Incorporating images of each kind of rock mentioned in the passage
c. Providing students with a word bank for reference at the end of the text
d. Assigning a series of comprehension questions to correspond with the text

70. During a spelling lesson for first-grade students, a teacher introduces the concept of consonant digraphs. Which of the following words best exemplifies a consonant digraph?

a. Bat
b. Flow
c. Run
d. Ship

71. After conducting a series of formative assessments, a first-grade teacher notices that many students in the class are struggling with phonemic awareness skills, particularly related to blending and segmenting sounds. Which of the following evidence-based instructional strategies would be most effective in addressing this issue to improve students' phonemic awareness skills?

a. Displaying multimorphemic vocabulary containing blends on a classroom word wall and reviewing them daily
b. Reviewing high-frequency sight words as a whole class using flash cards
c. Organizing students into small groups and implementing songs and rhyming games into instruction
d. Having students practice tapping out the syllables of multisyllabic words

72. A kindergarten teacher is preparing a unit on weather patterns. Planned activities include reading weather-related stories, creating drawings of different kinds of weather, singing weather-themed songs, as well as observing and logging daily weather on the class calendar. These activities align with which of the following instructional approaches for promoting the acquisition of academic vocabulary?

a. Direct instruction
b. Student-led learning
c. Differentiated instruction
d. Thematic unit

73. As part of a science unit on energy resources, a third-grade teacher quizzes students on several vocabulary words related to the unit. Below are the quiz results from one student in the class:

Spelling Word		Definitions	
1.	Renewable	a.	Energy that comes from flowing water
2.	Nonrenewable	b.	Energy that comes from wind
3.	Geothermal	c.	Energy that comes from sunlight
4.	Hydropower	d.	Energy that comes from burning fossils of plants and animals
5.	Biomass	e.	Non-replenishable energy that comes from finite resources
6.	Solar	f.	Energy that comes from plants and animals
7.	Wind	g.	Replenishable energy that comes from natural resources
8.	Fossil Fuel	h.	Energy that comes from heat found under the Earth's surface

Student's Responses:

1. A
2. G
3. F
4. H
5. E
6. C
7. B
8. D

Based on the student's performance, which of the following strategies would be most effective in supporting this student's development in understanding academic language?

a. Having the student review their errors and self-correct their quiz
b. Pairing the student with another that can help
c. Leading a whole-class vocabulary review game before the next vocabulary quiz
d. Implementing a targeted review of morphology concepts

74. A third-grade teacher aims to enhance students' acquisition and comprehension of academic language across subject areas. Which of the following approaches would be most effective in achieving this goal?

a. Incorporating vocabulary from different subject areas into weekly spelling tests
b. Integrating elements of language arts and literacy instruction into other content areas
c. Displaying new academic vocabulary on a class word wall and referring to it daily
d. Having students keep daily reflection journals to document their learning and areas for improvement

75. Which of the following instructional practices would be most effective for developing phonemic awareness in early readers, specifically focusing on the ability to manipulate individual sounds within words?

a. Teaching students to quickly recognize sight words
b. Providing opportunities for students to segment words into individual sounds and blend individual sounds to form words
c. Encouraging students to infer the meaning of new words from surrounding text
d. Teaching students to identify syllable patterns in multisyllabic words

76. During circle time a kindergarten teacher displays a large poster with a short poem written in big, clear letters. As the teacher reads the poem aloud, she points to each word in sequence. Which of the following best describes the primary benefit of this activity for the students' emergent reading development?

a. Improving their ability to recognize sight words
b. Reinforcing their understanding of phonological awareness
c. Enhancing their understanding of print directionality and word spacing
d. Developing their appreciation for rhyming patterns in language

77. Which of the following best describes why having students skim an informational text as a prereading strategy is effective in promoting overall comprehension and analysis?

a. It provides students with a general sense of the text's structure, main ideas, and key details
b. It enables students to read an informational text more efficiently
c. It sparks students' interest and engagement in reading
d. It prompts students to ask meaningful questions about the text before they engage in reading

78. A third-grade student struggling to recognize and decode both new and familiar vocabulary words when reading aloud would likely benefit most from targeted support in which of the following areas related to reading fluency development?

a. Prosody
b. Letter-sound correspondence
c. Expressive language skills
d. Automaticity

79. Which of the following scenarios best demonstrates an effective strategy for promoting development of critical analysis skills?

a. Assigning students to read an informational text and complete corresponding comprehension questions
b. Providing students with a story map to complete as they read a piece of historical fiction
c. Prompting students to circle unfamiliar vocabulary words in a text and look up the meanings in a dictionary
d. Having students participate in small-group literature circles to discuss a work of fictional literature

80. During a fluency check, a second-grade teacher notices that one student often mispronounces words and frequently loses his place while reading. Which of the following strategies would be most effective in supporting this student's development of accuracy when reading aloud?

a. Having the student track the text with his or her index finger as he or she reads aloud
b. Chunking the text into smaller, more manageable parts
c. Simplifying the text to align with the student's current reading fluency levels
d. Having the student practice pronouncing unfamiliar vocabulary words prior to reading the full text aloud

81. A first-grade teacher reads aloud a short nonfiction text about the first Thanksgiving. Afterward, she has students retell the events of the text using sentence starters beginning with *first, next, then,* and *finally*. This approach is most likely intended to develop which of the following reading comprehension skills?

a. Literal comprehension
b. Inferential comprehension
c. Evaluative comprehension
d. Overall comprehension

Refer to the following for questions 82–83:

A second-grade teacher is conducting reading fluency checks by having students individually read aloud from an assigned passage. Below is an excerpt from the text, followed by a transcript of one student reading the text. The sample is representative of the student's typical oral reading performance.

Text: As Emma wandered through the enchanted forest, she could not help but marvel at its beauty. It was extraordinary. All around, she saw flowing streams, big colorful flowers, and trees that nearly touched the sky.

Student: As Emma (pause) through the echoed fort (pause) ... forest, she could not help but (pause) marvel at its beauty. It was (pause). All around, she saw (pause) flowery streams, big color flowers, and trees that (pause) near touch, (pause) touched the sky.

82. Based on the information presented above, this student likely requires targeted intervention related to which of the following concepts related to reading comprehension and fluency?

a. Prosodic reading
b. Decoding multisyllabic words
c. Recognizing high-frequency sight words
d. Recalling information

83. Based on the information above, which of the following strategies would be most effective in supporting the development of this student's reading comprehension and fluency skills?

a. Incorporating additional opportunities for the student to practice reading passages that contain multisyllabic words
b. Providing the student with a word bank to accompany reading passages with complex vocabulary
c. Simplifying the complexity of assigned texts to align with the student's current reading comprehension and fluency skills
d. Implementing syllable division and word-building activities focused on multisyllabic words

84. Which of the following scenarios best exemplifies the use of heterogeneous flexible groupings to enhance reading comprehension skills?

a. Organizing temporary mixed-ability literature circle groups to facilitate discussion about an assigned novel
b. Pairing students with others of similar reading levels while reading an informational text
c. Grouping students based upon ability level using data collected from a reading comprehension pre-test
d. Placing students in mixed-ability groups at the beginning of the year and maintaining these groups over the whole year

85. Which of the following scenarios best exemplifies a summative assessment of students' reading comprehension skills?

a. Administering a multiple-choice test before having students read an informational text to assess prior knowledge
b. Tasking students with completing comprehension questions that correspond to an assigned text as they read
c. Forming literature circle groups for students to discuss and reflect upon their reading
d. Organizing students into small groups after reading a fictional text and having them act out the story

86. A first-grade teacher is conducting a unit on irregular plural nouns. As a practice activity, students are asked to complete a chart in which they attach the appropriate plural ending to a singular noun. Below is a chart completed by one of the students in the class.

Singular Form	Plural Form
Sky	Skyes
Foot	Feet
Monkey	Monkeys
Leaf	Leafs
Calf	Calfs

Based on the information in the chart above, which of the following strategies would be most effective for differentiating this lesson to support the student's development in morphemic analysis?

a. Scaffolding the activity to gradually increase in complexity, such as by providing the student with two options for irregular plurals and asking the student to circle the correct one
b. Reducing the number of irregular nouns that the student is asked to pluralize
c. Incorporating visuals into the singular noun list to promote sight word recognition
d. Providing small-group instruction to review and practice identifying and forming irregular plural nouns

87. During a science unit, a second-grade teacher assigns students to read an informational text on the water cycle. One student in the class has been identified as an intermediate-level English Language Learner. To support this student's understanding of the text, the teacher has provided a word bank containing key academic vocabulary and has paired the student with another student who can help. Which of the following additional strategies would be beneficial in helping facilitate this student's comprehension of the text?

a. Having the student complete an anticipatory reading guide prior to beginning the activity
b. Highlighting key vocabulary words throughout the text
c. Chunking the text into smaller, more manageable parts
d. Reading the text aloud individually to the student and addressing any questions the student may have

88. A third-grade teacher plans to have students work in guided reading groups to read a work of fictional literature. Before organizing students into guided reading groups for this and future texts, which initial step would be most effective in maximizing student comprehension and success?

a. Having students complete a KWL graphic organizer to focus their attention on specific information
b. Conducting a diagnostic test to assess students' reading comprehension skills
c. Assigning a pre-reading activity to familiarize students with new vocabulary and key concepts
d. Instructing students to complete an anticipation guide to leverage prior knowledge

89. During the first week of school, students in a kindergarten classroom are given a language and literacy skill assessment to determine their readiness for grade-level instruction and determine areas of individual need. This is an example of which of the following assessment approaches?

a. Norm-referenced
b. Screening
c. Criterion-referenced
d. Diagnostic

90. A second-grade teacher notices that a student continues to rely upon inventive spelling, even for familiar high-frequency sight words. Based upon this information, the student likely requires targeted remediation related to which of the following orthographic processing skills?

a. Decoding and encoding
b. Morphological awareness
c. High-frequency sight word recognition
d. Letter-sound correspondence

91. A kindergarten teacher is assessing students' emergent literacy skills. During each student's assessment, the teacher collects data on their performance. Below is a sample of the data collected from one student's assessment.

Literacy Skill Performance Indicator	Student Mastery
Recognizes upper case letters	Yes (80%)
Recognizes lower case letters	No (70%)
Identifies high-frequency sight words with 80% accuracy	Yes (90%)

Literacy Skill Performance Indicator	Student Mastery
Recognizes long vowel sounds	No (50%)
Recognizes short vowel sounds	No (30%)

Based on the chart above, this teacher is utilizing which of the following assessment approaches to evaluate students' emergent literacy skills?

a. Norm-referenced
b. Criterion-referenced
c. Screening
d. Formative

Refer to the following for questions 92–93:

A fourth-grade teacher is preparing a unit that will include having students read an advanced grade-level informational text. Many of the students in the class are identified as English Language Learners with varying levels of proficiency.

92. To best support the needs of English language learners in the classroom and promote reading comprehension skill development, which of the following measures should the teacher prioritize when planning the upcoming unit?

a. Allowing flexibility for student choice in learning activities
b. Offering a variety of pre-, during-, and post-reading activities to appeal to varying learning styles
c. Providing adequate linguistic aids aligned with ELL students' proficiency levels
d. Simplifying the complexity of the text to ensure it is accessible to ELL students

93. Which of the following additional strategies would be most effective in further promoting reading comprehension among English language learners during the upcoming unit?

a. Asking these students open-ended questions about their thoughts on the text to encourage increased vocabulary use
b. Pairing these students with others that can provide scaffolding while reading the text
c. Organizing these students into a small group to provide targeted individualized instruction
d. Prompting students to participate in a self-reflection activity to assess their own understanding and areas for improvement

Refer to the following for question 94:

During a language arts lesson, a fourth-grade teacher assigns students to read from a fictional text. While reading, one student encounters the sentence, "As she walked silently through the mystical ancient forest, she couldn't help but wonder how she would ever return to the hustle and bustle of her modern life." Unsure of the words *ancient* and *modern*, the student skips them and continues reading with the hope of grasping the main idea of the text despite their lack of understanding of these unfamiliar terms.

94. Based on the information in the above scenario, which of the following strategies would be most effective in promoting this student's comprehension of unfamiliar vocabulary words?

a. Providing the student with a word bank at the end of the passage
b. Incorporating illustrations into the text for reference
c. Chunking the text into smaller, more manageable parts
d. Having the student complete a semantic web to map out new vocabulary

95. Which of the following statements best describes the role of inventive spelling in early literacy development?

a. Inventive spelling is discouraged as it can lead to confusion and hinder spelling proficiency
b. Inventive spelling should be utilized sparingly, as excessive reliance on it may impede students' progress in mastering conventional spelling rules
c. Inventive spelling is a natural and beneficial stage in early writing development, allowing children to apply phonetic knowledge
d. Inventive spelling is ineffective and should be replaced with direct instruction on correct spelling from an early age

Refer to the following for question 96:

Prior to beginning a social studies unit focused on the United States Constitution, a fourth-grade teacher implements an introductory activity that includes several vocabulary words related to the unit, their definitions, and examples of their usage in sentences.

96. Which of the following additional strategies could the teacher implement to further strengthen students' understanding of academic language?

a. Assign a project in which students write their own version of a constitution
b. Conduct sentence dictation exercises using new vocabulary from the unit
c. Have students create their own flash cards based on the new vocabulary from the unit
d. Assign an expository essay assignment in which students write about the development of the United States Constitution

97. A first-grade teacher is beginning a new unit on mammals. As part of a whole-class activity, she has students participate in creating the following chart. This activity exemplifies which of the following strategies aimed at promoting students' word analysis skills?

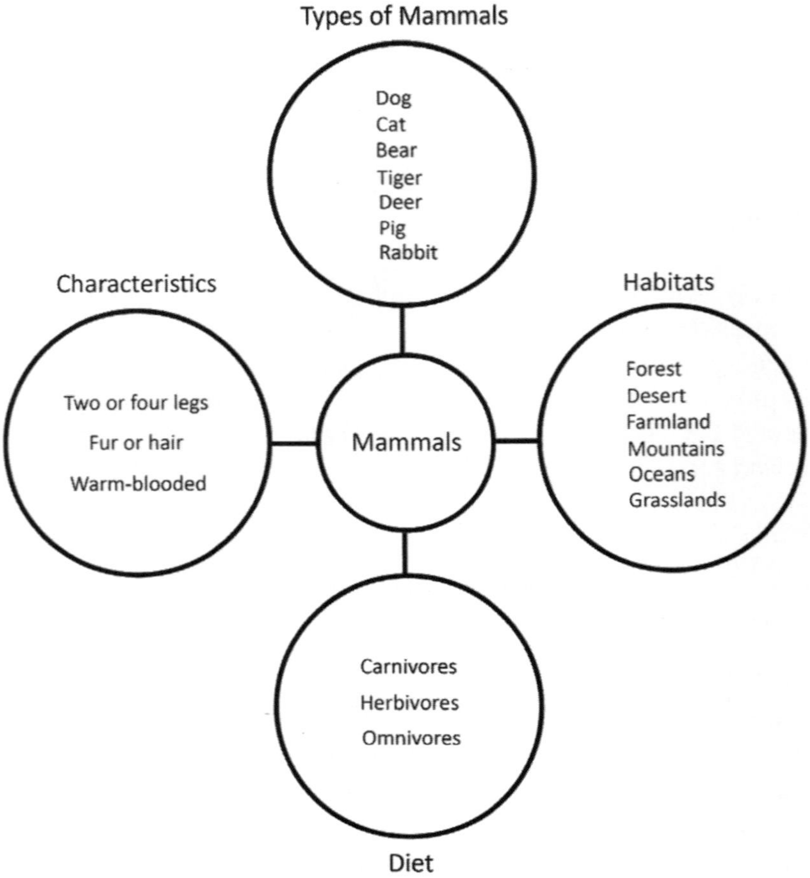

a. Brainstorming
b. Semantic mapping
c. Prewriting
d. Word sorting

Refer to the following for questions 98–99:

> A third-grade teacher is working to improve student reading comprehension and fluency skills. The class is comprised of students with a diverse range of skills, abilities, and needs, including those with learning disabilities and English language learners of varying proficiency levels. The teacher is currently preparing a lesson in which students will read a fictional short story and plans to differentiate learning by utilizing a flexible grouping approach.

98. Which of the following best describes the primary benefit of implementing flexible grouping during this lesson?

a. Encouraging students to work with others outside of their normal peer group
b. Enabling the teacher to adjust groupings based upon students' evolving needs
c. Allowing the teacher to ensure consistency in student groupings for the school year
d. Facilitating a student-led learning experience for increased engagement

99. Which of the following additional strategies would be most effective in differentiating this lesson to accommodate varying individual skills, abilities, and needs?

a. Providing each group with leveled versions of the text to align with their current abilities
b. Incorporating graphic organizers to support increased comprehension
c. Supplementing the fictional short story with visual aids
d. Prompting students to respond to a series of reflection questions after reading the text

100. A second-grade teacher is assessing students' oral reading fluency skills by timing them as they individually read aloud from an assigned passage. To accurately determine the number of words read correctly per minute for each student, which of the following steps must the teacher follow?

a. Subtract the number of errors from the total number of words in the passage, then divide by the total reading time in minutes.
b. Divide the total number of words the student reads correctly by one minute.
c. Subtract the total number of errors from the total number of words in the passage, then divide by one minute.
d. Divide the number of words in the reading passage by the time spent reading in minutes, then subtract the number of errors.

Integration of Knowledge and Understanding

101. Assignment:

Use the information in the exhibits provided to complete the following assignment:

Using the information presented in the exhibits and your understanding of foundational reading skills (e.g., phonemic awareness, phonics, high-frequency sight word recognition, morphemic analysis, syllabication, automaticity, reading fluency (i.e., accuracy, rate, and prosody), self-correcting), craft a response of approximately 150-300 words in which you:

- Identify one strength demonstrated by Kate related to foundational reading skills
- Identify one significant need demonstrated by Kate related to foundational reading skills
- Describe one effective instructional strategy, activity, or intervention that would adequately address the identified need
- Discuss why the instructional strategy, activity, or intervention you chose would be effective in addressing Kate's need and supporting the development of her foundational reading skills

Be sure to cite specific evidence from the exhibits and information provided to support your response.

A second-grade teacher conducts reading fluency checks by having students individually read aloud from an assigned passage. As they read, the teacher records notes about each student's performance to evaluate their progress in foundational reading skills. Below is an example of a fluency check of one student in the class, Kate.

Key:

Omission | Short pause ← Repetition © self-correction

Λ Insertion || Long pause [cat/cow] Substitution [t] Told by teacher

Exhibit:

Whether [cat/cow] (*water*) as a liquid ||, solid | , or gas, water is all around (us,) even if you cannot always see it. We use water for many things every single day. Did you know there are different || forms water can take? It can be liquid |, solid, or gas. Let us learn a little bit about each kind of water.

The most familiar [cat/cow] (*family*) © kind of water is in liquid form. This is the water we use every day to drink, clean, cook, and water our gardens. Liquid water falls from clouds when it rains. Oceans |, rivers, lakes, streams ← ©, and creeks [cat/cow] (*cracks*) © are all made up of liquid water too! Did you know that our planet is about 7(0%) water?

When the temperature || of liquid water falls below freezing [cat/cow] (*freeze*), it changes into the cold, hard solid that we know as ice. Ice covers frozen lakes and ponds in winter, forms icebergs | [cat/cow] (*icebugs*) © in the ocean, and even keeps our drinks cold in the summer ← ©!

Water can even be invisible [t]! This happens when water turns into a gas called water vapor ||. When water gets warm enough, its particles [t] turn into an invisible || vapor. This vapor rises and becomes part of the air. When lots of vapors rise together, they become || clouds and fall back down as raindrops |!

Water is always changing [cat/cow] (*changes*) its form. Whether it exists [cat/cow] (*exits*) as a solid, liquid, or invisible || vapor gas, we need water to sustain || life on Earth. All living things need water for survival [cat/cow] (*survive*). How many times have you used water today?

Exhibit:

After reading, the teacher determines Kate's oral reading fluency by calculating her words correct per minute (WCPM) and accuracy scores. This includes assigning Kate a holistic score of 1-4 in three domains related to oral reading performance, with 4 representing the highest possible score for that domain.

Indicator	Score
Words correct per minute	97
Accuracy	97%
Rate	2
Prosody	
• Smoothness	2
• Phrasing	3
Additional Notes	Second grade 50th percentile spring benchmark is 90 WCPM

102. Assignment:

Use the information in the exhibits provided to complete the following assignment:

Using the exhibits below and your knowledge of reading comprehension skills (e.g. vocabulary knowledge; knowledge of academic language structures, including conventions of standard English grammar; application of literal, inferential, or evaluative comprehension skills; use of comprehension strategies; application of text analysis skills to a literary or informational text, including determining key ideas and details, analyzing craft and structure, or integrating knowledge and ideas within a text or across texts), write a response of approximately 150-300 words in which you:

- Identify one significant strength that Blake demonstrates related to reading comprehension skills
- Identify one significant need that Blake demonstrates related to reading comprehension skills
- Describe one effective instructional strategy, activity, or intervention that would adequately address Blake's need
- Discuss why the instructional strategy, activity, or intervention you chose would be effective for developing Blake's reading comprehension skills

Be sure to use specific evidence from the reading passage and Blake's oral response to support all parts of your response.

Exhibit:

Reading Passage:

As part of a reading comprehension assignment, Blake, a fourth-grade student, reads a passage from the novel *The Wind in the Willows* by Kenneth Grahame. Before reading, the teacher explains that the story is about the adventures of Mole, Rat, and Badger as they try to help their friend Mr. Toad. The teacher has Blake read from the first four pages of the novel in which Mole decides to abandon spring cleaning in favor of leaving his home and going outside to enjoy the weather. Blake reads the passage aloud, then silently to himself. Below is the passage that Blake read.

> 'This is fine!' he said to himself. 'This is better than whitewashing!' The sunshine struck hot on his fur, soft breezes caressed his heated brow, and after the seclusion of the cellarage he had lived in so long the carol of the happy birds fell on his dulled hearing almost like a shout. Jumping off all his four legs at once, in the joy of living

and the delight of spring without its cleaning, he pursued his way across the meadow till he reached the hedge on the further side.

'Hold up!' said an elderly rabbit at the gap. 'Sixpence for the privilege of passing by the private road!' He was bowled over in an instant by the impatient and contemptuous Mole, who trotted along the side of the hedge chaffing with the other rabbits as they peeped hurriedly from their holes to see what the row was about. 'Onion-sauce! Onion-sauce!' he remarked jeeringly, and was gone before they could think of a thoroughly satisfactory reply. Then they all started grumbling at each other. 'How *stupid* you are! Why didn't you tell him----' 'Well why didn't *you* say----' 'You might have reminded him-----' and so on, in the usual way; but, of course, it was then much too late, as is always the case.

It all seemed too good to be true. Hither and thither through the meadows he rambled busily, along with the hedgerows, across the copses, finding everywhere birds building, flowers budding, leaves thrusting—everything happy, and progressive, and occupied. And instead of having an uneasy conscience pricking him and whispering 'whitewash!' he somehow could only feel how jolly it was to be the only idle dog among all these busy citizens. After all, the best part of a holiday is perhaps not so much to be resting yourself, as to see all the other fellows busy working.

He thought his happiness was complete when, as he meandered aimlessly along, suddenly he stood by the edge of a full-fed river. Never in his life had he seen such a river before---this sleek, sinuous, full-bodied animal, chasing and chuckling, gripping things with a gurgle and leaving them with a laugh, to fling itself on fresh playmates that shook themselves free, and were caught and held again. All was a-shake and a-shiver---glints and gleams and sparkles, rustle and swirl, chatter and bubble. The Mole was bewitched, entranced, fascinated. By the side of the river he trotted as one trots, when very small, by the side of a man who holds one spell-bound by exciting stories; and when tired at last, he sat on the bank, while the river still chattered on to him, a babbling procession of the best stories in the world, sent from the heart of the earth to be told at last to the insatiable sea.

Grahame, Kenneth. *The Wind in the Willows*. Charles Scribner's Sons, 1908. Pp. 1-4

Exhibit:

After Blake reads the passage to himself, the teacher asks him some questions about what he has read. Below is an excerpt of their conversation.

Teacher: Can you tell me what the passage was about?

Blake: First the Mole was cleaning his house but then he got tired of it.

Teacher: What in the passage makes you think he was tired of cleaning?

Blake: It said that he threw his broom on the floor and bolted outside.

Teacher: Good! What else happened?

Blake: Then he was really happy because he decided to go outside without a coat on because it was warm. Then he got stopped by a rabbit.

Teacher: What did the rabbit want?

Blake: Sixpence to pass the road, but I don't know what sixpence is.

Teacher: The rabbit wanted money to cross the road.

Blake: Yeah, but the Mole didn't give it to him. He ran away with the other rabbits.

Teacher: That's right. How do you think the Mole felt about being outside?

Blake: He was very very happy and glad to not be spring cleaning anymore.

Teacher: What details from the text tell you that he was happy?

Blake: The passage uses words like *jolly*, *happy*, and *fascinated* and the Mole said that being outside was *better than whitewashing*.

Teacher: Excellent. Can you tell me a little bit about the setting of the passage?

Blake: First the Mole was in his house, like I said. Then he climbed through a tunnel and went outside.

Teacher: What was outside like for the Mole?

Blake: Warm, and there were meadows, flowers, and leaves. And a river!

Teacher: What did the Mole think about the river?

Blake: I bet he liked the river too.

Teacher: Based on the description in the passage, what do you think the river was like?

Blake: Probably really big. It was talking to the Mole and the passage said there were animals in it, so a lot of animals probably go there to drink.

Answer Key and Explanations for Test #2

Multiple Choice Questions

1. D: The ability to recognize and analyze an author's point of view is an essential reading comprehension skill, as this enables students to interpret how the author's perspective affects the information presented in a text, analyze implications, and identify potential biases. To demonstrate this concept, educators should begin by providing students with multiple texts on the same topic, such as in the given scenario. When evaluating understanding, implementing an interactive activity, such as organizing students into teams and having them debate the main points from an assigned text, provides an authentic and engaging setting for demonstrating learning. This approach encourages students to interact meaningfully with the text and adopt the perspective of their assigned author, thus prompting them to critically analyze, discuss, and support their interpretations of the author's point of view. By having students engage in a debate after reading different texts about the same topic, the teacher can gain important feedback on students' ability to recognize the author's point of view while strengthening their understanding of the content material.

2. D: Orthographic mapping refers to a process in which readers employ knowledge of letter-sound correspondence to recognize and recall the spelling, pronunciation, and meaning of written words. This ability is foundational in developing the word recognition and automaticity skills required for developing reading fluency. Therefore, it is essential to incorporate strategies aimed at developing orthographic mapping skills into daily instruction, particularly when introducing new high-frequency vocabulary words. Effective strategies include utilizing word walls for new vocabulary and frequently referring to them throughout instruction, introducing word families to emphasize spelling patterns, and incorporating syllable clapping games to promote students' understanding of word structures and patterns. Among several others, these strategies are highly effective in developing students' ability to effortlessly employ orthographic mapping skills to recognize and internalize new words, thus promoting vocabulary acquisition, automaticity, and ultimately, reading fluency.

3. C: Implementing authentic tasks as a summative assessment strategy is beneficial in strengthening students' personal connections to learning to foster greater understanding and retention of content material. Authentic tasks are placed in a real-world context, thus providing students with a relevant, meaningful, and engaging avenue to express their learning. In the given scenario, having students complete an authentic task as a summative assessment would allow the teacher to effectively evaluate their grasp of both the historical time period and comprehension of the text. Having students create diaries from the perspective of a character in the text prompts them to become immersed in the historical period, ultimately allowing them to demonstrate learning in a manner that reflects deep engagement and a nuanced understanding of the text.

4. A: Understanding sentence structure is foundational in comprehending and utilizing academic language. As students advance to upper elementary school, this ability becomes vital in comprehending and expressing increasingly complex ideas and is therefore necessary for literacy skill development as well as overall academic achievement. Before introducing new sentence structures, such as compound-complex sentences, teachers should ensure that students have a solid grasp of related foundational concepts, such as parts of speech and conventions of grammar. This includes topics such as nouns, subjects, verbs, adjectives, and adverbs, as well as spelling, punctuation, and capitalization. By reviewing these, educators can ensure that students have a strong understanding of the fundamentals of the English language, thus promoting their success when encountering increasingly complex sentence structures and fostering their ability to recognize, understand, and apply various components within compound-complex sentences.

5. C: Inflectional morphemes are suffixes attached to the end of a word that changes its grammatical tense, quantity, or possession without altering the meaning of the root word itself. These linguistic units, such as *-ed*, *-ing*, *-s*, and *-est*, are bound to the root word and carry no independent semantic meaning. Understanding how to recognize, decipher, and utilize inflectional morphemes is integral in developing morphemic analysis skills, as they strengthen grasp of grammatical relationships, word structure, and word meanings. This grammatical concept can prove especially challenging for young readers to master. Therefore, targeted intervention is required when students struggle with this concept. In the given example, the student demonstrates difficulty in properly utilizing inflectional morphemes in their writing. This is apparent in several instances, such as when the student incorrectly uses the words *liones* and *monkies*, as well as when they attached incorrect inflectional morphemes to the ends of words, such as in writing *taked* rather than *taking*, and *sleeped* instead of *sleeping*. Providing this student with targeted support, therefore, is necessary in improving their skills in effectively using inflectional morphemes, and ultimately developing their writing proficiency.

6. A: Understanding how to recognize and properly use inflectional morphemes, such as *-ed*, *-ing*, *-s*, and *-est*, can prove especially difficult for young learners, as they typically involve slight changes to the end of a word that alters its grammatical tense, quantity, or possession. This skill is crucial for developing morphemic analysis skills, as it is foundational for understanding grammatical patterns, word structure, and word meanings, and therefore, must be addressed promptly and explicitly when a student exhibits difficulty. In this scenario, having the student participate in a word-building activity focused on manipulating word endings would effectively target this student's difficulty related to inflectional morphemes. By engaging in this activity, the student can kinesthetically explore how inflectional morphemes alter the meanings of words, thus promoting internalization of this concept and ultimately enhancing their morphemic analysis skills.

7. B: The alphabetic principle is the understanding that written letters represent sounds in spoken language, forming a crucial concept in early literacy learning as it lays the groundwork for effective decoding and encoding skills. After introducing the letter *A* and its sound (/a/), a practical follow-up activity would be to implement a game where students match pictures of objects with their initial letter sound, focusing on items starting with *A*. This hands-on approach reinforces the alphabetic principle by connecting the visual representation of the letter *A* with its corresponding sound. Through this activity, students strengthen their grasp of letter-sound relationships and enhance phonemic awareness, essential for early literacy success.

8. A: An integral aspect of developing students' reading comprehension and literary analysis skills involves implementing effective pre-reading strategies. Doing so enhances student engagement in reading by calling upon prior knowledge and fostering personal connections. Furthermore, pre-reading activities prompt students to focus on specific aspects of a text, such as characters, setting, plot, themes, and literary techniques, thus fostering their ability to understand complex works of literature, analyze key elements, and employ critical thinking skills to consider the author's deeper implications. Anticipation guides are a highly effective pre-reading strategy for increasing comprehension and analysis skills. This versatile activity can be differentiated to align with a variety of texts across genres. When reading works of literature, anticipation guides typically prompt students to agree or disagree with a series of statements related to a given text, as well as formulate predictions prior to engaging in reading. This activity establishes a purpose for reading, directs students' attention to specific components of the text, and encourages them to think critically as they read for increased overall engagement. By implementing anticipation guides, educators can encourage students to interact meaningfully with a text and reflect upon their original thoughts after reading, thus strengthening reading comprehension and literary analysis skills.

9. D: Understanding the author's purpose is an important component of comprehending and analyzing informational texts. This enables students to understand why a text was written, how the author's viewpoint may impact the content of the text and analyze any potential biases while forming their own conclusions. Cultivating this skill in early elementary school establishes the foundation necessary for promoting understanding of increasingly complex informational texts as they progress academically. By implementing activities in which students categorize short informational passages based on their intent to inform, explain, or persuade, the teacher in this scenario effectively develops students' understanding of how to identify the author's purpose. Through this activity, students can begin to observe how differences in vocabulary, style, and tone impact the overall message and purpose of a text.

10. D: Reader's theaters are literacy activities in which students assume the roles and act out the dialogue of characters from familiar plays or stories with the intention of developing prosodic reading and ultimately, reading fluency skills. During these activities, students are encouraged to focus on expression, intonation, pace, and volume to reflect that of spoken language. Effective implementation of reader's theaters in the elementary classroom requires the teacher to be cognizant of varying reading fluency levels and to differentiate the activity accordingly. In the given scenario, the teacher differentiates the activity by grouping students based on ability and providing scripts aligned with their reading fluency skills. To further modify this activity, the teacher could incorporate guided reading sessions with each group to support struggling readers in mastering their lines and improving overall comprehension and fluency. Doing so would promote students' confidence and engagement in reading while providing the necessary support to ensure all students build upon their reading fluency skills.

11. D: Phonological awareness refers to the ability to recognize and manipulate the sounds of spoken language, such as identifying individual sounds within words, blending sounds to form words, and segmenting words into their constituent sounds. Sound processing skills encompass a range of abilities related to auditory processing, including discriminating between similar sounds, remembering sound sequences, and understanding the relationship between sounds and letters. These skills are integral for successful reading and spelling development, as they provide the foundation for phonics instruction and word decoding. When a second-grade student struggles to distinguish individual sounds within words, it indicates a deficit in phonological awareness and sound processing abilities. Consequently, providing additional support in this area is essential to address the underlying difficulties hindering the student's progress in reading and spelling. By targeting phonological awareness and sound processing skills through evidence-based instructional practices, the teacher can help this student improve his or her phonemic proficiency and ultimately achieve success in building literacy skills.

12. B: Syllabication is the segmentation of words into syllables to help early readers build skills in pronunciation and spelling. This skill is integral in developing phonics skills, decoding abilities, and, ultimately, reading comprehension and writing fluency. By second grade, students can reasonably be expected to have mastered the syllabication of monosyllabic words and can begin working with increasingly complex two-syllable words, including those with prefixes or suffixes. Providing students with syllable cards to form words such as *apron*, *dislike*, *prepare*, and *drumstick* is therefore suitable for this age group, as each word contains two syllables, and the list includes a syllable card with a prefix. By implementing this activity, the teacher can engage students in building their syllabication skills in a developmentally appropriate manner that prepares them for increasingly complex multisyllabic words.

13. A: Regularly monitoring students' progress and development in phonics is crucial for effective literacy instruction and promptly addressing areas of difficulty. Phonics skills lay the groundwork for reading and writing, and as such, it is imperative to identify and assist students struggling in this aspect. Through consistent assessment of students' phonics knowledge and performance, educators obtain valuable insights into their strengths and areas requiring improvement, enabling tailored intervention to foster overall literacy growth. In the given scenario, the student's performance on two spelling assessments underscores the significance of ongoing monitoring. While demonstrating improvement in recognizing consonant blends, short vowel sounds, and the silent *e* rule, the student encountered ongoing challenges with long vowel sounds and vowel patterns, evident in inaccuracies in spelling words like *grain* and *boat*. Recognizing the student's progress in consonant blends alongside persistent difficulties in long vowel sounds and vowel patterns, the teacher can adapt instruction to provide additional support and encourage further development. Through targeted intervention and focused instruction, the teacher plays a pivotal role in helping the student enhance their phonics skills and ultimately boost overall literacy proficiency.

14. D: Providing students with context as they engage in reading is highly beneficial in promoting academic vocabulary development. Doing so helps students formulate connections to their reading and serves as a framework for reference when encountering new vocabulary. Specifically, when reading words of historical fiction, students may be unfamiliar with the time period, potentially impeding overall comprehension and vocabulary acquisition. In this scenario, the teacher can best promote students' academic vocabulary acquisition and development by leading class discussions about the historical context of the text they are reading and the significance of new vocabulary as it relates to that context. Doing so would provide students with an overall sense of the time period of the piece as well as a greater understanding of the characters, setting, plot, and events. This approach would provide students with a foundation for understanding the meaning of unfamiliar words in context, thus increasing comprehension and developing their ability to accurately utilize these words.

15. C: Rhyming plays a crucial role in phonological awareness because it involves the repetition of similar sounds at the ends of words. Recognizing rhymes is foundational for phonemic awareness and requires attention when students face challenges in this area. By grasping rhyme patterns, students develop a better understanding of language sounds. Those struggling with rhyming benefit greatly from nursery rhymes and rhyming games integrated into daily literacy activities. These exercises offer valuable opportunities for students to hear, identify, and use rhyming words in context, reinforcing their phonological awareness and improving overall literacy skills, thus establishing a strong foundation for emergent literacy development.

16. C: Reading comprehension and fluency development is reliant on students' ability to apply contextual analysis skills to determine the meaning of unfamiliar vocabulary words. Contextual analysis, as it relates to language and literacy development, involves locating and using clues within a text to infer the meaning of new vocabulary. Various strategies can effectively promote the development of students' contextual analysis skills. For example, students can look for definition words related to new vocabulary within a text, deduce meaning from pictures or illustrations, or search for clue words, such as synonyms, antonyms, or explanations of unfamiliar terms. By guiding students in locating clue words within a text to decipher the meaning of unfamiliar vocabulary, the teacher in this scenario can effectively develop students' contextual analysis skills by prompting them to utilize context clues in making educated guesses about the meaning of new vocabulary words.

17. A: Morphological awareness is the ability to recognize and interpret individual morphemes, or units of language, which comprise words. This ability allows young children to build phonological and orthographic processing skills and is therefore essential for all aspects of language and literacy development, including vocabulary acquisition, spelling, writing, speaking, and listening. As students develop morphological awareness, they build foundational skills such as identifying root words and affixes, including prefixes and suffixes, to decode both new and familiar vocabulary. Advanced proficiency in this area is exemplified by the ability to apply this knowledge to writing, as it demonstrates a strong understanding and internalization of word structure and semantic relationships to accurately convey meaning. Therefore, of the given options, a student's ability to accurately attach prefixes and suffixes to form multisyllabic words when writing demonstrates the most advanced level of skill related to morphological awareness.

18. B: Implementing multiple strategies and approaches to develop students' spelling proficiency and having them apply phonics knowledge to spell words accurately are crucial in fostering well-rounded literacy skills. By incorporating activities that explore word families, analyze spelling patterns, and apply phonics rules, this teacher provides students with diverse opportunities to reinforce their understanding of phonics principles and develop their spelling abilities. These instructional activities encourage active engagement with language and provide students with the tools and strategies necessary to spell words accurately in various contexts. Through word banks, word sorts, and spelling practice, students not only deepen their phonics knowledge but also gain confidence in their spelling abilities, ultimately enhancing their overall literacy proficiency. The described instructional activities primarily target improving spelling proficiency by providing students with opportunities to apply their understanding of phonics principles to spell words accurately. These activities engage students in active learning experiences that reinforce their phonics knowledge and develop their spelling skills. By incorporating multiple strategies and approaches, this teacher effectively supports students' spelling development and promotes their overall literacy proficiency.

19. B: Phonics instruction is vital for early literacy development as it teaches the relationship between letters and their corresponding sounds. Teaching phonics explicitly helps students understand how letters represent sounds, aiding them in decoding words while reading and encoding them while writing. In the given scenario, the introduction of the silent *e* rule focuses on a specific phonics concept relevant to CVCe (consonant-vowel-consonant-silent *e*) words. By having students practice segmenting CVCe words into individual phonemes, they engage in an interactive activity to reinforce their understanding of words with the silent *e* pattern. Segmenting words into phonemes allows students to isolate and identify the sounds within the word, thus helping them apply phonics rules accurately. Through this approach, the teacher effectively reinforces the silent *e* phonics rule and supports beginning readers' phonemic awareness and decoding skills.

20. B: Activating prior knowledge is a highly effective strategy for contextualizing complex academic language. This allows students to establish personal connections between their own experiences and the new vocabulary, thus enhancing comprehension and retention. For English language learners this approach facilitates comprehension despite potential language barriers and helps these students form connections between new and familiar vocabulary. Educators can tap into students' prior knowledge through a variety of methods. For ELLs, visual aids, such as pictures, are particularly helpful, as they allow for association of new academic vocabulary with familiar images, thus promoting retention. In the given scenario, providing students with images representing new vocabulary is helpful in promoting their ability to recognize and categorize goods and services, thus promoting attachment of the new terms to concrete representations. This association will allow these students to connect their experiences and materials with goods and services, thus enhancing their understanding of the concept and their acquisition of academic vocabulary.

21. A: Print awareness is a multifaceted concept that encompasses an understanding of what constitutes printed language, its function in daily life, as well as the notion that print conveys meaning. This includes recognizing the features and structure of printed material, such as books, and how to navigate them. Although prekindergarten students typically are unable to read fluently, it is essential to develop an early sense of print awareness to establish the foundation necessary for building reading fluency. In the given scenario, the teacher achieves this by pointing out book features during read-aloud sessions such as the title, author, and illustrator, as well as by demonstrating print directionality by modeling left-to-right and top-to-bottom reading. These practices develop students' understanding of text structure and the notion that printed words convey meaning, thus promoting early reading fluency and comprehension. In addition, by using her finger to track as she reads, the teacher emphasizes the relationship between spoken and written language, further strengthening early fluency and comprehension skills.

22. B: Phoneme substitution consists of replacing one phoneme, which is the smallest unit of sound, in a word with another to form a new word. This is an essential phonological awareness skill that helps students understand letter-sound relationships, contributing to their ability to distinguish and manipulate sounds in spoken language. In the given scenario the teacher's use of magnet tiles to spell a word and then substituting one letter tile to form a new word encourages students to engage in phoneme substitution. For example, changing the *c* in *can* to *p* transforms the word into *pan*. By recognizing and articulating this new word, students demonstrate their understanding of how changing one sound can alter the meaning of a word, thereby strengthening their phonemic awareness skills. Therefore, the teacher is likely aiming to develop phoneme substitution skills among students through this strategy, fostering their phonological awareness and literacy development.

23. A: Phonological awareness refers to the ability to identify, distinguish, and manipulate sounds in spoken language. Proficiency in this integral early literacy skill by a first-grade student would best be exemplified by the ability to listen to a word such as *bat*, break it down into individual phonemes, and then substitute one of those phonemes to create a new word, such as changing the *b* to *c* to make *cat*. This action demonstrates a deep understanding of the phonetic structure of language and the ability to manipulate individual sounds within words. Such skills are foundational for reading and writing development, as they allow students to understand how sounds relate to letters and how changing those sounds can alter word meanings; therefore, the ability to do so represents a high level of proficiency in phonological awareness.

24. C: Structural analysis skills refer to the ability to recognize, understand, and manipulate parts of words, including root words, prefixes, and suffixes. This ability is necessary for vocabulary acquisition, spelling proficiency, decoding unfamiliar words, and reading comprehension and fluency. This skill becomes imperative as older students encounter increasingly complex new vocabulary, as it enables them to examine the parts of unfamiliar words to decipher meaning. While there are variations for individual differences in skill levels and ability, third-grade students are typically developing more advanced structural analysis skills, and as such, can reasonably be expected to work with increasingly complex multisyllabic words, including those with prefixes, suffixes, or both. Therefore, providing a list of words that contain both prefixes and suffixes attached to their root, such as *preheated*, *disliking*, *unkindness*, and *pre-reading*, during a word-building activity would be appropriate for students in this grade level.

25. A: Prosodic reading is the ability to read aloud with a tone, pace, and level of expression akin to spoken language. This skill is indicative of reading fluency development, as it demonstrates the ability to recognize and articulate the relationship between written and spoken language. Strengthening prosodic reading skills is essential for fluency development because it fosters understanding of the connection between written and spoken language, thus enhancing comprehension and oral reading fluency. Echo reading, a strategy in which the teacher reads aloud from a text and pauses throughout to have students repeat it back with the same level of expression, is an effective strategy for developing prosodic reading skills among young readers. Through this approach, students are prompted to imitate the teacher's pace, volume, intonation, and rhythm, thus fostering a natural flow that mirrors spoken language. Utilizing works of poetry is particularly conducive to echo reading activities. Poetry often incorporates changes in rhythm, rhyme, meter, and cadence, thus allowing students to practice variations in intonation, expression, and timing that naturally reflect the sound of spoken language.

26. B: Variances in reading comprehension abilities will invariably occur in any classroom. Differentiating literacy instruction is essential to meeting students where they are in terms of skill level and providing adequate support for continuous development and growth. In the given scenario, the teacher plans to differentiate the upcoming unit by organizing students into guided reading groups based upon ability. To further ensure student comprehension and promote skill development, this teacher should consider also differentiating the complexity of the text according to skill level. Students in groups that require additional support would benefit from a simplified rendition of the text aligned with their abilities, while more advanced students will be challenged by a more complex version. By implementing this strategy, the teacher can ensure all students' needs are met while promoting reading comprehension skill development at a variety of levels.

27. B: The ability to recognize synonyms and antonyms in a text is highly beneficial for helping students employ contextual analysis skills to determine the meaning of unfamiliar vocabulary and ultimately, improve reading comprehension. Synonyms are two or more words that have the same meaning, whereas antonyms are words that have opposite meanings. Understanding this concept is essential to deciphering the meaning of new words in context. Students that struggle in this area may skip unfamiliar terms when reading, thus hindering overall reading comprehension. In this scenario, the student skips over the antonyms *ancient* and *modern*, despite contextual synonyms, thus indicating the need for a targeted review. Doing so would strengthen the student's recognition of similar and opposite words around unfamiliar vocabulary within a text, thus improving their ability to make educated inferences about meaning and enhancing their overall reading comprehension skills.

28. A: Encountering new academic vocabulary can pose a significant challenge for young children, particularly as they reach upper elementary school where language becomes increasingly complex. As such, implementing strategies to help students decipher unfamiliar terms is essential in fostering academic language acquisition and reading fluency skills. Encouraging students to utilize context clues when encountering unfamiliar vocabulary is an effective strategy for helping them derive meaning. One such strategy involves prompting students to refer to pictures or illustrations in a text to determine the meaning of an unfamiliar word. Visual images in a text provide students with contextual information, including tone, setting, actions, or objects associated with a new word, thus allowing them to infer meaning and attach a tangible example to the unfamiliar vocabulary. By encouraging students to refer to images in a text as context clues, teachers can promote improved comprehension and retention of academic language. Using the text surrounding an unknown word is also a strategy students can employ when encountering new words. Often, the context of a sentence can be enough for the student to guess the meaning of the word. This strategy becomes especially useful in texts without pictures.

29. A: Developmentally appropriate practice requires early elementary educators to acknowledge students' general abilities relative to their age group while recognizing that each student progresses at their own pace and tailoring support accordingly. At the kindergarten level, developmentally appropriate reading instruction typically entails a phonics-based curriculum to begin developing emergent literacy skills. While most students in this age group can be expected to grasp these concepts, educators must be aware of individual differences in skill, prior knowledge, and learning styles that may require additional support. In the given scenario, students struggling with letter-sound correspondence should be provided with targeted small-group instruction to develop their skills in this area. This approach allows the teacher to accommodate individual needs more effectively in a personalized setting, thus ensuring each student receives the support necessary to continuously build upon phonics skills at a grade-level pace.

30. D: Phonics instruction is a fundamental component of early literacy education, focusing on the relationship between letters and their corresponding sounds. Emerging readers must grasp these foundational phonics skills to decode words accurately and efficiently while reading. Explicit phonics instruction involves systematically teaching students the rules and patterns of the English language, such as letter-sound correspondences and syllable structures. This approach provides clear, structured guidance for students to understand how letters represent sounds in words. By explicitly teaching phonics rules and patterns, students develop the necessary skills to decode unfamiliar words independently, leading to improved fluency and comprehension. Systematic, sequential phonics programs guide students through a logical progression of skills, beginning with basic letter-sound relationships and gradually advancing to more complex phonics concepts. Therefore, this approach would be most effective in developing phonics skills among students and fostering their overall reading proficiency.

31. B: Tier II provides targeted small-group interventions for students who are not meeting grade-level benchmarks, making it the correct answer for students who meet twice a week for focused fluency instruction with a reading specialist. Response to intervention (RTI) is a three-tiered support model that provides increasingly intensive interventions for students who are struggling academically. Tier I includes universal classroom instruction provided to all students. Tier III provides more intensive, individualized support for students who do not respond adequately to Tier II interventions. An individualized education program (IEP) is a special education plan for students who meet eligibility criteria and is not a tier within the RTI model.

32. C: Identification of high-frequency words reflects students' ability to swiftly recognize commonly encountered words without the need to sound out each letter separately. This capability is integral in the early stages of literacy development, as it empowers students to read smoothly and comprehend text more effectively. By instantly identifying high-frequency words, students can dedicate their focus to grasping the overall meaning of the text rather than grappling with decoding individual words, thereby enhancing their reading fluency. Integrating high-frequency words into meaningful sentences serves as a highly beneficial instructional approach for fostering automatic recognition. Reading these words within sentences aids students in grasping their usage and context, thus reinforcing their recognition and promoting retention. Furthermore, exposure to high-frequency words in various contexts allows students to encounter them repeatedly, thereby solidifying their recognition skills and bolstering overall reading proficiency.

33. A: Decoding, a crucial reading skill, entails breaking words into individual sounds and recognizing the corresponding letters or letter combinations. This proficiency allows students to effectively decipher unfamiliar words and comprehend text. For first-grade students, who are in the early stages of decoding development, engaging in kinesthetic activities can significantly enhance their learning. These hands-on activities involve physical movement and tactile experiences, which are particularly beneficial for young learners as they encourage active participation and sensory engagement. In this scenario, introducing an activity where students build multisyllabic words using letter tiles serves as an effective continuation of clapping out multisyllabic words. By manipulating letter tiles to construct words, students not only reinforce their grasp of letter-sound relationships but also gain practical experience in manipulating word components. This interactive approach fosters active learning and reinforces decoding skills in first-grade students.

34. C: Onset and rime are essential phonological awareness skills that significantly contribute to reading fluency development. Onset refers to the initial consonant or consonants of a word that begin the syllable, while the rime is comprised of the following vowels and consonants. Understanding this concept is integral in reading fluency development, as it allows young readers to identify patterns, recognize word families, and decode unfamiliar vocabulary with greater rate and accuracy. Introducing word families, which are groups of words that are spelled and pronounced similarly, is an effective strategy for teaching onset and rime. In the given scenario, the teacher introduces the *-all* word family by displaying a chart that demonstrates how changing the onset while keeping the *-all* rime creates new words. By implementing this strategy, the teacher develops students' ability to quickly decode words within the same word family, thus building essential reading fluency skills.

35. B: Understanding the concepts of onset and rime is essential to developing word recognition skills, vocabulary acquisition, and ultimately, reading fluency. Use of word families is a highly effective strategy for introducing this concept to young readers, at it helps them to identify patterns, recognize words within the same family, and comprehend how changing the onset creates new words. To further reinforce this concept, it is important to provide students with ample opportunities to practice and manipulate new vocabulary. One effective strategy for achieving this includes implementing word-building activities using magnetic letter tiles. For example, in the given scenario, the teacher would provide students with letter tiles based on the displayed chart and the *-all* word family. This kinesthetic approach allows students to physically manipulate the onset and rime of new vocabulary words, thus strengthening their understanding and building foundational reading fluency skills.

36. A: Consonant blends refer to combinations of two or more consonants that appear together in a word, with each retaining its individual sound. They are a fundamental aspect of phonics instruction, as they play an integral role in helping emergent readers decode and read words accurately. Mastery of consonant blends enhances phonemic awareness and decoding skills, enabling students to recognize and manipulate the sounds within words effectively. When a student struggles with identifying words containing consonant blends, it indicates a need for targeted intervention to address this specific phonics concept. In this scenario, implementing a word sorting activity would be beneficial in focusing directly on the student's difficulty by providing them with hands-on practice in sorting words with and without consonant blends. This strategy would allow the student to differentiate between words containing consonant blends visually and kinesthetically and those without, thus helping them develop a deeper understanding of this phonics concept. By addressing the student's difficulty with consonant blends through targeted instruction, the teacher can support their progress in phonics and overall reading proficiency.

37. B: Derivational morphemes are linguistic units that are attached to root words, typically as prefixes and suffixes. Examples of derivational morphemes include *-er*, *-un*, and *-dis*. In contrast to inflectional morphemes, which do not change the meaning of the root word, adding derivational morphemes typically changes the meaning and part of speech of a word. This distinction can prove especially difficult for young children to grasp, and therefore, it is essential to provide ample opportunities for students to practice and develop their morphological awareness skills in this area. After introducing derivational morphemes through a word family exploration, an effective strategy to reinforce this concept would be to have students create word matrices in which they attach prefixes and suffixes to root words. Doing so would provide students with the opportunity to explore firsthand how attaching derivational morphemes transforms the meaning of words, therefore strengthening their understanding of this complex morphemic concept.

38. D: Understanding the author's viewpoint is an important part of comprehending and analyzing informational texts, as it enables readers to think critically about the author's intent, perspective, and potential biases. Having students complete a Venn diagram as they read two articles about the same topic is an effective strategy for demonstrating variances in perspective among authors. Through this approach, students can focus their attention on key details as they read and identify similarities and differences in opinion, tone, language, and content with a graphic organizer as a visual aid. This will allow students to recognize how different perspectives can impact the presentation of material in an informational text, thus strengthening their ability to critically analyze and comprehend their reading on a deeper level.

39. C: When planning reading instruction, educators must consider students' abilities relative to their developmental levels and scaffold activities accordingly. This ensures that instruction is appropriately challenging while providing the support necessary to make learning accessible. The ability to retell key events from a fictional story is fundamental to reading comprehension development, as it allows young learners to form connections between different parts of the text and ultimately, construct meaning. By providing students with a graphic organizer, such as a story map, to complete as they read, the teacher in this scenario can effectively scaffold this lesson to promote student understanding and success. This strategy will allow students to visually organize their ideas and record events from the story as they occur, ultimately fostering their ability to accurately retell events in sequential order while building reading comprehension skills.

40. B: The ability to segment words into individual phonemes and blending them back together is a skill that usually needs to be present before students can be taught to decode multisyllabic words. Option A would likely occur too early and would not indicate readiness to begin instruction in decoding multisyllabic words. Option C would likely occur after decoding multisyllabic words. Option D describes students who can already decode multisyllabic words.

41. D: Prioritizing oral proficiency skills in the early elementary classroom is fundamental for successful language and literacy development. Doing so establishes the foundation necessary for helping young learners understand how language is used in various forms and contexts, such as speaking and listening, and ultimately, reading and writing. Students with strong oral language skills typically have a richer vocabulary, can effectively express themselves, and have a stronger grasp of English grammatical patterns. To develop these skills, early elementary educators should incorporate multiple opportunities for students to practice speaking and listening throughout daily activities as well as in language and literacy instruction. This can be achieved by such strategies as verbally communicating directions, conducting daily read-alouds, asking open-ended questions during discussions, incorporating songs and rhymes into instruction, and facilitating collaborative learning opportunities. By prioritizing the development of oral language skills, early elementary educators can ensure that students are well-equipped to participate in grade-level language and literacy instruction.

42. B: Sequencing, as it relates to language arts, refers to the ability to accurately recall events from a story according to the order in which they occurred. This important reading comprehension skill is necessary for recalling major events and key information, recognizing cause and effect, and developing literary analysis skills, and therefore, must be integrated into early childhood literacy instruction. Providing young learners with visual aids, such as picture cards that correspond with events from the story, is an effective strategy for promoting the development of sequencing skills. By asking students to work in groups to sort the cards according to the story's events, this teacher provides a collaborative, hands-on setting that promotes arranging story events in sequential order.

43. C: Facilitating identification and analysis of similarities and differences between texts is beneficial for helping students make connections between them. Such connections allow students to consider various perspectives, identify common elements, and synthesize information, thus strengthening their overall understanding of a concept. In the given scenario, providing students with a Venn diagram to compare and contrast texts focused on European colonization would be most suitable in supporting their development of this skill. This format will allow students to visually identify and analyze both common and distinct components of the texts, thus promoting critical thinking and a deeper understanding of the time period.

44. C: Dr. Hollis Scarborough developed the reading rope to demonstrate processes that occur in reading fluency development. According to this model, reading fluency is developed through a combination of factors related to language comprehension and word recognition. Over time, language comprehension becomes strategic and comprises the learner's background and literacy knowledge, vocabulary skills, verbal reasoning, and understanding of language structure. Word recognition becomes primarily automatic with development and consists of the learner's phonological awareness, decoding and spelling skills, as well as sight recognition. In order for reading fluency to eventually occur, both language comprehension and word recognition must be explicitly developed through effective instructional practices. This model serves as a framework for educators to use when planning language and literacy instruction to ensure all necessary components of reading fluency development are included.

45. C: Decoding refers to the ability to recognize letter-sound correspondences to accurately decipher written words into spoken language. This early phonics skill is foundational for language and literacy development, as it is necessary for building automaticity and reading fluency. An effective strategy for evaluating students' decoding skills involves assessing their accuracy in reading aloud from a list of words. The list may include high-frequency sight words, new vocabulary, as well as nonsense words. Nonsense words are those which are spelled and pronounced phonetically but convey no actual meaning. Incorporating nonsense words into an assessment of students' decoding skills is beneficial in providing educators with comprehensive feedback regarding students' strengths and areas for improvement. Unlike high-frequency sight words, these words are unfamiliar and therefore require students to carefully notice and articulate each phoneme individually, thus providing a more thorough evaluation of their decoding abilities.

46. B: An integral aspect of cultivating reading comprehension and critical analysis skills involves the ability to interact with a text, recognize key elements, make inferences, and formulate opinions. This enables students to engage meaningfully in reading, formulate connections between ideas, and integrate information. Close readings are an effective strategy for encouraging students to delve deeply into a text. This activity prompts students to thoroughly examine and analyze a text, often by marking symbols throughout to signify various elements, such as unfamiliar vocabulary, questions or thoughts, and key information. Performing close readings is beneficial in helping students focus intentionally on specific aspects of a text to derive meaning, strengthening reading comprehension and critical analysis skills. In the above example, the student's markings throughout the assigned text to signify unfamiliar vocabulary, key information, and questions indicate a close reading activity.

47. B: Implementing effective pre-reading strategies is essential to helping students navigate complex and often content-specific informational texts. Such strategies typically engage students' prior knowledge, which serves as a framework for reference when students begin reading to foster personal connections and strengthen understanding. Effective pre-reading strategies also encourage meaningful interaction with a text, as this helps focus students' attention on specific information as they read, thus promoting deeper analysis and improved comprehension. KWL charts are effective in achieving both goals. This activity includes three columns, categorized as what students know about a given topic prior to reading, what they want to know, and what they learned after reading. Having students record what they already know about a topic, such as agriculture, taps into their prior knowledge and experiences. Prompting students to list what they want to learn before reading focuses their attention on looking for specific information as they read, thus promoting greater analysis and active engagement with the text. By having students in this scenario complete the first two columns of a KWL chart before reading a text about agriculture, this teacher can establish a strong foundation for promoting students' comprehension and analysis skills.

48. D: High-frequency words, those commonly encountered in written texts, are essential for developing reading fluency and comprehension. Unlike regular phonetic patterns, these words can prove difficult for young readers, as they pose challenges in phonetic decoding. Examples include sight words such as *and*, *with*, *one*, *your*, and *said*. Mastering these words is integral for young readers as they constitute a significant portion of written text, enhancing reading speed and accuracy, thereby bolstering overall comprehension. Promptly addressing difficulties with high-frequency words is essential as they can impede reading progress and academic achievement across subjects and genres. In the provided scenario, targeted interventions are key to supporting the struggling student in acquiring foundational reading skills. An effective strategy involves integrating high-frequency words into meaningful contexts through guided reading sessions. Such sessions would offer the student exposure to these words within authentic reading experiences, thus facilitating comprehension of their usage and application in sentences and passages, ultimately fostering recognition and retention.

49. A: Reading comprehension is typically categorized into three levels: literal, inferential, and evaluative, with evaluative requiring the most complex degree of thought. This level entails the ability to connect reading content to previous experiences and to formulate personal thoughts and opinions about the information presented. To develop this skill, it is important that educators ask students questions that prompt them to think critically about their own interpretations of a text. For example, asking students whether they agree with an author's viewpoint and encouraging them to elaborate on their opinion fosters independent critical thinking to evaluate the text based on their own judgements. By asking such a question after having students read an informational text, this teacher can leverage students' higher order thinking skills to promote deeper analysis and comprehension.

50. C: Understanding concepts of print is fundamental for emergent readers, as it establishes the foundation for early literacy development. Concepts of print encompass various aspects of how written language functions, including understanding the organization and features of printed materials. One important aspect includes recognizing elements such as the cover, title, and author of a book. This awareness signifies an understanding of where the text begins, the key information provided by the title, and the creators behind the content. For instance, when preschoolers identify these components during a shared reading activity, they demonstrate an emerging understanding of how print functions. Engaging in such activities exposes children to the conventions of print and helps them grasp concepts such as left-to-right progression and the role of punctuation, which are essential for becoming proficient readers. Therefore, the scenario described exemplifies a foundational understanding of concepts of print and their significance in fostering emergent literacy skills.

51. D: Mastering academic language becomes increasingly complex as students begin incorporating it into their writing. As academic language is often formal and complex, young learners may struggle to use this type of language when engaging in writing activities. However, developing this skill is an essential component of building writing fluency, as it demonstrates a deeper understanding of the nuances of language. Educators can begin fostering students' ability to incorporate academic language by providing them with sentence frames to guide their writing. Sentence frames scaffold learning by serving as a structural and contextual framework for students to utilize when crafting sentences, thus prompting them to properly utilize academic language. This strategy promotes internalization of how to incorporate increasingly advanced vocabulary into writing, thus strengthening student understanding and promoting writing fluency development.

52. C: Mastering academic language can be challenging for young learners, as it is content-specific, formal in nature, and often complex. However, academic language acquisition is an essential component of literacy development and, therefore, educators must implement methods to promote student understanding and retention. One effective approach to achieve this involves contextualizing academic language prior to beginning a new unit. Doing so provides students with a framework for reference as they encounter unfamiliar vocabulary throughout a unit. In this scenario, the teacher contextualizes new vocabulary related to the upcoming social studies unit by implementing an introductory activity that includes the new words, their definition, and examples of their usage. Through this approach, the teacher establishes a foundation for understanding the new academic language included in the unit, thus facilitating increased student understanding and acquisition.

53. C: Interacting with complex informational texts can prove especially challenging for young English language learners. Specifically, when asked to summarize what they have read, these students may struggle due to limited academic vocabulary comprehension and inability to accurately recall and articulate the main ideas or key details within a text. The ability to effectively summarize is integral for developing reading comprehension and analysis skills, and therefore, it is important that educators implement appropriate linguistic aids to support the needs of English language learners. In the given scenario the teacher differentiates the planned lesson by providing the English language learner with a simplified version of the informational text. While this strategy will aid in comprehension, the teacher can further scaffold the lesson by providing the student with a summary frame to complete after they read the text. Summary frames are versatile and can be differentiated to align with varying reading comprehension skill levels. This support serves as a template, typically consisting of sentence starters, to guide students in summarizing the main ideas and important details found in a text. By incorporating this linguistic aid, the teacher can effectively facilitate the student in recalling and restating key information from the informational text, thus developing their summarization skills and promoting enhanced comprehension.

54. D: Reading comprehension skills are typically categorized into three levels of complexity: literal comprehension, inferential comprehension, and evaluative comprehension. Literal reading comprehension occurs first and is the ability to grasp the surface-level meaning of the word in a text. As students master this skill, they can begin comprehending text on an inferential level, which requires use of critical thinking skills and application of context clues to determine the author's intent or implication. Evaluative comprehension is the most complex and refers to the ability to connect a text to one's own experiences to formulate personal opinions. In the given scenario, the teacher is planning instruction aimed at development of inferential reading skills. Scaffolding this lesson can provide students with valuable support as they begin expanding their reading comprehension abilities. By incorporating a story map, this teacher can provide students with a visual aid in the form of a graphic organizer to help facilitate inferential understanding. Story maps are versatile, and typically prompt students to record key information from a fictional text, such as main characters, setting, plot, conflict, resolution, and character attributes or motivations. Such an activity helps students make connections between story events, identify themes, and draw conclusions, thus strengthening their understanding and helping them make inferences about implications within the text.

55. C: Providing students with active, hands-on learning opportunities provides differentiation, promotes engagement, and enhances overall understanding of content material. Kinesthetic activities offer a multisensory approach to instruction, as they encourage students to physically interact with learning materials. This ultimately strengthens students' connections to learning for increased comprehension and retention. In the given scenario, the teacher demonstrates knowledge of this concept by incorporating kinesthetic learning opportunities into four activity stations aimed at reinforcing comprehension of a fictional short story. Each station prompts students to physically engage with a different concept related to the story, thus providing a multifaceted kinesthetic learning experience to strengthen understanding and build reading comprehension skills.

56. C: Encouraging active reading is a crucial component of developing reading comprehension skills, as it prompts students to engage and interact meaningfully with a text, thus strengthening overall understanding. To facilitate active reading, it is important that educators implement effective pre-, during, and post-reading activity, as this fosters consistent participation with the text. Implementing reader's response journals is a highly effective strategy for promoting active engagement during reading. This method provides students with the opportunity to reflect on their reading, discuss their thoughts and reactions, and ask questions as they read. Reader's response journals should incorporate open-ended question prompts, as this promotes active engagement by prompting students to employ critical-thinking skills to analyze a text on a deeper level. In the given scenario the teacher can foster active reading by asking students open-ended questions to answer in their reader's response journals, such as whether they would do anything differently if they were the main character, and whether it would impact the overall story. This type of question asks students to consider the character's perspective, evaluate the outcomes of their actions, and determine what changes they would make. Furthermore, by prompting students to visualize themselves as the main character, the teacher fosters personal connections to the story, thus strengthening engagement, active reading, and ultimately, comprehension.

57. A: The four-part processing model for word recognition outlines the necessary components for the development of reading comprehension and fluency skills. According to this model, the phonological, orthographic, context, and meaning processors must collaborate to facilitate word recognition and understanding. The phonological processor allows learners to distinguish and comprehend spoken words and sounds, while the orthographic processor facilitates the recognition and recall of written language and associated sounds. The context processor is necessary for applying prior knowledge and context clues to derive meaning, while the meaning processor is responsible for vocabulary knowledge, semantics, and recognizing potential multiple meanings of words. Applying the four-part processing model for reading instruction is highly beneficial for promoting reading comprehension and fluency skill development in the elementary classroom. By using this model as a framework, educators can plan instruction that incorporates all four processors in the brain to strengthen understanding, promote retention, and foster continuous development.

58. D: In assessing students' ability to segment phonemes orally for phonemic awareness, certain words will present more significant challenges than others. Among the options provided, the word *crunch* poses the greatest challenge in segmenting individual phonemes. This is because *crunch* contains consonant clusters, specifically the *cr* blend at the beginning and the final consonant cluster *-nch*. Consonant clusters consist of two or more consonants grouped together without an intervening vowel sound, making it more difficult for students to segment the word into individual phonemes. In contrast, words such as *trunk*, *spoon*, and *globe* have more straightforward phonetic structures with easily identifiable phonemes, thus making them less challenging for students to segment orally. Therefore, when designing a phonemic awareness activity, selecting words such as *crunch* can allow the teacher to effectively gauge students' proficiency in segmenting phonemes, as they require more advanced phonetic analysis.

59. D: Effective comprehension and analysis of informational texts requires students to identify the main idea of a passage and its supporting details. While identifying the main idea helps students understand the purpose of a text, recognizing key details is essential for finding explanations, examples, and evidence to clarify and expand upon the main idea. This is integral for helping students strengthen understanding, forge connections, and formulate conclusions about their reading. In the given scenario, the students' responses to the comprehension questions after reading a text on the life cycle of plants indicate difficulty in recalling supporting details. While the student accurately identifies the main idea of the text and the stages of the life cycle that were presented in the topic sentence of each paragraph, they struggled to explain the details of each stage in the plant life cycle or why understanding the concept was important. As such, this student likely requires a targeted intervention to support their ability to recognize and recall key details in an informational text so as to develop their overall comprehension and analytical skills.

60. A: Teaching students to actively engage with informational texts is necessary for developing their ability to recognize and recall key details that support the main idea, thus fostering deeper analysis and comprehension. Students that struggle to do so will likely require targeted support to improve upon their skills in this area. One effective approach involves guiding these students through annotating the text as they engage in reading. This may include strategies such as having students write notes or questions in the margins, highlighting key points and main ideas, or using sticky notes to mark important information. This approach fosters a close reading of the text, thus promoting meaningful interaction with it and focusing students' attention on essential details. By guiding the student in the given scenario through the process of text annotation, this teacher can effectively support their development of reading comprehension and analysis skills in relation to informational texts.

61. A: As students progress to upper elementary school, understanding increasingly complex literary devices becomes crucial in continuously developing reading comprehension and analysis skills. Figurative language is one such literary device that is commonly used throughout fictional texts. Examples include similes, metaphors, hyperboles, and idiomatic expressions. Interpreting figurative language requires students to employ higher-order thinking skills, and is essential to formulating connections between ideas, understanding the author's intent, and engaging with a text on a deeper level. In the given scenario, the passage chosen by the teacher contains several examples of figurative language, particularly in the form of similes, such as "soft bright eye which was black like a dewdrop" and "they're almost as friendly as dogs." Prior to beginning this lesson, the teacher should review examples and types of figurative language with a particular focus on similes. Doing so would help ensure students have a framework for reference as they engage in reading that will enable them to identify and interpret the meaning of figurative language throughout the text, thus strengthening overall comprehension.

62. B: Choral reading is an activity in which an entire class or group of students simultaneously read aloud together from the same text. This instructional strategy promotes reading fluency development, as it improves comprehension, prosodic reading, and overall engagement with a text. In addition, this approach is particularly helpful for struggling readers who may lack self-confidence when reading aloud among their peers. Through choral reading, these students have the opportunity to actively participate and practice reading aloud in a comfortable setting while also benefiting from modeling by their peers, thus promoting the development of their reading fluency skills.

63. B: Frequently assessing students' progress is an essential component of language and literacy skill development. This allows educators to identify gaps in understanding and adjust instruction accordingly to meet students' individual needs. In the given scenario, the teacher assesses students' ability to spell high-frequency sight words and records their performance according to several categories. Based on the data presented in the chart, Student 2 is categorized correctly because their response, *sed* for the high-frequency sight word *said* reflects a spelling error resulting from phonemic awareness difficulties. In this case, the student has substituted the correct vowel sound *ai* with the incorrect vowel sound *e*, indicating a challenge in accurately perceiving and reproducing the phonemes presented in the word *said*. Student 1 is categorized incorrectly, as although they spelled the sight word correctly, they were categorized as having incorrect spelling due to orthographic processing errors. Student 3's performance is also incorrectly categorized, as the chart indicates that they correctly spelled the sight word *here*, whereas their omission of the silent *e* at the end of the word indicates an orthographic processing difficulty. Student 4 was categorized as having incorrectly spelled the word *come* due to code-based difficulties. However, their use of inventive spelling is indicative of a lack of understanding due to orthographic processing. Therefore, Student 2's response is the only one categorized correctly according to the kindergarten teacher's key.

64. D: Automaticity in reading refers to one's ability to decode written words quickly and accurately. This is essential for building reading fluency, as it allows young readers to focus their attention on understanding the whole text rather than sounding out individual words. Frequent practice and assessment of automaticity in the early childhood classroom are essential for gauging reading proficiency levels and identifying areas of need for additional support. One effective strategy for evaluating automaticity involves timing students as they individually read aloud from a grade-level text. This method allows teachers to determine students' speed in correctly identifying and comprehending words in a text, providing measurable data on each individual's progress. In the above example, the teacher utilizes this approach to assess automaticity by having students individually read a passage aloud from *The Secret Garden* for one minute. In doing so, the teacher is able to determine how many words each student read, how many errors were made, and how many words per minute the student accurately recognizes and comprehends, thus providing a comprehensive assessment of each student's automaticity skills.

65. A: When planning summative assessments, it is important that educators ensure that the assessment itself and all instructional practices, learning activities, and formative assessments align with learning objectives specified by state and district academic standards. These standards outline expectations regarding student progress and achievement according to their grade level at varying points in the school year. Adhering to these standards when planning assessments and instruction is integral to ensuring that students are equipped to advance to the next grade level. In doing so, educators can make informed decisions about instructional strategies, activities, and assessments to provide appropriately challenging learning experiences that adequately prepare students for achieving academic benchmarks.

66. A: Creating activities that emphasize blending individual sounds to decode words plays a crucial role in promoting phonemic awareness, a cornerstone of early literacy acquisition. Phonemic awareness refers to the capacity to discern and manipulate individual phonemes, or sounds, within spoken language. Through participation in tasks that necessitate merging sounds to construct words, students cultivate a deeper comprehension of the phonetic structure inherent in language. This proficiency establishes the foundation for proficiency in decoding and encoding words, thereby facilitating overall proficiency in reading and writing.

67. A: Orthographic processing skills refer to the ability to recognize and recall written words, as well as how to properly utilize the conventions of writing. These skills are crucial for developing reading and writing fluency, as they are foundational for decoding both new and familiar vocabulary, and using proper spelling, punctuation, and capitalization. Students at the second-grade level who exhibit proficiency in orthographic processing are easily able to identify misspelled words due to their understanding of word structure and components. Therefore, a second-grade student who accurately identifies misspelled words from a vocabulary list best showcases strong orthographic processing skills.

68. D: Providing students with effective graphic organizers promotes comprehension of complex informational texts. This learning tool allows students to organize their thoughts while reading, focus on specific details, and visualize important information for greater retention. Graphic organizers are versatile and can be tailored to align with nearly any style of text. In the given scenario, the teacher plans to assign an expository text about different kinds of rocks and their characteristics. Considering each paragraph in the passage focuses on a specific type of rock, an outline would be the most suitable style of graphic organizer. This format will allow students to specify the main idea of each paragraph and record important information, thus focusing their attention on categorizing the names of each kind of rock and their unique features.

69. B: Informational texts, particularly those rich in complex and content-specific academic language, can prove especially difficult for young readers to comprehend. As such, it is important that educators recognize these potential challenges and incorporate necessary supports to facilitate comprehension. Doing so helps ensure that students maintain continuous understanding and avoid becoming overwhelmed or confused during the reading process. Supplementing informational texts with visual aids is a highly effective strategy for enhancing student comprehension. This strategy provides students with a concrete representation of concepts presented in the text, thus making the information more digestible, accessible, and ultimately increasing retention. In this scenario, the teacher should consider including an image of each kind of rock mentioned in the passage, as this would provide students with a reference to correspond with their reading. This would allow students to visualize the characteristics of each type of rock, thus strengthening their grasp of the learning material and improving overall comprehension.

70. D: Consonant digraphs refer to pairs of consonants that represent a single sound. Understanding this concept plays a crucial role in early literacy development, as it helps young readers decode and spell words accurately. Specifically, mastering consonant digraphs enhances students' phonemic awareness and decoding skills, enabling them to recognize and manipulate the sounds within words effectively. In the given question, *ship* exemplifies a consonant digraph because the letters *sh* together represent the singular /sh/ sound, rather than each letter representing its individual sound. By correctly identifying *ship* as containing the *sh* digraph, students demonstrate their understanding of this phonics concept and their ability to apply it to spelling words accurately.

71. C: Phonemic awareness consists of identifying, comprehending, and manipulating spoken language, including the ability to blend and segment individual sounds. This emergent literacy skill is integral for building word recognition, decoding, and reading comprehension skills, and therefore must be addressed when students are experiencing difficulty. In the given scenario, the teacher notices that many students in the class are struggling with blending and segmenting sounds after conducting a series of formative assessments. To support development in this area, the teacher should consider incorporating songs and rhyming games into small-group instruction. Rhymes and songs often emphasize individual sounds within words, thus promoting students' ability to recognize them in context. This interactive strategy encourages active engagement while allowing students to actively practice blending and segmenting sounds, thus strengthening their ability to identify and manipulate phonemes. Further, by organizing students into small groups, the teacher can more effectively provide targeted support based upon individual student needs and address specific difficulties related to phonemic awareness skills. This approach allows the teacher to support both individual and whole-class areas for improvement to develop phonemic awareness skills and ultimately build reading comprehension skills.

72. D: Thematic units are an instructional technique in which a given concept is incorporated into learning across subject areas. This multifaceted approach allows young learners to explore new topics in-depth by participating in several activities related to a central idea. Furthermore, by utilizing thematic units, educators can promote the acquisition and retention of academic language by incorporating new vocabulary across content areas and in multiple contexts. In this scenario, the teacher is preparing a thematic unit focused on weather patterns, as related activities are integrated into language arts, music, art, and science. By using this approach, the teacher can incorporate new weather-related academic vocabulary into multiple activities, thus strengthening students' understanding and retention.

73. D: Understanding academic language requires that students possess foundational morphological skills. This includes the ability to analyze prefixes, suffixes, and base words to decipher unfamiliar vocabulary. In the given scenario, the student's performance on the vocabulary quiz indicates a lack of understanding related to word structure. This is evident in his incorrect matching of words that contained prefixes and suffixes, while words that do not contain affixes are correctly matched to their definitions. By providing the student with a targeted review of morphology concepts, the teacher can enhance the student's understanding of how to analyze prefixes and suffixes to decipher complex vocabulary, thus promoting their understanding of academic language.

74. B: Comprehension of academic language is an essential component of language and literacy development, as it impacts student learning and achievement across subject areas. Academic language can often prove challenging for young learners, as it is content-specific, formal, and complex in nature, and is primarily used within a classroom setting. By integrating language and literacy activities throughout the curriculum however, educators can strengthen students' understanding and mastery of academic language. Doing so exposes students to academic language in context while providing them with opportunities to engage with, utilize, and manipulate the new vocabulary themselves. Through this approach, educators promote students' internalization of academic language and their ability to apply it across subject areas, thus enhancing language and literacy development and overall academic achievement.

75. B: Phonemic awareness refers to the ability to hear, identify, and manipulate individual sounds, or phonemes, in spoken words. To effectively foster this skill, it is important to provide early readers with ample opportunities to practice segmenting words into their individual sounds and blending individual sounds to form complete words. By breaking words down into their constituent sounds, then blending those sounds to form complete words, students gain a fundamental understanding of the phonetic structure of language. This practice helps students grasp the concept that words are made up of individual sounds, which is foundational in both reading and writing. Through activities such as phoneme segmentation and blending, students can become more adept at recognizing and manipulating phonemes, thus enhancing their overall phonemic awareness and reading abilities.

76. C: Understanding print directionality and word spacing are integral components of grasping concepts of print, as they form the basic rules governing how written language is structured on a page. This knowledge is fundamental for emergent readers as it lays the groundwork for navigating and comprehending written texts effectively. By reading a poem aloud while pointing to each word, the kindergarten teacher fosters her students' emergent reading development by reinforcing their understanding of print directionality and word spacing. By observing the consistent left-to-right and top-to-bottom movement of the teacher's finger along the words, students internalize the organizational structure of written language. Furthermore, the clear spacing between words helps them discern individual word boundaries, thus facilitating their ability to recognize and decode words as they progress in their reading journey. Therefore, activities that emphasize print directionality and word spacing play a vital role in building emergent readers' foundational understanding of how written language functions, thus establishing the foundation for their future reading success.

77. A: Implementing effective prereading strategies is essential for supporting comprehension and analysis of informational texts. Doing so helps establish a purpose and context for reading, thus promoting increased engagement and fostering critical thinking that ultimately results in deeper understanding. One effective prereading strategy involves having students skim through an informational text prior to reading to identify main ideas, supporting details, and key vocabulary. This approach helps students tap into prior knowledge while providing them with a general overview of the structure, content, tone, and overall message of the text. Engaging in this activity serves as a framework for reference and establishes a foundation for deeper understanding as students begin to closely read a text, thus enhancing comprehension and analysis.

78. D: Automaticity is the ability to quickly recognize written words, particularly when reading aloud. This skill is crucial for building reading fluency and is best developed through exposure to new vocabulary, printed words, and patterns of phonics. Students struggling with automaticity typically have difficulty identifying and decoding both new and familiar vocabulary, reading with expression, and retaining what they have read. These students may read slowly, mechanically, and may skip over difficult words, thus impeding overall comprehension. As this skill is integral to language and literacy development, it is imperative to provide struggling students with necessary interventions and targeted support. Strategies may include individualized instruction and remediation, dedicated practice activities, and repeated exposure to new vocabulary in a variety of contexts. Students that continue to exhibit difficulty with automaticity may require specialized reading programs or evaluations for potential learning disabilities.

79. D: At the elementary level critical analysis skills encompass the ability to think critically about a text, including interpreting textual elements, making inferences, and formulating opinions. This is integral for effectively reading, analyzing, and understanding texts across subject areas, and therefore, it is important that educators incorporate strategies throughout instruction to promote critical analysis skills. One effective strategy for achieving this involves having students participate in small-group literature circles as they read a fictional text. Literature circles are a student-led instructional approach in which small groups of students gather to discuss a particular piece of literature. In this collaborative setting each student is typically assigned a role, such as summarizer, questioner, and discussion leader, and is given the opportunity to ask questions, discuss ideas, and build upon one another's interpretations of the text. This approach prompts students to explore elements of the text, gather evidence to support their thoughts, and analyze it on a deeper level, thus enhancing their overall reading comprehension and critical analysis skills.

80. A: Accuracy is the ability to read and understand text with minimal errors. Students struggling with accuracy benefit significantly from targeted support aimed at developing their ability to accurately decode and comprehend text at a grade-level pace. One effective strategy involves having these students use their index finger to physically track a given text while reading aloud. This helps students focus on individual words as they read aloud, thus improving accuracy in decoding and comprehension. This also helps students maintain their place in a text. While pre-teaching pronunciation of vocabulary could help this student, tracking with the finger addresses both the pronunciation issues that can arise from inaccurate reading and the issues the student has with losing his or her place.

81. A: Developing young readers' early comprehension skills is integral to establishing the foundation necessary for success as they interact with increasingly complex texts. This begins with building literal reading comprehension skills. Literal comprehension encompasses understanding the meaning of a text, the ability to recall basic facts or information, and the ability to retell events in the correct sequence. In the given scenario, the teacher asks students to recall events from a text about the first Thanksgiving by guiding them with sentence starters beginning with *first*, *next*, *then*, and *finally*. In doing so, the teacher focuses students' attention on recalling facts and events from the text in sequential order, thus promoting the development of literal reading comprehension skills.

82. B: Regularly assessing students' oral reading proficiency provides educators with an overview of their strengths and areas for improvement. Having students individually read aloud from an assigned passage provides insight into areas of individual need and allows educators to implement the necessary support to ensure proper language and literacy skill development. In the given scenario, the student appears to have difficulty in decoding multisyllabic words, particularly those containing affixes. This is evident in the student's frequent pauses, omissions, and mispronunciations when encountering these words. Such frequent errors indicate a pattern in struggling to identify and accurately decode multisyllabic words, likely requiring a targeted intervention to build the student's skills in this area and ultimately improve their reading comprehension and fluency skills.

83. D: Assessing students' oral reading proficiency skills allows educators to identify areas of individual need and provide the support necessary for proper language and literacy skill development. In the given scenario, the student's performance during an oral reading fluency check indicates difficulty in decoding multisyllabic words, particularly those containing affixes. To develop the student's skills in this area, it is important that the teacher implements targeted intervention strategies focused on decoding multisyllabic words. This may include having the student complete syllable division and word-building activities to familiarize them with words containing more than one syllable. Syllable division activities will prompt the student to identify, distinguish, and articulate parts of multisyllabic words, including prefixes, root words, and suffixes to enhance recognition and pronunciation. Furthermore, interactive word-building activities will provide a kinesthetic opportunity for the student to physically manipulate, create, and decode multisyllabic words. By implementing these targeted interventions, the teacher can effectively develop the student's ability to decode multisyllabic words when reading aloud, ultimately improving their reading comprehension and fluency.

84. A: Heterogeneous flexible grouping refers to a strategy in which students of varying abilities, skill levels, and needs are temporarily grouped to participate in a learning activity. These groups are dynamic and can be adjusted based on student progress, individual needs, and learning goals to promote continuous development. Heterogeneous flexible groupings are beneficial in promoting collaboration and providing students with the opportunity to support one another, build upon one another's knowledge, and learn from different experiences and perspectives. Literature circles are an example of an activity that can be grouped heterogeneously. In such an activity, students of varying abilities work in small groups to discuss ideas, ask questions, and share knowledge about an assigned work of literature. This strategy promotes active participation and engagement with the text while allowing students to support one another in understanding and analyzing their reading, thus strengthening comprehension skills.

85. D: Summative assessments take place at the end of a lesson or unit to evaluate students' understanding and mastery of learning objectives. These assessments provide valuable feedback regarding whole-class and individual strengths and needs, thus driving future instruction by allowing educators to implement remediation and additional supports, as necessary. Summative assessments can be conducted through a variety of methods. For example, after having students read a fictional text as part of an English language arts unit, educators can evaluate students' overall comprehension by having them work in small groups to act out the story, such as in a reader's theatre. This interactive approach allows students to demonstrate their interpretation and understanding of the text, including their ability to recall key information and identify important text elements, such as plot, characters, setting, and theme. By having students act out the events of a story after reading it, educators can gain a comprehensive and holistic assessment of students' comprehension of the text.

86. A: Irregular plural nouns are nouns that do not follow the general rule of attaching *-s* or *-es* to pluralize them and therefore must be memorized individually. This concept can prove especially challenging for young learners, as these words do not follow conventional grammatical patterns. Students experiencing difficulty in grasping irregular plural nouns will benefit significantly from differentiation to support their morphemic analysis development. This can best be achieved by scaffolding instruction and practice activities to gradually increase in complexity. In the given scenario, an effective strategy for doing so may include providing the student with two options for pluralizing irregular singular nouns and having them circle the correct choice. This would help the student to visually analyze both the correct and incorrect spellings of each plural irregular noun. By scaffolding learning through this approach, the student can begin to internalize individual irregular plural nouns, thus allowing the student to engage in increasingly complex practice activities and promoting their morphemic analysis skills.

87. C: English language learners often require additional support to facilitate their comprehension and acquisition of complex academic language. As these students are still developing English language proficiency, academic language can be especially challenging. These students typically require linguistic support throughout instruction and particularly when introducing new academic vocabulary. In this scenario, the teacher supports an ELL student's understanding of an informational text by providing a word bank with key vocabulary, as well as by pairing the student with another who can provide assistance. To further facilitate this student's comprehension of academic language, the teacher should consider chunking the text into smaller, more manageable parts. Chunking allows students to focus on one part of a text at a time, thus preventing the students from becoming overwhelmed and allowing them to process new information more effectively, identify new vocabulary, and formulate connections between ideas. Further, this method allows for repeated exposure to new academic vocabulary in context, thus improving comprehension and promoting acquisition.

88. B: A diagnostic reading-comprehension assessment is the appropriate initial step before forming guided reading groups because it provides the information needed to group students according to their instructional reading levels and comprehension needs. Pre-reading activities, such as introducing vocabulary, completing a KWL chart, or using an anticipation guide, can improve comprehension of a specific text, but they are most effective after groups have been formed and appropriate texts have been selected.

89. B: In early elementary education screening assessments are often conducted at the beginning of the school year to evaluate students' preparedness to participate in grade-level instruction. These assessments usually focus on core content areas such as English language arts, and cover learning targets that students will be expected to achieve throughout the school year. For kindergarten students, a screening assessment in English language arts will generally include early literacy concepts such as letter recognition, high-frequency sight words, and basic comprehension. These assessments provide educators with insights into students' strengths, previous knowledge, and areas of individual need. This allows for informed instructional planning to accommodate students' individual needs and promote positive learning outcomes throughout the school year.

90. C: Orthographic processing skills encompass the ability to recognize, recall, and manipulate written letters, words, and word combinations, including proper spelling, punctuation, and capitalization. Overreliance on inventive spelling for familiar high-frequency words reflects insufficient automatic recognition of these words. In the given scenario, the student continues to spell common sight words phonetically, suggesting a need for targeted remediation in high-frequency sight word recognition. Improving this skill will strengthen the student's ability to recognize and recall the visual letter symbols associated with units of sound, ultimately improving their spelling abilities and overall writing proficiency.

91. B: Criterion-referenced assessments are those that evaluate students' progress and abilities in relation to predetermined criteria. Unlike norm-referenced assessments, which compare students' performance to that of grade-level peers, criterion-referenced assessments focus solely on individual mastery of learning objectives. The objective data provided from these assessments provides educators with valuable feedback regarding students' strengths, ability levels, and individual need. In the given example, the teacher assesses the student's proficiency in various tasks related to emergent literacy skills and records their performance against established criteria, thus making it a criterion-referenced assessment.

92. C: Recognizing individual learning needs and implementing supports accordingly is integral to effective reading instruction. This includes acknowledging variances in English language proficiency levels among ELL students, its potential impact on reading comprehension, and incorporating appropriate linguistic supports into instruction. Most school districts outline specific linguistic aids that coincide with each identified level of proficiency and can be implemented into learning, such as visuals, word banks, and leveled texts. While planning an upcoming unit that includes a reading of an advanced grade-level informational text, it is important that the teacher includes linguistic aids that align with the unique proficiency levels of their ELL students. This will help ensure that learning is accessible to these students while providing the support necessary to facilitate the development of English language proficiency and reading comprehension skills.

93. B: Collaborative learning opportunities are highly beneficial for enhancing understanding, as they allow students to build upon each other's knowledge, learn about different perspectives, and guide one another through the learning process. This strategy is particularly effective when pairing students in need of support with others that can provide scaffolding. In these situations, more advanced students can offer assistance during learning activities, provide clarification, and aid in comprehension. Specifically, pairing English language learners with peers who can offer support while reading an advanced text is helpful in strengthening reading comprehension. This approach allows native English-speaking students to guide English language learners in navigating complex vocabulary and concepts, thus fostering their ability to interact meaningfully with the text. By pairing the English language learners in the class with others that can provide scaffolding, the teacher in this scenario can help ensure that these students grasp the main ideas and key points presented in the text while developing reading comprehension skills in the English language.

94. D: Recognizing and understanding synonyms and antonyms within a text is an important part of developing contextual analysis skills necessary for vocabulary acquisition and reading comprehension. This ability allows students to make educated guesses about the meaning of new vocabulary, and therefore, must be addressed when a student experiences difficulty. In the given scenario, the student's omission of the words *ancient* and *modern* despite contextual synonyms and antonyms strongly indicates a need for a targeted review. One effective strategy for promoting understanding of this concept involves having the student complete a semantic web to map out new vocabulary. Semantic webs are an analysis strategy aimed at helping students build word recognition and comprehension skills by prompting them to categorize the features of new vocabulary using a graphic organizer. This method allows students to visualize relationships between words, including synonyms and antonyms, thus strengthening their ability to connect contextual clues with unfamiliar vocabulary and improving overall reading comprehension.

95. C: Inventive spelling, also known as phonetic spelling, refers to the stage in early literacy development where children attempt to spell words based on their understanding of phonetic principles, often using unconventional letter combinations to represent sounds. This stage is integral in early literacy development as it allows children to apply their knowledge of letter-sound correspondences and phonemic awareness in a meaningful context. Inventive spelling serves as a bridge between spoken language and conventional written language, enabling children to experiment with spelling independently as they explore the alphabetic principle. This process fosters a deeper understanding of how letters represent sounds in words, as it allows children to actively engage with language and develop their understanding of spelling patterns and phonemic awareness. Therefore, of the given options, the statement, "Inventive spelling is a natural and beneficial stage in early writing development, allowing children to apply phonetic knowledge," most accurately captures the significance of inventive spelling in early literacy instruction. By allowing children to experiment with spelling independently, educators support the development of their literacy skills while fostering creativity and confidence in their writing abilities.

96. A: Incorporating new and complex academic language into meaningful contexts is integral to promoting acquisition and retention. Doing so provides students with a framework for reference when encountering unfamiliar vocabulary, thus facilitating their comprehension. An effective strategy for achieving this involves providing students with authentic tasks focused on newly learned academic language. Authentic tasks are those which prompt students to apply new concepts in real-world situations, thus strengthening their personal connections to make learning relevant and meaningful. In the given scenario, assigning students to create their own version of a constitution provides an authentic opportunity for utilizing newly acquired academic language in an engaging and meaningful context, thus reinforcing their understanding and internalization of the new vocabulary.

97. B: Word analysis skills refer to students' ability to deconstruct and comprehend words, including decoding unfamiliar vocabulary, recognizing the components of words, and deciphering the meanings of words in various contexts. Developing these skills is integral for vocabulary acquisition, spelling proficiency, and reading comprehension, as they allow students to decode new vocabulary, infer meanings based on context, and formulate connections between words and their meanings. One effective strategy for developing word analysis skills among young readers is semantic mapping. Semantic mapping is an analysis strategy aimed at helping students develop word-learning skills by having them categorize the features of new vocabulary using a graphic organizer format. Implementing this approach allows students to visualize the characteristics of and the relationship between new words associated with a particular concept, such as mammals in the given scenario, thus strengthening their understanding of word meanings, relationships, and structure and ultimately promoting vocabulary acquisition and reading comprehension. In the given scenario, having students participate in creating a semantic map focused on mammals is beneficial in developing students' word analysis skills to build their understanding of new vocabulary.

98. B: Flexible grouping is an instructional strategy intended to accommodate varying skills, abilities, and needs that exist within the classroom, as well as develop specific skills in a given content area. With this approach, students are temporarily grouped and provided with scaffolded supports, instructional modalities, and activities aligned with their learning needs to promote growth and development. In the given scenario, the teacher plans to utilize flexible grouping in a class with students of varying abilities, including those with learning disabilities and English language learners, during a reading of a fictional short story. By implementing this approach, the teacher can continuously adapt and adjust student groupings as their skills and learning needs evolve to best support reading comprehension and fluency skill development.

99. A: Leveled texts are those that vary in complexity to align with diverse reading abilities and needs. These texts allow educators to align reading materials with students' current skills to provide appropriately challenging learning experiences while supporting reading comprehension skill development at a suitable pace. In the given scenario, the teacher plans to implement flexible grouping to accommodate students with differing skills and needs as they read a fictional short story. To further differentiate this lesson, the teacher should consider providing each group with a leveled version of the text aligned with their current abilities. Doing so would ensure that the content of the short story is made accessible for each student, thus promoting engagement and ensuring comprehension while fostering language and literacy skill development.

100. A: Calculating the number of words that a student can read correctly per minute is an effective strategy for measuring progress and identifying areas of individual need in language and literacy development. By conducting this assessment frequently throughout the school year, teachers can identify patterns, adjust instruction as necessary, and implement targeted support to promote improvement for each student. Determining a student's words read correctly per minute involves completing a series of specific steps. To begin, the teacher assigns students to read aloud individually from an assigned grade-level passage. While reading, the teacher times students and records the number of words read correctly versus incorrectly. Then, the teacher must subtract the number of errors the student made while reading from the total number of words in the passage and divide the answer by the number of minutes spent reading. This strategy allows the teacher to determine the student's number of words read correctly per minute, or WCPM, thus providing quantifiable data regarding their oral reading proficiency.

Integration of Knowledge and Understanding

101. Sample Strong Response:

In reviewing Kate's performance on her reading fluency assessment, it is evident that she possesses several strengths as well as areas that require additional support. One such strength lies in Kate's ability to self-correct as she reads aloud. Throughout the fluency check, she frequently corrects herself on words such as *familiar*, *creeks*, and *icebergs*, as well as repeats herself but eventually self-corrects when she encounters the words *streams* and *summer*. This ultimately results in accurate word identification and pronunciation, as is evidenced in her score of 97 words correct per minute.

However, Kate demonstrates a need for additional support related to automaticity, particularly when encountering multisyllabic words with affixes. This is evident in several instances as she reads the passage, such as in long pauses before reading *temperature* and *liquid*, as well as frequent substitutions of multisyllabic words, such as *freezing*, *changing*, and *survival*. She also appears to have been told by the teacher how to pronounce complex multisyllabic words such as *invisible* and *particles*. This ultimately affected her automaticity and pace when reading, as is reflected in her overall score of "2" in rate and smoothness. To address this issue, the teacher should provide Kate with a targeted review to strengthen her recognition and comprehension of these words. One effective strategy for achieving this would be to have Kate participate in a word-building activity using cards with prefixes, suffixes, and root words. This would provide Kate with a kinesthetic opportunity to interact with different parts of words visually and physically as she creates them, thus improving her grasp of morphological structure. Through this hands-on approach, the teacher can help Kate more accurately and efficiently recognize and read aloud multisyllabic words with affixes, ultimately improving her reading comprehension and fluency skills.

102. Sample Strong Response:

After reading the assigned passage both aloud to the teacher and independently, Blake demonstrates several strengths related to reading comprehension as well as some areas that need improvement. One of the strengths Blake exhibits is the ability to recall key specific details from a text. This is evident throughout his conversation with the teacher, as he mentions the Mole bolting from his home after becoming tired of spring cleaning, leaving his home without a coat because it was warm, and recalls specific vocabulary to describe how the Mole feels about being outside, such as *jolly*, *happy*, and *fascinated*. He also accurately recalls the flowers, meadows, leaves, and rivers mentioned in the passage.

However, Blake struggles to comprehend figurative language in a fictional text. This is apparent in his inability to accurately describe the river based on the description from the passage. Rather than interpreting descriptive language such as *chatter*, *chuckling*, and *full-bodied animal* as referring to a lively flowing river, Blake stumbles at this point in his conversation with the teacher, stating that the river was "probably really big" and mistakenly thinking that there were animals in it. If left unaddressed, Blake's struggle to interpret figurative language will ultimately hinder his inferential reading comprehension skills, making it difficult for him to interact meaningfully with increasingly complex fictional texts.

Blake would benefit significantly from a targeted intervention to improve his ability to recognize and interpret figurative language. This can be achieved by prompting Blake to look for context clues while reading to improve his understanding. Doing so can help Blake make connections about the tone and implication of the figurative language, thus allowing him to infer meaning. The teacher can also support Blake during this process by providing him with a reference guide that indicates and describes various kinds of figurative language, such as imagery, symbolism, personification, similes, and metaphors. This would serve as a visual aid for Blake to refer to when engaging in reading to clarify any misunderstanding of figurative language, thus improving his recognition, interpretation, and ultimately, comprehension of this literary device.

Mometrix
TEST PREPARATION

Georgia

Milestones

Grade 7 English Language Arts Success Strategies

I0878281

Dear Future Exam Success Story

First of all, **THANK YOU** for purchasing Mometrix study materials!

Second, congratulations! You are one of the few determined test-takers who are committed to doing whatever it takes to excel on your exam. **You have come to the right place.** We developed these study materials with one goal in mind: to deliver you the information you need in a format that's concise and easy to use.

In addition to optimizing your guide for the content of the test, we've outlined our recommended steps for breaking down the preparation process into small, attainable goals so you can make sure you stay on track.

We've also analyzed the entire test-taking process, identifying the most common pitfalls and showing how you can overcome them and be ready for any curveball the test throws you.

Standardized testing is one of the biggest obstacles on your road to success, which only increases the importance of doing well in the high-pressure, high-stakes environment of test day. Your results on this test could have a significant impact on your future, and this guide provides the information and practical advice to help you achieve your full potential on test day.

Your success is our success

We would love to hear from you! If you would like to share the story of your exam success or if you have any questions or comments in regard to our products, please contact us at **800-673-8175** or **support@mometrix.com**.

Thanks again for your business and we wish you continued success!

Sincerely,
The Mometrix Test Preparation Team

Written and edited by the Mometrix Test Preparation Team
Printed in the United States of America

TABLE OF CONTENTS

Introduction

Thank you for purchasing this resource! You have made the choice to prepare yourself for a test that could have a huge impact on your future, and this guide is designed to help you be fully ready for test day. Obviously, it's important to have a solid understanding of the test material, but you also need to be prepared for the unique environment and stressors of the test, so that you can perform to the best of your abilities.

For this purpose, the first section that appears in this guide is the **Success Strategies**. We've devoted countless hours to meticulously researching what works and what doesn't, and we've boiled down our findings to the most impactful steps you can take to improve your performance on the test. We start at the beginning with study planning and move through the preparation process, all the way to the testing strategies that will help you get the most out of what you know when you're finally sitting in front of the test.

We recommend that you start preparing for your test as far in advance as possible. However, if you've bought this guide as a last-minute study resource and only have a few days before your test, we recommend that you skip over the first two Success Strategies since they address a long-term study plan.

If you struggle with **test anxiety**, we strongly encourage you to check out our recommendations for how you can overcome it. Test anxiety is a formidable foe, but it can be beaten, and we want to make sure you have the tools you need to defeat it.

Strategy #1 – Plan Big, Study Small

There's a lot riding on your performance. If you want to ace this test, you're going to need to keep your skills sharp and the material fresh in your mind. You need a plan that lets you review everything you need to know while still fitting in your schedule. We'll break this strategy down into three categories.

Information Organization

Start with the information you already have: the official test outline. From this, you can make a complete list of all the concepts you need to cover before the test. Organize these concepts into groups that can be studied together, and create a list of any related vocabulary you need to learn so you can brush up on any difficult terms. You'll want to keep this vocabulary list handy once you actually start studying since you may need to add to it along the way.

Time Management

Once you have your set of study concepts, decide how to spread them out over the time you have left before the test. Break your study plan into small, clear goals so you have a manageable task for each day and know exactly what you're doing. Then just focus on one small step at a time. When you manage your time this way, you don't need to spend hours at a time studying. Studying a small block of content for a short period each day helps you retain information better and avoid stressing over how much you have left to do. You can relax knowing that you have a plan to cover everything in time. In order for this strategy to be effective though, you have to start studying early and stick to your schedule. Avoid the exhaustion and futility that comes from last-minute cramming!

Study Environment

The environment you study in has a big impact on your learning. Studying in a coffee shop, while probably more enjoyable, is not likely to be as fruitful as studying in a quiet room. It's important to keep distractions to a minimum. You're only planning to study for a short block of time, so make the most of it. Don't pause to check your phone or get up to find a snack. It's also important to **avoid multitasking**. Research has consistently shown that multitasking will make your studying dramatically less effective. Your study area should also be comfortable and well-lit so you don't have the distraction of straining your eyes or sitting on an uncomfortable chair.

The time of day you study is also important. You want to be rested and alert. Don't wait until just before bedtime. Study when you'll be most likely to comprehend and remember. Even better, if you know what time of day your test will be, set that time aside for study. That way your brain will be used to working on that subject at that specific time and you'll have a better chance of recalling information.

Finally, it can be helpful to team up with others who are studying for the same test. Your actual studying should be done in as isolated an environment as possible, but the work of organizing the information and setting up the study plan can be divided up. In between study sessions, you can discuss with your teammates the concepts that you're all studying and quiz each other on the details. Just be sure that your teammates are as serious about the test as you are. If you find that your study time is being replaced with social time, you might need to find a new team.

Strategy #2 – Make Your Studying Count

You're devoting a lot of time and effort to preparing for this test, so you want to be absolutely certain it will pay off. This means doing more than just reading the content and hoping you can remember it on test day. It's important to make every minute of study count. There are two main areas you can focus on to make your studying count.

Retention

It doesn't matter how much time you study if you can't remember the material. You need to make sure you are retaining the concepts. To check your retention of the information you're learning, try recalling it at later times with minimal prompting. Try carrying around flashcards and glance at one or two from time to time or ask a friend who's also studying for the test to quiz you.

To enhance your retention, look for ways to put the information into practice so that you can apply it rather than simply recalling it. If you're using the information in practical ways, it will be much easier to remember. Similarly, it helps to solidify a concept in your mind if you're not only reading it to yourself but also explaining it to someone else. Ask a friend to let you teach them about a concept you're a little shaky on (or speak aloud to an imaginary audience if necessary). As you try to summarize, define, give examples, and answer your friend's questions, you'll understand the concepts better and they will stay with you longer. Finally, step back for a big picture view and ask yourself how each piece of information fits with the whole subject. When you link the different concepts together and see them working together as a whole, it's easier to remember the individual components.

Finally, practice showing your work on any multi-step problems, even if you're just studying. Writing out each step you take to solve a problem will help solidify the process in your mind, and you'll be more likely to remember it during the test.

Modality

Modality simply refers to the means or method by which you study. Choosing a study modality that fits your own individual learning style is crucial. No two people learn best in exactly the same way, so it's important to know your strengths and use them to your advantage.

For example, if you learn best by visualization, focus on visualizing a concept in your mind and draw an image or a diagram. Try color-coding your notes, illustrating them, or creating symbols that will trigger your mind to recall a learned concept. If you learn best by hearing or discussing information, find a study partner who learns the same way or read aloud to yourself. Think about how to put the information in your own words. Imagine that you are giving a lecture on the topic and record yourself so you can listen to it later.

For any learning style, flashcards can be helpful. Organize the information so you can take advantage of spare moments to review. Underline key words or phrases. Use different colors for different categories. Mnemonic devices (such as creating a short list in which every item starts with the same letter) can also help with retention. Find what works best for you and use it to store the information in your mind most effectively and easily.

Strategy #3 – Practice the Right Way

Your success on test day depends not only on how many hours you put into preparing, but also on whether you prepared the right way. It's good to check along the way to see if your studying is paying off. One of the most effective ways to do this is by taking practice tests to evaluate your progress. Practice tests are useful because they show exactly where you need to improve. Every time you take a practice test, pay special attention to these three groups of questions:

- The questions you got wrong
- The questions you had to guess on, even if you guessed right
- The questions you found difficult or slow to work through

This will show you exactly what your weak areas are, and where you need to devote more study time. Ask yourself why each of these questions gave you trouble. Was it because you didn't understand the material? Was it because you didn't remember the vocabulary? Do you need more repetitions on this type of question to build speed and confidence? Dig into those questions and figure out how you can strengthen your weak areas as you go back to review the material.

Additionally, many practice tests have a section explaining the answer choices. It can be tempting to read the explanation and think that you now have a good understanding of the concept. However, an explanation likely only covers part of the question's broader context. Even if the explanation makes perfect sense, **go back and investigate** every concept related to the question until you're positive you have a thorough understanding.

As you go along, keep in mind that the practice test is just that: practice. Memorizing these questions and answers will not be very helpful on the actual test because it is unlikely to have any of the same exact questions. If you only know the right answers to the sample questions, you won't be prepared for the real thing. **Study the concepts** until you understand them fully, and then you'll be able to answer any question that shows up on the test.

It's important to wait on the practice tests until you're ready. If you take a test on your first day of study, you may be overwhelmed by the amount of material covered and how much you need to learn. Work up to it gradually.

On test day, you'll need to be prepared for answering questions, managing your time, and using the test-taking strategies you've learned. It's a lot to balance, like a mental marathon that will have a big impact on your future. Like training for a marathon, you'll need to start slowly and work your way up. When test day arrives, you'll be ready.

Start with the strategies you've read in the first two Success Strategies—plan your course and study in the way that works best for you. If you have time, consider using multiple study resources to get different approaches to the same concepts. It can be helpful to see difficult concepts from more than one angle. Then find a good source for practice tests. Many times, the test website will suggest potential study resources or provide sample tests.

Practice Test Strategy

If you're able to find at least three practice tests, we recommend this strategy:

Untimed and Open-Book Practice

Take the first test with no time constraints and with your notes and study guide handy. Take your time and focus on applying the strategies you've learned.

Timed and Open-Book Practice

Take the second practice test open-book as well, but set a timer and practice pacing yourself to finish in time.

Timed and Closed-Book Practice

Take any other practice tests as if it were test day. Set a timer and put away your study materials. Sit at a table or desk in a quiet room, imagine yourself at the testing center, and answer questions as quickly and accurately as possible.

Keep repeating timed and closed-book tests on a regular basis until you run out of practice tests or it's time for the actual test. Your mind will be ready for the schedule and stress of test day, and you'll be able to focus on recalling the material you've learned.

Strategy #4 – Pace Yourself

Once you're fully prepared for the material on the test, your biggest challenge on test day will be managing your time. Just knowing that the clock is ticking can make you panic even if you have plenty of time left. Work on pacing yourself so you can build confidence against the time constraints of the exam. Pacing is a difficult skill to master, especially in a high-pressure environment, so **practice is vital**.

Set time expectations for your pace based on how much time is available. For example, if a section has 60 questions and the time limit is 30 minutes, you know you have to average 30 seconds or less per question in order to answer them all. Although 30 seconds is the hard limit, set 25 seconds per question as your goal, so you reserve extra time to spend on harder questions. When you budget extra time for the harder questions, you no longer have any reason to stress when those questions take longer to answer.

Don't let this time expectation distract you from working through the test at a calm, steady pace, but keep it in mind so you don't spend too much time on any one question. Recognize that taking extra time on one question you don't understand may keep you from answering two that you do understand later in the test. If your time limit for a question is up and you're still not sure of the answer, mark it and move on, and come back to it later if the time and the test format allow. If the testing format doesn't allow you to return to earlier questions, just make an educated guess; then put it out of your mind and move on.

On the easier questions, be careful not to rush. It may seem wise to hurry through them so you have more time for the challenging ones, but it's not worth missing one if you know the concept and just didn't take the time to read the question fully. Work efficiently but make sure you understand the question and have looked at all of the answer choices, since more than one may seem right at first.

Even if you're paying attention to the time, you may find yourself a little behind at some point. You should speed up to get back on track, but do so wisely. Don't panic; just take a few seconds less on each question until you're caught up. Don't guess without thinking, but do look through the answer choices and eliminate any you know are wrong. If you can get down to two choices, it is often worthwhile to guess from those. Once you've chosen an answer, move on and don't dwell on any that you skipped or had to hurry through. If a question was taking too long, chances are it was one of the harder ones, so you weren't as likely to get it right anyway.

On the other hand, if you find yourself getting ahead of schedule, it may be beneficial to slow down a little. The more quickly you work, the more likely you are to make a careless mistake that will affect your score. You've budgeted time for each question, so don't be afraid to spend that time. Practice an efficient but careful pace to get the most out of the time you have.

Test-Taking Strategies

This section contains a list of test-taking strategies that you may find helpful as you work through the test. By taking what you know and applying logical thought, you can maximize your chances of answering any question correctly!

It is very important to realize that every question is different and every person is different: no single strategy will work on every question, and no single strategy will work for every person. That's why we've included all of them here, so you can try them out and determine which ones work best for different types of questions and which ones work best for you.

Question Strategies

✓ Read Carefully

Read the question and the answer choices carefully. Don't miss the question because you misread the terms. You have plenty of time to read each question thoroughly and make sure you understand what is being asked. Yet a happy medium must be attained, so don't waste too much time. You must read carefully and efficiently.

✓ Contextual Clues

Look for contextual clues. If the question includes a word you are not familiar with, look at the immediate context for some indication of what the word might mean. Contextual clues can often give you all the information you need to decipher the meaning of an unfamiliar word. Even if you can't determine the meaning, you may be able to narrow down the possibilities enough to make a solid guess at the answer to the question.

✓ Prefixes

If you're having trouble with a word in the question or answer choices, try dissecting it. Take advantage of every clue that the word might include. Prefixes can be a huge help. Usually, they allow you to determine a basic meaning. *Pre-* means before, *post-* means after, *pro-* is positive, *de-* is negative. From prefixes, you can get an idea of the general meaning of the word and try to put it into context.

✓ Hedge Words

Watch out for critical hedge words, such as *likely, may, can, often, almost, mostly, usually, generally, rarely,* and *sometimes.* Question writers insert these hedge phrases to cover every possibility. Often an answer choice will be wrong simply because it leaves no room for exception. Be on guard for answer choices that have definitive words such as *exactly* and *always.*

✓ Switchback Words

Stay alert for *switchbacks.* These are the words and phrases frequently used to alert you to shifts in thought. The most common switchback words are *but, although,* and *however.* Others include *nevertheless, on the other hand, even though, while, in spite of, despite,* and *regardless of.* Switchback words are important to catch because they can change the direction of the question or an answer choice.

⊘ FACE VALUE

When in doubt, use common sense. Accept the situation in the problem at face value. Don't read too much into it. These problems will not require you to make wild assumptions. If you have to go beyond creativity and warp time or space in order to have an answer choice fit the question, then you should move on and consider the other answer choices. These are normal problems rooted in reality. The applicable relationship or explanation may not be readily apparent, but it is there for you to figure out. Use your common sense to interpret anything that isn't clear.

Answer Choice Strategies

⊘ ANSWER SELECTION

The most thorough way to pick an answer choice is to identify and eliminate wrong answers until only one is left, then confirm it is the correct answer. Sometimes an answer choice may immediately seem right, but be careful. The test writers will usually put more than one reasonable answer choice on each question, so take a second to read all of them and make sure that the other choices are not equally obvious. As long as you have time left, it is better to read every answer choice than to pick the first one that looks right without checking the others.

⊘ ANSWER CHOICE FAMILIES

An answer choice family consists of two (in rare cases, three) answer choices that are very similar in construction and cannot all be true at the same time. If you see two answer choices that are direct opposites or parallels, one of them is usually the correct answer. For instance, if one answer choice says that quantity x increases and another either says that quantity x decreases (opposite) or says that quantity y increases (parallel), then those answer choices would fall into the same family. An answer choice that doesn't match the construction of the answer choice family is more likely to be incorrect. Most questions will not have answer choice families, but when they do appear, you should be prepared to recognize them.

⊘ ELIMINATE ANSWERS

Eliminate answer choices as soon as you realize they are wrong, but make sure you consider all possibilities. If you are eliminating answer choices and realize that the last one you are left with is also wrong, don't panic. Start over and consider each choice again. There may be something you missed the first time that you will realize on the second pass.

⊘ AVOID FACT TRAPS

Don't be distracted by an answer choice that is factually true but doesn't answer the question. You are looking for the choice that answers the question. Stay focused on what the question is asking for so you don't accidentally pick an answer that is true but incorrect. Always go back to the question and make sure the answer choice you've selected actually answers the question and is not merely a true statement.

⊘ EXTREME STATEMENTS

In general, you should avoid answers that put forth extreme actions as standard practice or proclaim controversial ideas as established fact. An answer choice that states the "process should be used in certain situations, if..." is much more likely to be correct than one that states the "process should be discontinued completely." The first is a calm rational statement and doesn't even make a definitive, uncompromising stance, using a hedge word *if* to provide wiggle room, whereas the second choice is far more extreme.

⊘ Benchmark

As you read through the answer choices and you come across one that seems to answer the question well, mentally select that answer choice. This is not your final answer, but it's the one that will help you evaluate the other answer choices. The one that you selected is your benchmark or standard for judging each of the other answer choices. Every other answer choice must be compared to your benchmark. That choice is correct until proven otherwise by another answer choice beating it. If you find a better answer, then that one becomes your new benchmark. Once you've decided that no other choice answers the question as well as your benchmark, you have your final answer.

⊘ Predict the Answer

Before you even start looking at the answer choices, it is often best to try to predict the answer. When you come up with the answer on your own, it is easier to avoid distractions and traps because you will know exactly what to look for. The right answer choice is unlikely to be word-for-word what you came up with, but it should be a close match. Even if you are confident that you have the right answer, you should still take the time to read each option before moving on.

General Strategies

⊘ Tough Questions

If you are stumped on a problem or it appears too hard or too difficult, don't waste time. Move on! Remember though, if you can quickly check for obviously incorrect answer choices, your chances of guessing correctly are greatly improved. Before you completely give up, at least try to knock out a couple of possible answers. Eliminate what you can and then guess at the remaining answer choices before moving on.

⊘ Check Your Work

Since you will probably not know every term listed and the answer to every question, it is important that you get credit for the ones that you do know. Don't miss any questions through careless mistakes. If at all possible, try to take a second to look back over your answer selection and make sure you've selected the correct answer choice and haven't made a costly careless mistake (such as marking an answer choice that you didn't mean to mark). This quick double check should more than pay for itself in caught mistakes for the time it costs.

⊘ Pace Yourself

It's easy to be overwhelmed when you're looking at a page full of questions; your mind is confused and full of random thoughts, and the clock is ticking down faster than you would like. Calm down and maintain the pace that you have set for yourself. Especially as you get down to the last few minutes of the test, don't let the small numbers on the clock make you panic. As long as you are on track by monitoring your pace, you are guaranteed to have time for each question.

⊘ Don't Rush

It is very easy to make errors when you are in a hurry. Maintaining a fast pace in answering questions is pointless if it makes you miss questions that you would have gotten right otherwise. Test writers like to include distracting information and wrong answers that seem right. Taking a little extra time to avoid careless mistakes can make all the difference in your test score. Find a pace that allows you to be confident in the answers that you select.

⊘ Keep Moving

Panicking will not help you pass the test, so do your best to stay calm and keep moving. Taking deep breaths and going through the answer elimination steps you practiced can help to break through a stress barrier and keep your pace.

Final Notes

The combination of a solid foundation of content knowledge and the confidence that comes from practicing your plan for applying that knowledge is the key to maximizing your performance on test day. As your foundation of content knowledge is built up and strengthened, you'll find that the strategies included in this chapter become more and more effective in helping you quickly sift through the distractions and traps of the test to isolate the correct answer.

Now that you're preparing to move forward into the test content chapters of this book, be sure to keep your goal in mind. As you read, think about how you will be able to apply this information on the test. If you've already seen sample questions for the test and you have an idea of the question format and style, try to come up with questions of your own that you can answer based on what you're reading. This will give you valuable practice applying your knowledge in the same ways you can expect to on test day.

Good luck and good studying!

English Language Arts

The Writing Process

Brainstorming

When choosing what to write about, activities like brainstorming can help inspire new ideas or help writers see how their ideas go together. **Brainstorming** means considering a variety of topics or ideas and is mainly used to find a creative approach to a subject or problem. A good first step in brainstorming is simple **free-association** with a topic. One way of doing this is sitting down with paper and pen and writing every thought that comes to mind about the topic in a word or phrase. It does not matter how helpful or good the thought seems at first; the writer should write down everything that comes to mind about the topic. Then, the writer should read the list over a few times. Next, he or she should look for patterns, repetitions, and clusters of ideas. This allows a variety of fresh ideas to come as the writer thinks about the topic.

Free Writing

Free writing is a more organized form of brainstorming. **Free writing** means taking a limited amount of time, like 2 to 3 minutes, to write everything that comes to mind about a topic in complete sentences. When the time is up, the writer should review everything he or she has written down. Many of the sentences may not make sense, but they may contain ideas and details that help the writer organize his or her ideas and prepare to plan the composition. Usually, free writing results in more useful ideas than brainstorming because the writer's thoughts and connections are written in complete sentences. However, both methods can be used together to help the writer prepare to plan and write a composition.

Mapping

One specific way to use graphic organizers is to map an essay. There are many different types of graphic organizers. One easy method to create one is to draw a circle in the middle of the page and write a broad topic in it. Then, draw smaller circles with related topics and ideas, or with topics that fit within the broad topic, written inside and draw line to connect each circle to the main circle. This method can show ideas that fit within the broad topic and will help guide the essay, or it can show which ideas may work better as the main topic of the essay.

Once the main idea and other ideas and details for the essay have been chosen, they can be used to map the essay. Mapping is another word for using a certain type of graphic organizer. These graphic organizers look like a map and organize ideas and details as they will appear in the essay. The essay map can have the main idea at the top or in the center. If the main idea is at the top, the supporting ideas will appear below it in a row, and any additional details will appear under the supporting idea they go with. If the main idea appears in the center, the supporting ideas may appear around it, and the additional details will appear around the supporting ideas they go with.

Planning

Planning is the process of organizing a piece of writing before writing a draft. At the beginning of planning, writers should decide **why they are writing** and **who will read what they write**. The writer must also choose a **genre**, which is the **type** of composition he or she will write. There are fiction genres, such as comedy, folklore, action, and mystery. There are also nonfiction genres, such as essays, reports, poems, and journals. To plan his or her composition, a writer may create an outline or a graphic organizer, such as a Venn diagram, a spider-map, or a flowchart. These methods should help the writer choose their topic, main ideas, and how to organize the composition. If the writer needs to do research for the composition, he or she may also do so as they plan. Planning helps writers organize all of their ideas and decide if they have enough information to begin their first draft. However, writers should remember that the decisions they make during planning may change later, so their plan does not have to be perfect.

DRAFTING

Writers may then use their plan, outline, or graphic organizer to compose their first draft. They may write more drafts after the first one to improve their writing. Writing multiple drafts can help writers think of different ways to state their ideas and correct mistakes that may be hard to fix without rewriting a section of the composition, or the whole composition. There is no "right" number of drafts, so different writers may write a different number of drafts. Writing drafts also makes it easier to write freely because a writer can improve his or her composition with each draft they write.

REVISING, EDITING, AND PROOFREADING

Once a writer completes a draft, he or she can move on to revising, editing, and proofreading to improve the draft. **Revising** is making sure that the composition is right for the audience, is not missing important information, is on topic, and is well organized. The writer should also consider the composition's style when revising and ensure that it is appropriately formal or serious. Revising may happen after the first draft so that errors are not repeated in the next draft. Each draft should be revised before the next one is written so that no mistakes are missed. **Editing** comes next. Editing a composition includes steps like improving transitions between paragraphs and making sure each paragraph is on topic. While editing, the writer must pay attention to the words he or she uses and the way the information in each paragraph is organized. Writers may also fix grammar mistakes in the editing phase, since some errors will require a writer to rewrite large parts of their work. **Proofreading** means fixing misspelled words, errors in grammar, and any other small mistakes in the composition.

During the revising, editing, and proofreading steps, it can be helpful for writers to ask a peer to read their work, since he or she may notice mistakes or problems the writer missed before. A writer may also choose to read his or her own work aloud, or listen to someone else read it. Hearing a composition aloud can help writers find mistakes or opportunities for improvement in their work more easily. This happens because when something is read aloud, the person reading the text must pay closer attention to the words on the page. When a writer or a peer reads the composition, they should point out any sentence that confuses them the first time they read it. Most of these sentences can be revised in a way that makes it easier to read and understand.

ADDING AND REMOVING INFORMATION

While both revising and editing may involve changing the words in a composition, they can also involve adding or taking away words. When a writer has completed a draft and reread it, he or she may notice that something, such as a transition, important details, or an explanatory sentence, is missing. Simply changing the words to make the passage sound better will not solve this problem, so the writer must **add** whatever words and information is needed to make the passage make sense and achieve the writer's purpose.

In other cases, a writer may have words, a sentence, or sometimes an entire paragraph that gives unnecessary information or explains the information in a way that is confusing. When this happens, the extra words and information weaken the composition and must be **removed**. Sometimes, this is difficult for writers to do because it may require them to remove writing they are proud of or a fact they find interesting. Despite this, revising and editing are steps meant to improve and strengthen a composition, so the writer should change, add, or remove parts of his or her writing in a way that makes it better and achieves his or her purpose.

Revising Sentences

Sentence variety is important to consider when writing an essay. A variety of sentence lengths and types can make an essay more engaging, and different types of sentences can sometimes help readers better understand information. For example, a sentence containing a list may make more sense when written with a simple sentence structure, since writing a compound sentence containing a list may give the reader too much information at once. On the other hand, information that is closely related and can be connected with a conjunction should be written in a compound sentence, rather than a simple sentence, since a compound sentence helps the reader see that the information goes together.

Using only simple sentences often makes writing boring and bothersome to read. Writing using only compound sentences makes it difficult for writers to explain information well and difficult for readers to understand, since every sentence will include a coordinating conjunction. To check an essay for sentence variety, it is helpful to look at whether the essay contains different sentence structures and lengths. It is also important to pay attention to the way each sentence starts and avoid beginning with the same words or phrases.

Revising Vocabulary

When writing informational or argumentative texts, it is important to use **precise vocabulary**, or **word choice**, to explain your main idea and supporting details. Generalized vocabulary will not help the audience fully understand the points that you are attempting to make because it will not accurately explain your main idea and supporting details. Precise vocabulary is important to use because it will accurately describe the ideas that are central to your text. When you research a subject, make sure to familiarize yourself with any vocabulary that is involved in its explanation. Use context clues, dictionaries, or, if necessary, a technical dictionary to decode any words that you are not familiar with. Precise vocabulary also impacts the effectiveness of narrative text. Carefully choosing vocabulary to describe sensory details, or imagery, helps writers paint the best possible picture of the events they are describing through their writing.

Recursive Writing Process

Brainstorming, planning, drafting, revising, editing, and proofreading are all steps in the **writing process**. This process is helpful to remember when beginning a new composition, but once a writer has practiced these steps in this order, he or she can use the **recursive writing process**. The recursive writing process is the same as the normal writing process, but the steps in the recursive writing process do not have to happen in the same order. For example, one writer may need to repeat steps after completing other steps. A different writer may discover that he or she can practice the planning and revising steps as he or she writes a draft. The recursive writing process involves moving back and forth between planning, drafting, and revising, followed by more planning, more drafting, and more revising until the writer is happy with his or her work. Each writer can use the recursive writing process in their own way, as long as it helps them improve their work and write the best they can.

Review Video: Recursive Writing Process
Visit mometrix.com/academy and enter code: 951611

Essay Structure and Organization

Central Ideas and Supporting Details

In the first paragraph of a composition, writers include a sentence that explains the **central idea.** This sentence is also known as the **thesis**. The rest of the paragraph shows the reader why the topic of the essay is interesting and includes details that support the central idea. One way to understand the relationship between the central idea and supporting information is to think about a table: the tabletop is the central idea, and each of the table's legs is a supporting detail or group of details. All of the legs work together to support the tabletop and create a table, just like the supporting details work together to support the central idea and create a composition.

Introduction

The introduction is used to capture the reader's attention and announce the essay's central idea. Normally, the introduction contains about 3-5 sentences. An introduction can begin with an interesting quote, a question, a strong opinion, or something else that will **interest** the reader's and prompt them to keep reading. If the composition has a prompt, the introduction should **restate** or **summarize** some part of the prompt so that the reader will have an idea of what information will be in the essay. Finally, your introduction should include the **central idea**, the primary thing the essay will tell the reader.

Review Video: Introduction
Visit mometrix.com/academy and enter code: 961328

Body

In an essay's introduction, the writer states the central idea and prepares the reader for the information in the rest of the composition. In the body of the composition, the writer **explains**, **demonstrates**, and **gives more information about** the **central idea**. This is done using supporting details and examples that are relevant to the central idea of the composition. For example, if the composition's central idea is a vacation the writer took, the body will include descriptions of where the writer went, what they experienced, and what they thought of the trip. If the composition's central idea is the writer's opinion, the body will include examples and facts that show why he or she has formed that opinion. If composition's central idea is a topic and the writer wants to instruct the reader, the body will contain facts, explanations, and examples that help teach the reader about the central idea. A writer will use supporting details to explain the central idea throughout the body.

The body should also contain multiple paragraphs, and the order the writer puts these paragraphs in is important. Each paragraph should include at least one supporting detail, but a paragraph may include more than one if two or more supporting details work together to support the central idea. If the central idea is to describe something that happened, the paragraphs should match the order in which the events occurred. If the central idea is to present an opinion or instruct the reader, the paragraphs should be ordered in the way that would make the most sense to the reader. The order of body paragraphs is important because it can impact how easy a composition is to read.

Review Video: Drafting Body Paragraphs
Visit mometrix.com/academy and enter code: 724590

Choosing Supporting Details and Examples

When writing an informative or argumentative text, writers must choose supporting details carefully. Including details that are irrelevant, inaccurate, or vague does not strengthen the author's writing, while relevant, accurate, provable, and specific details do strengthen the author's writing. These details can make the writer's meaning clearer or give evidence that the author's points are true or logical. Such details may include examples or facts, such as statistics, statements from others who have authority on the subject, and common events or experiences. Choosing appropriate supporting details can also help the author show that they put effort into forming their ideas. This can also make the composition more intriguing and enjoyable to read, since the writer's own interest and insight will be apparent to the reader.

Paragraphs

After the introduction of a passage, the body paragraphs will explain and elaborate upon the central idea. While each paragraph should relate to the central idea of the composition, each paragraph should focus on one point or supporting detail. Normally, a paragraph has a good topic sentence that summarizes the paragraph's main point. A topic sentence is a sentence that gives an introduction to the paragraph and its contents. Topic sentences should contain information that is more specific than what is in the introduction and may include a supporting detail, but they should not contain explanations or examples.

The next sentences in the paragraph should support the topic sentence. These sentences can contain examples, explanations, or other specific information that supports the topic sentence, which supports the central idea of the composition. While a paragraph may be structured in any way, as long as it logically provides information that supports the central idea, it can be best to use a template or pattern to make sure that each paragraph is complete and well organized. For example, a good template to follow is topic sentence, evidence, explanation, conclusion. This means that after the topic sentence, the next sentence should provide evidence, like a quote or example, that supports the paragraph's main point. Next, the paragraph should include a sentence that explains how that evidence supports the paragraph's main point. If there are multiple examples or quotes, more than one sentence may be used to explain them. Finally, there should be a concluding sentence that helps the reader understand the paragraph and prepares them for the next one.

A paragraph must contain enough information to support its main point and the composition's central idea. A paragraph of two or three sentences will most likely not support the main point or central idea because it is not likely to contain enough information, explanation, or evidence. When a paragraph does not support the main point or central idea, it does not help the writer achieve their purpose or goal for writing the essay. A helpful, informative paragraph will often have somewhere from three to five sentences. Also, it is important that the sentences within the paragraph lead the reader through the information. Each paragraph should flow logically and stay on topic throughout.

Starting a New Paragraph

For most forms of writing, you will need to use multiple paragraphs. This means that deciding when to start a new paragraph is very important. Reasons for starting a new paragraph include:

- To separate the introduction and conclusion from the body paragraphs
- To move from one supporting detail or point to another
- To indicate an important shift in time or place
- To show a comparison, contrast, or cause and effect relationship

Transitions

Transitions between sentences and paragraphs guide readers from idea to idea and show relationships between sentences and paragraphs. Writers should use transitions carefully and only when they are truly helpful. They should also be selected to fit the author's purpose. Transitions can show relationships such as time, comparison, an order of events, and cause and effect. Transitions are often used at the beginning of a phrase, sentence, or paragraph, since this helps prepare the reader for the next piece of information.

Review Video: Transitions in Writing
Visit mometrix.com/academy and enter code: 233246

Types of Transitional Words

Time	Afterward, immediately, earlier, meanwhile, recently, lately, now, since, soon, when, then, until, before, etc.
Sequence	too, first, second, further, moreover, also, again, and, next, still, besides, finally
Comparison	similarly, in the same way, likewise, also, again, once more
Contrasting	but, although, despite, however, instead, nevertheless, on the one hand... on the other hand, regardless, yet, in contrast.
Cause and Effect	because, consequently, thus, therefore, then, to this end, since, so, as a result, if... then, accordingly
Examples	for example, for instance, such as, to illustrate, indeed, in fact, specifically
Place	near, far, here, there, to the left/right, next to, above, below, beyond, opposite, beside
Repetition, Summary, or Conclusion	as mentioned earlier, as noted, in other words, in short, on the whole, to summarize, therefore, as a result, to conclude, in conclusion
Addition	and, also, furthermore, moreover

Review Video: Transition Words
Visit mometrix.com/academy and enter code: 707563

Conclusion

The conclusion of a composition should summarize the central idea and show that it has been explained well. A good conclusion shows the reader why the author's central idea is meaningful and important and how the supporting details should help the reader understand the central idea. The conclusion should also give the reader something to think about that is related to the central idea. For example, in the conclusion, the author can invite readers to think about how they feel or what they think after reading the composition. Some things to avoid when writing conclusions include:

- Introducing a completely new idea
- Apologizing for one's opinions or writing
- Repeating the central idea word for word rather than summarizing them
- Using the conclusion to summarize every detail in the composition

Review Video: Drafting Conclusions
Visit mometrix.com/academy and enter code: 209408

Grammar

Subjects and Predicates

Subjects

Every sentence needs a subject and a predicate. The **subject** of a sentence names who or what the sentence is about. The subject may be directly stated in a sentence, or the subject may be implied. The **complete subject** includes the simple subject and any **modifiers**, such as adjectives, articles, prepositions, and adverbs, that go with it. To find the complete subject, ask *Who* or *What* before the verb to complete the question. The answer, including any modifiers, is the complete subject. To find the **simple subject**, remove all of the modifiers in the complete subject.

Examples:

simple subject

The small, red car is the one that he wants for Christmas.

complete subject

simple subject

The young artist is coming over for dinner.

complete subject

Review Video: Subjects in English
Visit mometrix.com/academy and enter code: 444771

An imperative sentence is a sentence that gives someone instructions or makes a request to someone. In **imperative** sentences, the verb's subject is understood, but is not actually present in the sentence. For example, this about the sentence *Drive to the store*. This sentence is a command, and the subject is *you*. If the subject were directly stated, the sentence would be *You, drive to the store*. Another fact to consider is that, normally, the subject comes before the verb. However, the subject comes after the verb in sentences that begin with *There are* or *There was*.

Direct:

John knows the way to the park.	Who knows the way to the park?	John
The cookies need ten more minutes.	What needs ten minutes?	The cookies
By five o'clock, Bill will need to leave.	Who needs to leave?	Bill
There are five letters on the table for him.	What is on the table?	Five letters
There were coffee and doughnuts in the house.	What was in the house?	Coffee and doughnuts

Implied:

Go to the post office for me.	Who is going to the post office?	You
Come and sit with me, please?	Who needs to come and sit?	You

PREDICATES

In a sentence, there is always a predicate and a subject. The subject tells what the sentence is about, and the **predicate** explains or describes the subject.

Think about the sentence *He sings.* In this sentence, we have a subject, *He*, and a predicate, *sings.* This is all that is needed for a sentence to be complete. Most sentences contain more information, but if this is all the information that is given in a sentence, then it is a complete sentence.

Now, let's look at another sentence: *John and Jane sing on Tuesday nights at the dance hall.*

subject: John and Jane — predicate: sing on Tuesday nights at the dance hall.

John and Jane sing on Tuesday nights at the dance hall.

SUBJECT-VERB AGREEMENT

Verbs **agree** with their subjects in number. In other words, singular subjects need singular verbs. Plural subjects need plural verbs. **Singular** is for **one** person, place, or thing. **Plural** is for **more than one** person, place, or thing. Subjects and verbs must also share the same point of view, as in first, second, or third person.

Review Video: Subject-Verb Agreement Visit mometrix.com/academy and enter code: 479190

NUMBER AGREEMENT EXAMPLES:

Single Subject and Verb: Dan (singular subject) calls (singular verb) home.

Dan is one person. So, the singular verb *calls* is needed.

Plural Subject and Verb: Dan and Bob (plural subject) call (plural verb) home.

More than one person needs the plural verb *call.*

PERSON AGREEMENT EXAMPLES:

First Person: I *am* walking.

Second Person: You *are* walking.

Third Person: He *is* walking.

COMPLICATIONS WITH SUBJECT-VERB AGREEMENT

WORDS BETWEEN SUBJECT AND VERB

Words that come between the simple subject and the verb do not affect subject-verb agreement.

Examples:

The joy (singular subject) of my life returns (singular verb) home tonight.

The phrase *of my life* does not affect the verb *returns.*

singular subject / singular verb

The question that still remains unanswered is "Who are you? "

Don't let the phrase "*that still remains…*" confuse you. The subject *question* goes with the verb *is.*

Compound Subjects

A compound subject is formed when two or more nouns joined by *and*, *or*, or *nor* act together as the subject of the sentence.

Joined by And

When a compound subject is joined by *and*, it is treated as a plural subject and requires a plural verb.

Examples:

plural subject / plural verb

You and Jon are invited to come to my house.

plural subject / plural verb

The pencil and paper belong to me.

Joined by Or/Nor

For a compound subject joined by *or* or *nor*, the verb must agree in number with the part of the subject that is closest to the verb.

Examples:

subject / verb

Today or tomorrow is the day.

subject / verb

Stan or Phil wants to read the book.

subject / verb

Neither the pen nor the book is on the desk.

subject / verb

Either the blanket or pillows arrive this afternoon.

Indefinite Pronouns as Subject

An indefinite pronoun is a pronoun that does not refer to a specific noun. Different indefinite pronouns are used as a singular noun, a plural noun, or change depending on how they are used.

Always Singular

Pronouns such as *each*, *either*, *everybody*, *anybody*, *somebody*, and *nobody* are always singular. This is because these pronouns always stand in for one person, place, or thing.

Examples:

Each (singular subject) of the runners has (singular verb) a different bib number.

Is (singular verb) either (singular subject) of you ready for the game?

Note: The words *each* and *either* can also be used as adjectives. For example, *each* person is unique. When one of these adjectives modifies the subject of a sentence, it is always a singular subject.

Everybody (singular subject) grows (singular verb) a day older every day.

Anybody (singular subject) is (singular verb) welcome to bring a tent.

ALWAYS PLURAL

Pronouns such as *both*, *several*, and *many* are always plural. This is because these pronouns always stand in for more than one person, place, thing, or idea.

Examples:

Both (plural subject) of the siblings were (plural verb) too tired to argue.

Many (plural subject) have tried (plural verb), but none have succeeded.

DEPEND ON CONTEXT

Pronouns such as *some*, *any*, *all*, *none*, *more*, and *most* can be either singular or plural depending on what they are representing in the context of the sentence.

Examples:

All (singular subject) of my dog's food was (singular verb) still there in his bowl.

By the end of the night, all (plural subject) of my guests were (plural verb) already excited about coming to my next party.

OTHER CASES INVOLVING PLURAL OR IRREGULAR FORM

Some nouns are **singular in meaning but plural in form**: news, mathematics, physics, and economics.

The *news is* coming on now.

Mathematics is my favorite class.

Some nouns are plural in form and meaning, and have **no singular equivalent**: scissors and pants.

> Do these *pants come* with a shirt?
>
> The *scissors are* for my project.

Note: Look to your **dictionary** for help when you aren't sure whether a noun with a plural form has a singular or plural meaning.

Example

Which word should go in the blank?

> If Kelly if going to the party, Joan and Susan ____ going to the store.

a. Is
b. Are
c. Am
d. Was

Try using each choice in the sentence. Choice A, *is*, forms this sentence: If Kelly is going to the party, Joan and Susan is going to the store. There are two people, Joan and Susan, who are going to the store. This makes the subject of the clause plural. *Is* is a singular verb, meaning it does not agree with the subject and cannot be the answer.

Choice B, *are*, forms this sentence: If Kelly is going to the party, Joan and Susan are going to the store. The subject of the clause is still plural. But *are* is a plural verb! The subject and verb agree, so *are* is the correct answer.

Choice C, *am*, forms this sentence: If Kelly is going to the party, Joan and Susan am going to the store. *Am* is a singular verb, and it is also only used in first person, when the writer or speaker is referring to themself. The subject of the clause is plural, and the sentence is in third person, so *am* is not the correct answer.

Choice D, *was*, forms this sentence: If Kelly is going to the party, Joan and Susan was going to the store. *Was* is a singular verb, so it does not agree with the plural subject in this clause.

Complements

A complement is a noun, pronoun, or adjective that is used to give more information about the subject or verb in the sentence.

Direct Objects

A direct object is a noun or pronoun that takes or receives the **action** of a verb. A complete sentence does not need a direct object, so not all sentences will have them. When you are looking for a direct object, find the verb and ask *who* or *what.*

Examples:

> I took *the blanket.*
>
> Jane read *books.*

Indirect Objects

An indirect object is a word or group of words that show how an action had an **influence** on someone or something. If there is an indirect object in a sentence, then you always have a direct object in the sentence. When you are looking for the indirect object, find the verb and ask *to*, *for*, *whom*, or *what*.

Examples:

We taught the old dog (indirect object) a new trick (direct object).

I gave them (indirect object) a math lesson (direct object).

Review Video: Direct and Indirect Objects
Visit mometrix.com/academy and enter code: 817385

Pronoun-Antecedent Agreement

The **antecedent** is the noun that has been replaced by a pronoun. A pronoun and its antecedent **agree** when they have the same number (singular or plural) and gender (male, female, or neutral).

Examples:

Singular agreement: John (antecedent) came into town, and he (pronoun) played for us.

Plural agreement: John and Rick (antecedent) came into town, and they (pronoun) played for us.

To determine which is the correct pronoun to use in a compound subject or object, try each pronoun **alone** in place of the compound in the sentence. Your knowledge of pronouns will tell you which one is correct.

Example:

Bob and (I, me) will be going.

Test: (1) *I will be going* or (2) *Me will be going*. The second choice cannot be correct because *me* cannot be used as the subject of a sentence. Instead, *me* is used as an object.

Answer: Bob and I will be going.

When a pronoun is used with a noun immediately following (as in "we boys"), try the sentence **without the added noun**.

Example:

(We/Us) boys played football last year.

Test: (1) *We played football last year* or (2) *Us played football last year*. Again, the second choice cannot be correct because *us* cannot be used as a subject of a sentence. Instead, *us* is used as an object.

Answer: We boys played football last year.

Review Video: Pronoun Usage
Visit mometrix.com/academy and enter code: 666500

Review Video: Pronoun-Antecedent Agreement
Visit mometrix.com/academy and enter code: 919704

A pronoun should point clearly to the **antecedent**. Here is how a pronoun reference can be unhelpful if it is puzzling or not directly stated.

Unhelpful: Ron and Jim (antecedent) went to the store, and he (pronoun) bought soda.

Who bought soda? Ron or Jim?

Helpful: Jim (antecedent) went to the store, and he (pronoun) bought soda.

The sentence is clear. Jim bought the soda.

EXAMPLE

Tom printed his ticket to the concert, but he forgot ____ at home.

Which pronoun should go in the blank?

a. It
b. Them
c. Him
d. He

What is the antecedent that the missing pronoun must match? There are only four nouns in the sentence. They are *Tom*, *ticket*, *concert*, and *home*. Which one should the missing pronoun refer to? Tom is the one who forgot something, so the pronoun does not refer to Tom. The concert is not at Tom's home, so he cannot forget the concert at home. It is also not logical to say that Tom forgot his home at home The antecedent must be *ticket*.

Choice A says that the missing pronoun is *it*. The pronoun refers to *ticket*, which is a singular noun. A ticket is also a nonliving thing. The missing pronoun is also the object in the second clause. *It* is singular, refers to nonliving nouns, and can be used as the object. Choice A is correct.

Choice B says that the missing pronoun is *them*. The pronoun refers to the singular noun *ticket*. While *them* can be used to refer to nonliving nouns and can be the object of a sentence, it is a plural pronoun. Choice B is incorrect.

Choice C says that the missing pronoun is *him*. The missing pronoun refers to a nonliving thing, not a human or animal. *Him* is an objective personal pronoun and is singular, but it only refers to living nouns. *Him* cannot represent *ticket*, so choice C is incorrect.

Choice D says that the missing pronoun is *he*. The missing pronoun refers to a nonliving noun and is the object of the second sentence. While *he* is a singular pronoun, it can only be used as the subject of a sentence and only refers to living nouns. Choice D is incorrect.

PHRASES

A phrase is a group of words that functions as a single part of speech, usually a noun, adjective, or adverb. A **phrase** is not a complete thought, and does not contain a subject, but it adds detail or explanation to a sentence, or renames something within the sentence.

CLAUSES

A clause is a group of words that contains both a subject and a predicate (verb). There are two types of clauses: independent and dependent. An **independent clause** contains a complete thought, while a **dependent (or subordinate) clause** does not. A dependent clause includes a subject and a verb, and may also contain additional information, but it cannot stand as a complete thought without being joined to an independent clause. Dependent clauses function within sentences as adjectives, adverbs, or nouns.

Example:

independent clause	dependent clause
I am running	because I want to stay in shape.

The clause *I am running* is an independent clause: it has a subject and a verb, and it gives a complete thought. The clause *because I want to stay in shape* is a dependent clause: it has a subject and a verb, but it does not express a complete thought. This is due to the fact that it begins with *because*, which shows that there is more information needed to complete the thought. This dependent clause adds detail to the independent clause to which it is attached.

Review Video: Independent and Dependent Clauses
Visit mometrix.com/academy and enter code: 556903

SENTENCE STRUCTURE

Sentence structure is based on the type and number of clauses in the sentence. Two common sentence structures are simple sentences and compound sentences:

Simple: A simple sentence has one independent clause with no dependent clauses. A simple sentence may have a **compound subject** or a **compound verb**, or both.

Examples:

Judy (single subject) watered (single verb) the lawn.

Judy and Alan (compound subject) watered (single verb) the lawn.

Judy (single subject) watered (compound verb) the lawn and pulled (compound verb) weeds.

Judy and Alan (compound subject) watered (compound verb) the lawn and pulled (compound verb) weeds.

Compound: A compound sentence has two or more independent clauses with no dependent clauses. Usually, the independent clauses are joined with a comma and a coordinating conjunction or with a semicolon.

Examples:

The time has come, (independent clause) and we are ready. (independent clause)

I woke up at dawn (independent clause); the sun was just coming up. (independent clause)

Complex: A complex sentence has one independent clause and at least one dependent clause.

Examples:

Although he had the flu, (dependent clause) Harry went to work. (independent clause)

Marcia got married (independent clause) after she finished college. (dependent clause)

Review Video: Sentence Structure
Visit mometrix.com/academy and enter code: 700478

Sentence Fragments

Recall that a group of words must contain at least one **independent clause** in order to be considered a sentence. If it doesn't contain even one independent clause, it is called a **sentence fragment**.

Choosing the best steps for **repairing** a sentence fragment depends on what type of fragment it is. If the fragment is a dependent clause, it can sometimes be fixed by simply removing a subordinating word, such as *when*, *because*, or *if*, from the beginning of the fragment. Alternatively, a dependent clause can be joined to a closely related neighboring sentence. If the fragment is missing some required part, like a subject or a verb, it may be fixed by simply adding the missing part.

Examples:

Fragment: Because he wanted to sail the Mediterranean.

Removed subordinating word: He wanted to sail the Mediterranean.

Combined with another sentence: Because he wanted to sail the Mediterranean, he booked a Greek island cruise.

EXAMPLE

Which of the following changes will NOT correct this sentence fragment?

Although she had found the coin first.

a. Remove *Although.*
b. Add a comma and *she let her brother keep it* after *first.*
c. Add *She let her brother keep the coin* before *although.*
d. Remove *first.*

Choice A suggests removing the word *although* to form the following sentence: She found the coin first. This option removes the subordinating conjunction to make the clause independent. The resulting sentence is complete, so removing *although* is an acceptable way to correct the fragment. Choice A is incorrect.

Choice B forms the following sentence: Although she had found the coin first, she let her brother keep it. A comma and an independent clause have been added to the sentence fragment to form a complex sentence. The resulting sentence is complete and written correctly, so choice B is incorrect.

Choice C forms the following sentence: She let her brother keep the coin although she had found the coin first. An independent clause has been added before the sentence fragment to form a complex sentence. This sentence is correctly written and complete, so choice C is an acceptable way to correct the fragment. Choice C is incorrect.

Choice D removes the word *first,* leaving *Although she had found the coin.* This is still a sentence fragment, since it is a single dependent clause. Choice D does not correct the fragment, so D is correct.

RUN-ON SENTENCES

Run-on sentences consist of multiple independent clauses that have not been joined together properly. Run-on sentences can be corrected in several different ways:

Join clauses properly: This can be done with a comma and coordinating conjunction, with a semicolon, or with a colon or dash if the second clause is explaining something in the first clause.

Example:

Incorrect: I went on the trip, we visited lots of castles.

Corrected: I went on the trip, and we visited lots of castles.

Split into separate sentences: This correction is best to use when the independent clauses are very long or when they are not closely related.

Example:

Incorrect: The drive to New York takes ten hours, my uncle lives in Boston.

Corrected: The drive to New York takes ten hours. My uncle lives in Boston.

Make one clause dependent: This is the easiest way to make the sentence correct and more interesting at the same time. It's often as simple as adding a subordinating word between the two clauses or before the first clause.

Example:

Incorrect: I finally made it to the store and I bought some eggs.

Corrected: When I finally made it to the store, I bought some eggs.

Reduce to one clause with a compound verb: If both clauses have the same subject, remove the subject from the second clause, and you now have just one clause with a compound verb.

Example:

Incorrect: The drive to New York takes ten hours, it makes me very tired.

Corrected: The drive to New York takes ten hours and makes me very tired.

Note: While these are the simplest ways to correct a run-on sentence, often the best way is to completely reorganize the thoughts in the sentence and rewrite it.

COMMA SPLICES

A comma splice is a specific error that may appear in a run-on sentence. When a sentence has two independent clauses, but the clauses are joined with only a comma, a **comma splice** is formed. Remember that if two independent clauses are joined with a comma, a coordinating conjunction is also needed. Most of the solutions for fixing run-on sentences can also be used to correct a comma splice.

Review Video: Fragments and Run-on Sentences
Visit mometrix.com/academy and enter code: 541989

EXAMPLE

Rick wants to go see a movie tomorrow he would miss his sister's recital.

Identify the change that would NOT correct this run-on sentence.

a. Add a comma after *tomorrow*.
b. Split it into two sentences between *tomorrow* and *he*.
c. Add a comma and *but* after *tomorrow*.
d. Add a subordinating conjunction to make one of the clauses dependent.

Choice A says to add a comma after *tomorrow*. This forms the following sentence: Rick wants to go see a movie tomorrow, he would miss his sister's recital. A comma has been used to join two independent clauses, but there is no coordinating conjunction. This choice forms a comma splice, so it is not an acceptable correction for this sentence. Choice A is the correct answer.

Choice B says to split the sentence into two sentences. This forms the following two sentences: Rick wants to go see a movie tomorrow. He would miss his sister's recital. Both of these sentences are complete. This is an acceptable way to correct the run-on sentence, so choice B is incorrect.

Choice C says to add a coordinating conjunction after *tomorrow*. This forms the following sentence: Rick wants to go see a movie tomorrow, but he would miss his sister's recital. A comma and a coordinating conjunction have been added between the two independent clauses. This is an acceptable way to correct a run-on sentence. Choice C is incorrect.

Choice D says to add a subordinating conjunction to make one of the sentences dependent. There are many new sentences that could be created by adding a subordinating conjunction. For example, consider the following sentence: Although Rick wants to go see a movie tomorrow, he would miss his sister's recital. Alternatively, the following sentence could also be created: Rick wants to go see a movie tomorrow even though he would miss his sister's recital. Both of these sentences have an independent clause and a dependent clause. These sentences are both complete and written correctly, so choice D is incorrect.

Example

Identify the sentence that has a comma splice.

a. Tom stopped at the store to buy supplies and his family met him at the campsite.
b. The ball rolled into the living room quietly, but it still startled the dog.
c. Theresa brought her mom some flowers, her mom did not have a vase.
d. Sweet potatoes, pecans, and brown sugar are all ingredients in my cousin's sweet potato casserole.

Choice A has two independent clauses joined by a coordinating conjunction. This is incorrect because there should be a comma before the coordinating conjunction. While the sentence is written incorrectly, there is no comma, so this sentence does not have a comma splice. Choice A is incorrect.

Choice B has two independent clauses joined by a comma and a coordinating conjunction. This is the correct way to write a compound sentence, so there is no error here. Choice B is incorrect.

Choice C has two independent clauses joined by a comma. This is incorrect because independent clauses should be joined together by a comma and a coordinating conjunction. When the comma is present without a coordinating conjunction between two independent clauses, a comma splice is formed. This means that choice C is correct.

Choice D is a simple sentence that contains one independent clause. The only commas used in this sentence are used to separate items in a list. There are no clauses that need to be joined or errors related to commas, so choice D does not contain a comma splice. Choice D is incorrect.

The Eight Parts of Speech

Nouns

When you talk about a person, place, thing, or idea, you are talking about a **noun**. The two main types of nouns are **common** and **proper** nouns.

Common Nouns

Common nouns are generic names for people, places, and things. Common nouns are not usually capitalized.

Examples of common nouns:

People: boy, girl, worker, manager

Places: school, bank, library, home

Things: dog, cat, truck, car

Proper Nouns

Proper nouns name specific people, places, or things. All proper nouns are capitalized.

Examples of proper nouns:

People: Abraham Lincoln, George Washington, Martin Luther King, Jr.

Places: Los Angeles, California; New York; Asia

Things: Statue of Liberty, Earth, Lincoln Memorial

Note: When referring to the planet that we live on, capitalize *Earth*. When referring to the dirt, rocks, or land, lowercase *earth*.

Singular and Plural Nouns

Singular nouns name **one** person, place, thing, or idea. **Plural nouns** name **more than one** person, place, thing, or idea. Most nouns have both a singular and plural form. Many plural nouns are spelled like the singular noun with an *-s* at the end, but this is not true for all plural nouns. Singular nouns that already end in an *s*, *o*, *ch*, *sh*, or *x* usually end in *-es* when they are in the plural form. Singular nouns that end in a consonant followed by the letter *y* will usually lose the *y* and end in *-ies* in the plural form, and words that end with the letter *f* or *fe* will usually lose the *f* and end in *-ves*.

Some plural nouns have much different spellings than their singular form, and some plural nouns are spelled the same as their singular form. There are more rules for spelling plural nouns, but these are the most common spelling changes.

Examples of singular nouns:

Typical nouns: dog, pencil, girl, store, hope, stingray

Nouns ending in *s*, *o*, *ch*, *sh*, or *x*: mass, hero, lunch, polish, fox

Nouns ending in a consonant and *y*: puppy, baby, fairy, sky

Nouns ending in *f* or *fe*: self, life, calf, hoof

Examples of plural nouns:

Typical nouns: dogs, pencils, girls, stores, hopes, stingrays

Nouns ending in *s*, *o*, *ch*, *sh*, or *x*: masses, heroes, lunches, polishes, foxes

Nouns ending in a consonant and *y*: puppies, babies, fairies, skies

Nouns ending in a vowel and *f* or *fe*: selves, lives, calves, hooves

Collective Nouns

Collective nouns are the names for a group of people, places, or things that function like singular nouns. The following are examples of collective nouns: *class, company, dozen, group, herd, team,* and *public*. Collective nouns usually require an article, such as *a, an,* and *the*, which shows that the noun is a single unit. For example, a choir is a group of singers. Even though there are many singers in a choir, the word choir describes a single group. If we refer to the members of the group, and not the group itself, it is no longer a collective noun.

Incorrect: The *choir are* going to compete nationally this year.

Correct: The *choir is* going to compete nationally this year.

Incorrect: The *members* of the choir *is* competing nationally this year.

Correct: The *members* of the choir *are* competing nationally this year.

Pronouns

Pronouns are words that are used to stand in for nouns. There are several different types of pronouns, but the two main types are subjective and objective pronouns. **Subjective** nouns and pronouns that those that are the subject of a sentence. **Objective** nouns and pronouns are those that are an object in a sentence. Another important type of pronoun is the personal pronoun, which refers to people. Personal pronouns can be subjective or objective. **Possessive** nouns and pronouns show possession or ownership. Pronouns can also be singular or plural.

Singular

Subjective	Objective	Possessive
I	Me	My, Mine
You	You	Your, Yours
He	Him	His
She	Her	Her, hers
It	It	Its
Who	Whom	Whose

Plural

Subjective	Objective	Possessive
we	us	our, ours
you	you	your, yours
they	them	their, theirs

Reflexive: Reflexive pronouns are pronouns that function as the object of a sentence and refer to the subject. Examples of reflexive pronouns include *myself, yourself, himself, herself, itself, ourselves, yourselves*, and *themselves.*

Indefinite: Indefinite pronouns are used to refer to multiple nouns or an undefined noun. Examples of indefinite nouns include *all, any, each, everyone, either/neither, one, some*, and *several.*

Relative: Relative pronouns are used to connect relative clauses that specify or describe a noun to the rest of the sentence. Examples of relative pronouns include *which, who, whom,* and *whose.*

Review Video: Nouns and Pronouns
Visit mometrix.com/academy and enter code: 312073

Verbs

If you want to write a sentence, then you need a verb. Without a verb, you have no sentence. The verb of a sentence indicates action or being. In other words, the verb shows something's action or state of being or the action that has been done to something.

Action Verbs and Linking Verbs

Action verbs show what the subject is doing. In other words, an action verb shows action. **Linking verbs** link the subject of a sentence to a noun or pronoun. They can also link a subject to an adjective, so the linking verb helps create a description. You always need a verb if you want a complete sentence. However, linking verbs on their own cannot be a complete sentence. Any verb that shows a condition and connects to a noun, pronoun, or adjective that describes the subject of a sentence is a linking verb.

Action: He sings. | Run! | Go! | I talk with him every day. | She reads.

Linking:

Incorrect: I am.

Correct: I am John. | I smell roses. | I feel tired.

Review Video: Action Verbs and Linking Verbs
Visit mometrix.com/academy and enter code: 743142

Verb Tenses

A verb **tense** shows the different form of a verb to point to the time of an action. The present and past tense are indicated by the verb's form. An action in the present, *I talk,* can change form for the past: *I talked*. However, for future tense, an auxiliary, or helping, verb is sometimes needed to show the change in form. When writing a composition, it is important to use verb tenses consistently. Choose the best tense for the composition and do not switch to a different tense unless it is necessary or appropriate for a particular sentence or paragraph.

Present: I talk
Past: I talked
Future: I will talk

Present: The action happens at the current time.

Example: He *walks* to the store every morning.

Past: The action happened in the past.

Example: He *walked* to the store an hour ago.

Future: The action is going to happen later.

Example: I *will walk* to the store tomorrow.

Review Video: Verb Tenses
Visit mometrix.com/academy and enter code: 269472

IRREGULAR VERBS

While most verbs gain the suffix -ed when used in the past tense, irregular verbs receive different spelling changes when they are written in the past tense. For example, *walk* is a regular verb, and it becomes *walked* when written in the past tense. However, *run* is an irregular verb because it becomes *ran* when written in the past tense.

EXAMPLE

My mother _____ me about the big nest of ants near the sandbox. I thanked her for telling me!

Which of the following verbs should go in the blank?

a. Warn
b. Warned
c. Will warn
d. Warns

First, look at the sentences. The first sentence does not have enough information to show which tense it is in. However, the second sentence says that the child thanked the mother. The verb here is *thanked*, which is the past-tense form of *thank*. Because the second sentence is in the past tense, it makes sense to say that the first sentence is also in past tense.

Choice A says that the missing verb is *warn. Warn* is a present-tense verb, but it can be used in the future tense if a helping verb is present. However, this sentence is in past tense, so it needs a past-tense verb. Choice A is wrong.

Choice B says that the missing verb is *warned. Warned* is a past-tense verb, and it logically completes the sentence. Choice B is correct!

Choice C says that the missing verb is *will warn. Will warn* is a future-tense verb, meaning that it describes an action that will occur in the future. However, since the speaker already thanked his or her mother for the warning, it is not logical to use a future-tense verb in the blank. Choice C is incorrect.

Choice D says that the missing verb is *warns. Warn* is usually used with plural subjects, and *warns* used with single subjects. *Warns* can be used in the future or present tense, but it cannot be used in the past tense. Since the sentence is in the past tense, it needs a past-tense verb, so D is incorrect.

ADJECTIVES

An **adjective** is a word that is used to modify a noun or pronoun. An adjective answers a question: *Which one? What kind?* or *How many?* Usually, adjectives come before the words that they modify, but they may also come after a linking verb.

Which one? The *third* suit is my favorite.

What kind? This suit is *navy blue*.

How many? I am going to buy *four* pairs of socks to match the suit.

Review Video: Descriptive Text
Visit mometrix.com/academy and enter code: 174903

COMPARISON WITH ADJECTIVES

Some adjectives are relative, and other adjectives are absolute. Adjectives that are **relative** can show the comparison between things. **Absolute** adjectives can also show comparison, but they do so in a different way. Let's say that you are reading two books. You think that one book is perfect, and the other book is not exactly perfect. It is not possible for one book to be more perfect than the other. Either you think that the book is perfect, or you think that the book is imperfect. In this case, perfect and imperfect are absolute adjectives.

Relative adjectives will show the different **degrees** of something or someone to something else or someone else. The three degrees of adjectives include positive, comparative, and superlative.

The **positive** degree is the normal form of an adjective.

Example: This work is *difficult*. | She is *smart*.

The **comparative** degree compares one person or thing to another person or thing.

Example: This work is *more difficult* than your work. | She is *smarter* than me.

The **superlative** degree compares more than two people or things.

Example: This is the *most difficult* work of my life. | She is the *smartest* lady in school.

Review Video: Adjectives
Visit mometrix.com/academy and enter code: 470154

ADVERBS

An **adverb** is a word that is used to **modify,** or describe, a verb, adjective, or another adverb. Usually, adverbs answer one of these questions: *When? Where? How?* and *Why?* The negatives *not* and *never* are considered adverbs. Adverbs that modify adjectives or other adverbs **strengthen** or **weaken** the words that they modify.

Examples:

He walks *quickly* through the crowd.

The water flows *smoothly* on the rocks.

Note: Adverbs are usually indicated by the suffix *-ly*, which has been added to the root word. For instance, *quick* can be made into an adverb by adding *-ly* to construct *quickly*. Some words that end in *-ly* do not follow this rule and can function as other parts of speech. Examples of adjectives ending in *-ly* include: *early, friendly, holy, lonely, silly*, and *ugly*. To know if a word that ends in *-ly* is an adjective or adverb, check your dictionary. Also, while many adverbs end in *-ly*, you need to remember that not all adverbs end in *-ly*.

Examples:

He is *never* angry.

You are *too* irresponsible to travel alone.

Types of Adverbs

Different types of adverbs are used to describe particular aspects of a verb, adjective, or other adverb. The following are examples of common types of adverbs:

Time: Some adverbs show when something was done, such as *yesterday*, *today*, or *in two days*.

Manner: Some adverbs show the way something was done, such as *hurriedly*, *neatly*, *grumpily*, or *loudly*.

Frequency: Some adverbs show how often something was done, such as *seldom*, *often*, *never*, or *often*.

Degree: Some adverbs show how much or to what degree something was done, such as *completely*, *barely*, *highly*, or *halfway*.

Conjunctive: Conjunctive adverbs are used similarly to conjunctions, as they connect different ideas, but they can connect ideas from different clauses or sentences. Some examples of conjunctive adverbs are *however*, *alternatively*, *likewise*, and *then*.

Comparison with Adverbs

The rules for comparing adverbs are the same as the rules for adjectives.

The **positive** degree is the standard form of an adverb.

Example: He arrives *soon.* | She speaks *softly* to her friends.

The **comparative** degree compares one person or thing to another person or thing.

Example: He arrives *sooner* than Sarah. | She speaks *more softly* than him.

The **superlative** degree compares more than two people or things.

Example: He arrives *soonest* of the group. | She speaks the *most softly* of any of her friends.

Review Video: Adverbs
Visit mometrix.com/academy and enter code: 713951

EXAMPLE

Identify the conjunctive adverb in the following sentences.

> Every night, Savannah's brother loudly gets up to get a glass of water. Consequently, she has started sleeping with earmuffs on so that he does not wake her up at night.

a. Every night
b. Loudly
c. Consequently
d. At night

Choice A says that *every night* is a conjunctive adverb. What does *every night* describe in this sentence? It describes how often Savannah's brother loudly gets a glass of water. This means that *every night* shows the frequency that Savannah's brother does this action. Since *every night* is an adverb that shows frequency, choice A is incorrect.

Choice B says that *loudly* is a conjunctive adverb. In this sentence, what does *loudly* describe? It describes the way that Savannah's brother gets a glass of water each night. This means that *loudly* is an adverb that shows manner. *Loudly* is not a conjunctive adverb, so choice B is incorrect.

Choice C says that *consequently* is a conjunctive adverb. What function does *consequently* have in this sentence? It shows the reason that Savannah started wearing earmuffs while she sleeps. It also shows a connection between the information in the first sentence and the information in the second sentence. Since *consequently* connects the ideas in these sentences, it is a conjunctive adverb. Choice C is correct.

Choice D says that *at night* is a conjunctive adverb. *At* and *night* work together to form an adverbial phrase. Which type of adverb do they form? In this sentence, *at night* shows when Savannah wants to avoid being woken up by her brother. This makes *at night* an adverb that shows time, meaning that *at night* is not a conjunctive adverb and choice D is incorrect.

PREPOSITIONS

A **preposition** is a word placed before a noun or pronoun that shows the relationship between an object and another word in the sentence.

Common prepositions:

about	before	during	on	under
after	beneath	for	over	until
against	between	from	past	up
among	beyond	in	through	with
around	by	of	to	within
at	down	off	toward	without

Examples:

The napkin is *in* the drawer.

The Earth rotates *around* the Sun.

The needle is *beneath* the haystack.

Can you find "me" *among* the words?

Prepositional Phrases

One important thing to know about prepositions is that they form special phrases, called prepositional phrases. A **prepositional phrase** begins with a preposition and ends with a noun or pronoun that is the object of the preposition. Normally, the prepositional phrase functions as an **adjective** or an **adverb** within the sentence.

Examples:

The picnic is $\overbrace{\text{on the blanket}}^{\text{prepositional phrase}}$.

I am sick $\overbrace{\text{with a fever}}^{\text{prepositional phrase}}$ today.

$\overbrace{\text{Among the many flowers,}}^{\text{prepositional phrase}}$ John found a four-leaf clover.

Be careful not to mistake the object in a prepositional phrase as the subject of a sentence. The subject of the sentence will not be found in a prepositional phrase because a prepositional phrase is used to describe how an object is related to the subject. Prepositional phrases do not influence subject-verb agreement.

Review Video: Prepositions
Visit mometrix.com/academy and enter code: 946763

Example

Which of the following could NOT complete the sentence?

She went ____ the cave.

a. Sadly
b. Into
c. From
d. Through

Choice A says that the missing word is *sadly*. The blank is between *went* and *the cave*, meaning that the missing word will connect these pieces of the sentence. While *sadly* could be used here to show how the girl felt, there would still be missing information. A preposition is needed here to show whether she entered, exited, or stood outside of the cave. *Sadly* is an adverb, so A is the correct answer.

Choice B says that *into* would complete the sentence. Does *into* complete the sentence without leaving missing information? To say *she went into the cave* is a logical, complete sentence. Choice B is incorrect.

Choice C says that the missing word is *from*. This creates the sentence *she went from the cave*. Since she could have left the cave to go somewhere else, this is also a logical, complete sentence. Choice C is incorrect.

Choice D says that *through* would complete the sentence. The sentence would read *she went through the cave*. Since she could have explored the whole cave or found an exit on the other side of it, *through* can logically complete the sentence. Choice D is incorrect.

EXAMPLE

Identify the prepositional phrase in the following sentence.

Mable visited the store to buy some vegetables.

a. To buy
b. Visited the store
c. The store to buy
d. To buy some vegetables

Remember the pieces of a prepositional phrase. Prepositional phrases should begin with a preposition and end with a noun or pronoun. Considering these rules, can any of the answer choices be eliminated? Choice B and choice C can be eliminated because neither choice begins with a preposition!

That leaves choices A and D. Choice A says that the prepositional phrase is *to buy*. This does start with a preposition, and it does give more information about Mable's trip to the store. However, it does not end with a noun or pronoun. Choice D says that the prepositional phrase is *to buy some vegetables*. Choice D begins with a preposition and ends with a noun, and it explains why Mabel went to the store.

Choice D is the only choice that has all of the pieces of a prepositional phrase, so D is correct!

EXAMPLE

Read the sentence below and answer the following question.

A band with 15 members _____ performing at my restaurant tonight.

Identify the verb that best completes the sentence.

a. Were
b. Is
c. Are
d. Are not

This question is asking which verb should go in the blank. There are a couple of reasons why choosing the correct verb for this sentence may be confusing. First of all, there are two nouns that appear before the verb. Second, one of these nouns is singular and one is plural.

The first step is to determine which noun goes with the verb. The two nouns are *band* and *members*. While *members* is closest to the blank, it is part of a prepositional phrase that describes *band*. The subject of the sentence is *band*, so the verb must agree with *band*.

Is *band* singular or plural? The sentence says that the band has multiple members, but there is only one band. *Band* is a collective noun, meaning that it is a singular noun. This means that the correct verb will also be singular. With this in mind, can any of the answer choices be eliminated?

Choices A, C, and D are all plural verbs. Even though the blank appears after a plural noun, this noun is part of a prepositional phrase. The verb should match the singular subject *band*. The only choice with a singular verb is choice B, so B is the correct answer.

CONJUNCTIONS

Conjunctions join words, phrases, or clauses and they show the connection between the joined pieces. **Coordinating conjunctions** connect equal parts of sentences. Coordinating conjunctions can also be used to create compound subjects and compound predicates, in addition to compound sentences.

COORDINATING CONJUNCTIONS

The **coordinating conjunctions** include: *and, but, yet, or, nor, for,* and *so*

Compound Subjects:

compound subject

Terry *and* Marissa went to the movies last Saturday.

compund subject

Either pumpkin pie *or* apple pie would be a good dessert to bring to Thanksgiving dinner.

compound subject

Neither the clownfish *nor* the goldfish liked the new fish food very much.

Compound Predicates:

compound predicate

Veronica left school *and* picked up her sister from soccer practice.

compound predicate

The cat did not take a nap *or* play with the dog yesterday.

Compound Sentences:

The rock was small, *but* it was heavy.

She drove in the night, *and* he drove in the day.

Bill dressed nicely today, *for* he must give an important presentation this afternoon.

Correlative Conjunctions

Some examples of **correlative conjunctions** are: *either...or* | *neither...nor* | *not only...but also*. When one correlative conjunction is used, its matching correlative conjunction will be used later in the sentence.

Examples:

> *Either* you are coming *or* you are staying.
>
> He *not only* ran three miles *but also* swam 200 yards.

Review Video: Coordinating and Correlative Conjunctions
Visit mometrix.com/academy and enter code: 390329

Subordinating Conjunctions

Subordinating conjunctions link dependent clauses, clauses with either a subject or a predicate, to independent clauses, clauses with both a subject and a predicate, to form a complex sentence. The subordinating conjunction will always be at the beginning of the dependent clause. When the dependent clause is at the beginning of the sentence, it will end with a comma. When the independent clause is at the beginning of the sentence, no comma is needed.

Common **subordinating conjunctions** include:

after	since	whenever
although	so that	where
because	unless	wherever
before	until	whether
in order that	when	while

Examples:

> I am hungry *because* I did not eat breakfast.
>
> He went home *when* everyone left.
>
> *While* her brother ate dinner, she played his favorite video game.

Review Video: Subordinating Conjunctions
Visit mometrix.com/academy and enter code: 958913

Example

Which of the following is a complex sentence?

a. Joseph went grocery shopping and put all of the groceries away at home.
b. Joseph went grocery shopping, and he put all of the groceries away at home.
c. Joseph went grocery shopping and put all of the groceries away when he got home.
d. Joseph went grocery shopping; he put all of the groceries away at home.

Choice A contains one subject and a compound predicate. Because there is only one subject, Joseph, there is only one clause. Since the sentence is made of one independent clause and a prepositional phrase, it is a simple sentence, and choice A is incorrect.

Choice B contains two clauses. The clauses are separated by a comma and a coordinating conjunction, and both are independent clauses. This sentence contains a prepositional phrase and two independent clauses, so it is a compound sentence. Choice B is incorrect.

Choice C contains two clauses. There are two subjects in the sentence, *Joseph* and *he*. Even though one clause is much shorter than the other, these subjects each go with a different clause. The first clause is independent. The second clause is dependent, as it begins with the word *when*. Since the sentence is made of one independent clause and one dependent clause, it is a complex sentence. Choice C is correct.

Choice D contains two clauses. They are both independent clauses, because they both contain a subject and a predicate, and they both form complete thoughts. Since there is no coordinating conjunction, they are linked by a semicolon. Since the sentence is made from two independent clauses, it is a compound sentence. Choice D is incorrect.

Example

Identify the sentence that contains correlative conjunctions.

a. She can wait for her friend's letter to arrive, or she can call her now.
b. He must leave now, or he will end up in heavy traffic when he gets on the highway.
c. When your grandfather gets here, you can greet him with a handshake or a hug.
d. I can't decide whether to go to my brother's concert or to study for my test tomorrow.

Read the answer choices carefully. Remember that correlative conjunctions appear in pairs, so there will be at least two conjunctions in the sentence. Additionally, these conjunctions will go together. The information given immediately after the first conjunction will make little sense without the information that comes after the second conjunction.

Choice A contains the conjunction *or*. Though *or* can be a correlative conjunction, in this sentence, it is used by itself to connect two independent clauses. This means it is a coordinating conjunction. There are no correlative conjunctions in this sentence, so choice A is incorrect.

Choice B contains the conjunctions *or* and *when*. Again, *or* can be a correlative conjunction. However, the sentence could end after *traffic*. The information beginning with *when* is not needed to complete the thought, and *or* and *when* do not form a pair of correlative conjunctions. Choice B is incorrect.

Choice C contains the conjunctions *when* and *or*. *When* is used to begin a dependent clause. *Or* is used to form a compound object by linking *handshake* and *hug*. These conjunctions do not work together in this sentence, so they are not correlative conjunctions. Choice C is incorrect.

Choice D contains the conjunctions *whether* and *or*. *Whether* is used to introduce one choice the speaker can make, and *or* is used to introduce an alternative choice. If the sentence ended before *or*, it would be an incomplete thought. The conjunctions *whether* and *or* go together in this sentence, and they are correlative conjunctions. Choice D is correct.

End Punctuation

Periods

Use a period to end all sentences except direct questions and exclamations. Periods are also used for abbreviations.

Examples: 3 p.m. | 2 a.m. | Mr. Jones | Mrs. Stevens | Dr. Smith | Bill, Jr. | Pennsylvania Ave.

Note: An abbreviation is a shortened form of a word or phrase.

Question Marks

Question marks should be used following a **direct question**. A polite request can be followed by a period instead of a question mark.

Direct Question: What is for lunch today? | How are you? | Why is that the answer?

Polite Requests: Can you please send me the item tomorrow. | Will you please walk with me on the track.

Review Video: Question Marks
Visit mometrix.com/academy and enter code: 118471

Exclamation Marks

Exclamation marks are used after a word group or sentence that shows much feeling or has special importance. Exclamation marks should not be overused. They are saved for proper **exclamatory interjections**.

Example: We're going to the finals! | You have a beautiful car! | "That's crazy!" she yelled.

Review Video: Exclamation Points
Visit mometrix.com/academy and enter code: 199367

Commas

The comma is a punctuation mark that can help you understand connections in a sentence. Not every sentence needs a comma. However, if a sentence needs a comma, you need to put it in the right place. A comma in the wrong place or a missing comma will make a sentence's meaning unclear. These are some of the rules for commas:

Use Case	Example
Before a **coordinating conjunction** joining independent clauses in compound sentences	Bob caught three fish, and I caught two fish.
Between **items in a series**	I will bring the turkey, the pie, and the coffee.
After a **dependent clause** that **begins a complex sentence**	Before she left, Ashley turned off all of the lights in her house.
After **transition words**	Consequently, Joel's mother grounded him.
After an **introductory phrase**	After the final out, we went to a restaurant to celebrate.
After a **prepositional phrase** at the **beginning of a sentence**	At 10 in the evening, Georgia finally arrived home from work.
After an **adverbial clause**	Studying the stars, I was awed by the beauty of the sky.
Before and after **nonessential modifiers**	John Frank, who coaches the team, was promoted today.
Before and after **nonessential appositives**	Thomas Edison, an American inventor, was born in Ohio.
Before and after **nonrestrictive phrases** or **clauses**	His favorite movie, which premiered before he was born, is over three hours long.
After **absolute phrases**	Relieved the test was over, Leah dropped her pencil and slouched in her chair.

Commas for Setting Off Nonessential Words, Phrases, and Clauses

Identifying where to place commas for nonessential words, phrases, and clauses is sometimes tricky. If the word, phrase, or clause is necessary for the sentence to be complete or logical, then it is essential, or restrictive. Additionally, if the word, phrase, or clause cannot be removed without changing the meaning of the sentence, then it is essential. Nonessential words, phrases, and clauses are those that give unnecessary information or do not flow smoothly with the rest of the words in the sentence. These words usually can also be logically placed in more than one spot in the sentence. **Appositives** are often nonessential words or phrases. They are most often used to specify which person or thing is being discussed. An appositive is an additional name or description that may be essential or nonessential.

Review Video: When To Use a Comma
Visit mometrix.com/academy and enter code: 786797

Example

Ella's favorite stuffed animal Rory used to be her mother's.

Which word in the sentence is nonessential and should be set off by commas?

a. Be
b. Stuffed
c. Her
d. Rory

Choice A says that *be* should be set off by commas. Since *be* is a verb, it is unlikely that it is a nonessential word. In this sentence, the subject is *stuffed animal*, and *be* is the verb that shows the subject's action. *Be* is essential to the sentence, so choice A is incorrect.

Choice B says that *stuffed* should be set off by commas. *Stuffed* is an adjective, so it may be nonessential. However, it affects the meaning of this sentence. The word *stuffed* shows that the sentence is about a toy, not a live animal. *Stuffed* is essential to the meaning of the sentence, so choice B is incorrect.

Choice C says that *her* should be set off by commas. *Her* is a personal pronoun, so it is unlikely that it is nonessential. This sentence uses the word *her* to identify whose mother previously owned the stuffed animal. *Her* is essential to show who is being discussed. Choice C is incorrect.

Choice D says that *Rory* should be set off by commas. *Rory* is a name, so it could be a nonessential word, or even an appositive. In this sentence, the word tells the reader the name of Ella's favorite stuffed animal. The sentence can only be about one stuffed animal, because Ella can only have one favorite. This means that the stuffed animal's name is extra, or nonessential, information. *Rory* is a nonessential appositive, so choice D is correct.

Example

> The singer growing more exhausted with every song decided to stop dancing and stood still while singing.

Identify the nonrestrictive phrase that should be set off by commas in the above sentence.

a. The singer growing more exhausted
b. Decided to stop dancing
c. Growing more exhausted with every song
d. Stop dancing and stood still

Choice A says that *the singer growing more exhausted* is the nonrestrictive phrase. Is the sentence still a complete sentence without this phrase? No, because choice A includes the subject, *the singer*. Choice A is not the nonrestrictive phrase.

Choice B says that *decided to stop dancing* is the nonrestrictive phrase. Does the sentence make sense without this phrase? No, removing this phrase leaves the following sentence: The singer growing more exhausted with every song and stood still while singing. This is not a logical sentence, so choice B is not the nonrestrictive phrase.

Choice C says that *growing more exhausted with every song* is the nonrestrictive phrase. Removing this phrase leaves the following sentence: The singer decided to stop dancing and stood still while singing. This sentence makes sense and has the same meaning as the original sentence. This phrase gives extra information that is not essential to the sentence, so choice C is the nonrestrictive phrase. Choice C is correct.

Choice D says that *stop dancing and stood still* is the nonrestrictive phrase. Removing this phrase leaves the following sentence: The singer growing more exhausted with every song decided to while singing. This sentence is now missing important information. What did the singer decide to do while singing? The remaining sentence is now missing the verb. Removing choice D makes the sentence incomplete, so choice D is not the nonrestrictive phrase.

EXAMPLE

Where should a comma be added in the following sentence?

Though the mountain is very steep he is not afraid to scale it.

a. After *Though*
b. After *mountain*
c. After *steep*
d. After *afraid*

Choice A says there should be a comma after *though*. In this sentence, *though* is a subordinating conjunction that begins a dependent clause. Remember that a comma goes at the end of a dependent clause that appears at the beginning of a sentence. *Though* is at the beginning of the clause, and there is no other need for a comma right after it. Choice A is incorrect.

Choice B says there should be a comma after *mountain*. *Mountain* is the subject of the dependent clause in this sentence. The comma should go at the end of the dependent clause. *Mountain* appears in the middle of the dependent clause, not at the end of it. Choice B is incorrect.

Choice C says there should be a comma after *steep*. *Steep* is the last word in the dependent clause that begins the sentence. Adding a comma here would correctly separate the dependent clause from the following independent clause. This is the correct place for the comma, so choice C is correct.

Choice D says there should be a comma after *afraid*. *Afraid* is the verb in the independent clause, and there is no need to separate it from the rest of the sentence. Choice D is incorrect.

SEMICOLONS

The semicolon is used to connect major sentence pieces of equal value. Some rules for semicolons include:

Use Case	Example
Between closely connected independent clauses **not connected with a coordinating conjunction**	You are right; we should go with your plan.
Between independent clauses **linked with a transitional word**	I think that we can agree on this; however, I am not sure about my friends.
Between items in a **series that has internal punctuation**	I have visited New York, New York; Augusta, Maine; and Baltimore, Maryland.

Review Video: How to Use Semicolons
Visit mometrix.com/academy and enter code: 370605

EXAMPLE

Which of the following sentences is NOT written correctly?

a. My sister burned the lasagna we were going to eat for dinner; we went out to eat instead of cooking something else.
b. The ball rolled into the ditch, therefore, it was muddy and wet when he retrieved it.
c. She has lived in many cities, including Nashville, Tennessee; San Diego, California; and Salt Lake City, Utah.
d. He hung the picture in the wrong spot; now there is a distracting hole in the wall.

Choice A is a compound sentence. The semicolon is used to separate two independent clauses. There is no coordinating conjunction in the sentence. This sentence correctly uses a semicolon, so choice A is incorrect.

Choice B is a compound sentence. In a compound sentence, either a coordinating conjunction or a semicolon can be used to separate the independent clauses. This sentence includes a transitional word, but it uses neither a semicolon nor a coordinating conjunction. To revise this sentence, *therefore* can be replaced by a coordinating conjunction, or the first comma can be replaced with a semicolon This sentence is written incorrectly, so choice B is the correct answer.

Choice C is a sentence that includes a list. Remember that semicolons can be used to separate items in a list when at least one of the items includes a comma. In this sentence, a list of cities is given. Since a comma is required to separate the name of a city from the name of the state it is in, each of the items in the list contain a comma. This means that each full city name must be separated by a semicolon. This sentence is written correctly, so choice C is incorrect.

Choice D is a compound sentence and does not contain a coordinating conjunction. Semicolons can be used to separate independent clauses in a compound sentence instead of a coordinating conjunction. This sentence uses a semicolon correctly, so choice D is incorrect.

QUOTATION MARKS

Use quotation marks to close off **direct quotations** of a person's written or spoken words, which are also called **dialogue**. Do not use quotation marks around indirect quotations. An indirect quotation gives someone's message without using the person's exact words. Use **single quotation marks** to close off a quotation inside a quotation.

> **Direct Quote**: Nancy said, “I am waiting for Henry to arrive.”
>
> **Indirect Quote**: Henry said that he is going to be late to the meeting.
>
> **Quote inside a Quote**: The teacher asked, “Has everyone read Martin Luther King's ‘I Have a Dream’ speech?”

Quotation marks should be used around the titles of **short works**: newspaper and magazine articles, poems, short stories, songs, television episodes, and radio programs. Titles of **long works** should be italicized when they are part of a typed composition or underlined when they are part of a handwritten composition.

Examples:

> “Rip Van Winkle” (short story by Washington Irving)
>
> “O Captain! My Captain!” (poem by Walt Whitman)

Review Video: Quotation Marks
Visit mometrix.com/academy and enter code: 884918

Apostrophes

An apostrophe is used to show **possession** or the **deletion of letters in contractions**. An apostrophe is not needed with the possessive pronouns *his, hers, its, ours, theirs, whose*, and *yours*.

Singular Nouns: David's car | a book's theme | my brother's board game

Plural Nouns that end with -*s*: the scissors' handle | boys' basketball

Plural Nouns that end without -*s*: Men's department | the people's adventure

Review Video: Apostrophes
Visit mometrix.com/academy and enter code: 213068

Review Video: Punctuation Errors in Possessive Pronouns
Visit mometrix.com/academy and enter code: 221438

Apostrophes in Contractions

Contractions are combinations of words. Contractions involve taking two words, removing at least one letter from one of the words, putting an apostrophe in its place, and removing the space. For example, *does not* can be written as the contraction *doesn't*. The *o* is removed from *not* and is replaced with an apostrophe, which represents the removed letter, so it appears as *n't*. The space after does is then removed, turning *does not* into the contraction *doesn't*. Some more examples of contractions are listed below.

First Word	Second Word	Contraction
Can	Not	Can't
Do	Not	Don't
She	Will	She'll
They	Will	They'll
He	Is	He's
It	Is	It's
They	Are	They're
I	Am	I'm

Not all words can be used to form contractions, but many small, commonly used words can.

Capitalization

One important part of using correct grammar is properly capitalizing words. Usually, only nouns will be capitalized, but there are some exceptions. The most important capitalization rule is that the first word of every sentence, no matter what part of speech it is, should be capitalized. Another exception is that the pronoun *I* should always be capitalized.

Proper nouns are always capitalized, but sometimes it can be tricky to decide whether or not a noun is a proper noun. Some words that are usually common nouns may become proper nouns when used with other words or phrases. Also, when words that are not nouns are used with a noun, or when a group of words are used together as one noun, those words may also need to be capitalized.

Titles of Books, Stories, and Essays

Most of the words in titles of things like books, stories, and essays should be capitalized, but some should not. The very first word in a title should always be capitalized. Any other word in a title that is a noun, pronoun, adjective, verb or adverb should be capitalized. Articles, such as *a* or *the*, should not be capitalized. Short conjunctions and prepositions are usually not capitalized.

Abbreviations, Initials, and Acronyms

Abbreviations are shortened versions of other words. When an abbreviation shortens, or abbreviates, a word that should be capitalized, the abbreviation's first letter should also be capitalized. When the shortened word is a noun that is not capitalized, the abbreviation should be in lowercase. Initials are usually written using the first letter from multiple words. For example, John Fitzgerald Kennedy is commonly referred to by his initials, JFK. Acronyms also use the first letter from multiple words, but they are different from initials because they form words on their own. For example, NASA is an acronym for National Aeronautics and Space Administration. Some acronyms, like NASA, omit small words, such as *and*, *of*, and *for*. When initials and acronyms are used for proper nouns, each letter should be capitalized.

The types of words and phrases in the chart below are proper nouns and should always be capitalized:

	Description	**Example**
Historical Periods	A range of time in history that is related to specific events or circumstances	During the Romantic Period, many authors and poets wrote about their emotions.
Historical Events	Names of important events that happened in history	Napoleon Bonaparte led France after the French Revolution.
Historical Documents	Titles of important papers or compositions that are connected to historical events	The Mayflower Compact was written to create rules and expectations for the colony in Plymouth.
Languages	Names of the different languages that people speak	I want to learn to speak Cantonese, Spanish, and German.
Races and Ethnicities	Words often used to describe a person's heritage or cultural group	Malia taught her granddaughter how to hula so she could share a tradition of her Native Hawaiian heritage with her.
Nationalities	Words that describe which country a person is from	My teacher who moved to Canada last year is Romanian.
Organizations	Titles of official groups formed by people	Fewer than half of the states in America have a team in the National Basketball Association.

Example

Allison and Claire enjoy studying art from the beginning of the renaissance. They started a club so they and other students can learn more about it. Allison and Claire named the club Early Renaissance Art Club, which can be abbreviated to ERA Club. The students that joined elected Claire as the president and Allison as the vice president. The club's first meeting will take place after Christmas vacation.

Which of the following changes should be made in the passage?

a. In the first sentence, *Renaissance* should be capitalized.
b. In the third sentence, *ERA* should be written as *Era*.
c. In the fourth sentence, *president* and *vice president* should be capitalized.
d. In the last sentence, *Christmas* should be in lowercase.

Choice A says that *Renaissance* should be capitalized in the first sentence of the passage. The Renaissance is a historical period, so *Renaissance* is a proper noun that should always be capitalized. Choice A is correct.

Choice B says that *ERA* should be written as *Era*. In the third sentence of the passage, the word *era* is used as an acronym. Remember that all letters in an acronym should be capitalized. The correct capitalization is *ERA*, so choice B is incorrect.

Choice C says that *president* and *vice president* should be capitalized. Titles for people are capitalized when they are used as part of a person's name or in the place of a person's name. In this passage, these titles are not used as part of anyone's name or in place of anyone's name, so they should be in lowercase. Choice C is incorrect.

Choice D says that *Christmas* should be in lowercase. The passage says that the first meeting will be held after Christmas break. Even though *Christmas* is used to describe when the students are getting a vacation from school, it is the name of a holiday. Names of holidays are always capitalized, so choice D is incorrect.

Word Confusion

To, Too, and Two

To can be an adverb or a preposition for showing direction, purpose, and relationship. A dictionary can also be used to see the many other ways to use *to* in a sentence.

Examples: I went to the store. | I want to go with you.

Too is an adverb that means *also, as well, very,* or *in excess.*

Examples: I can walk a mile too. | You have eaten too much.

Two is a number.

Example: You have two minutes left.

There, Their, and They're

There can be an adjective, adverb, or pronoun. Often, *there* is used to show a place or to start a sentence.

Examples: I went there yesterday. | There is something in his pocket.

Their is a pronoun that is used to show ownership.

Examples: He is their father. | This is their fourth apology this week.

They're is a contraction of *they are.*

Example: Did you know that they're in town?

Its and It's

Its is a possessive pronoun that shows ownership.

Example: The guitar is in its case.

It's is a contraction of *it is.*

Example: It's an honor and a privilege to meet you.

Affect and Effect

There are two main reasons that *affect* and *effect* are so often confused: 1) both words can be used as either a noun or a verb, and 2) unlike most homophones, their usage and meanings are closely related to each other. Here is a quick explanation of the four usage options:

Affect (n): feeling, emotion, or mood that is displayed

Example: The patient had a flat *affect.* (i.e., his face showed little or no emotion)

Affect (v): to alter, to change, to influence

Example: The sunshine *affects* the plant's growth.

Effect (n): a result, a consequence

Example: What *effect* will this weather have on our schedule?

Effect (v): to bring about, to cause to be

Example: These new rules will *effect* order in the office.

Example

Choose the correct spelling from each pair of homophones in the following passage.

I found a unique tree in the forest. (It's/Its) trunk is blue, and it has (two/too) many branches to count. I brought some of my friends to see it, but the tree did not seem to (affect/effect) them. While (their/they're) not fascinated by the strange tree, I am!

The first pair of homophones is *it's* and *its.* Remember that the contraction *it's* is used in place of *it is. Its* is a possessive pronoun that shows a thing's ownership or possession. An easy way to decide whether *it's* or *its* is correct is to see how the sentence sounds with *it is,* instead. *It is trunk is blue* does not make sense. *Its trunk is blue* means that the tree has a blue trunk, so *its* is the correct choice.

The next pair of homophones is *two* and *too. Two* only means the number two. *Too* can mean *also* or *in excess.* Which of these makes the most sense in this sentence? *Two many branches to count* or *too many branches to count*? The correct meaning is that there is an abundance of branches, so *too* is the correct choice for this pair.

The third pair of homophones is *affect* and *effect*. Since both of these words can be used as a noun or verb, identifying the correct part of speech is a helpful first step. The part of speech is a verb, since the correct word will show what *the tree* does to *them*. *Affect* as a verb means to change or influence. *Effect* as a verb means to lead to or cause something to happen. Replace the homophone with these synonyms. Seeing the tree cannot cause or lead the speaker's friends to exist, but it can change them or influence them. *Affect* is the correct choice for this pair.

The last pair of homophones is *their* and *they're*. *Their* is a possessive pronoun used to show that multiple people or things own something. *They're* is a contraction used in place of *they are*. Replace the homophone with *they are*. Does the sentence make sense? It does because they, the speaker's friends, are not fascinated by the tree. Saying *their not fascinated* does not make sense. *They're* is the correct choice for this pair.

Types of Essays

Essays

Essays usually focus on one topic, subject, or goal. There are several types of essays, including informative, persuasive, and narrative. An essay's structure and formality depend on the type of essay and its goal. While narrative essays typically do not include outside sources, other types of essays often require some research and the use of primary and secondary sources.

The basic format of an essay typically has three major parts: the introduction, the body, and the conclusion. The body is further divided into the writer's main points. Most essays will have at least three main points, but essays that go into more depth can have almost any number of main points.

An essay's introduction should answer three questions:

1. What is the **subject** of the essay?

   If an essay is about a book, the answer would include the title and author of the book, as well as any additional information needed, such as the subject or argument of the book.

2. How does the essay **discuss** the subject?

   To answer this, the writer briefly summarizes the main points and the evidence supporting them to let readers know how the essay is organized and what information they can expect to read.

3. What will the essay **prove**?

   This information is in the thesis statement, usually the opening paragraph's last sentence, which clearly states the writer's message.

The body elaborates on all the main points related to the thesis, introducing one main point at a time, and includes supporting evidence with each main point. Each body paragraph should state the point in a topic sentence, which is usually the first sentence in the paragraph. The paragraph should then explain the point's meaning, support it with quotations or other evidence, and then explain how this point and the evidence are related to the thesis. The writer should then repeat this procedure in a new paragraph for each additional main point.

The conclusion restates the content of the introduction, including the thesis, to remind the reader of the essay's main argument or subject. The essay writer may also summarize the highlights of the argument or description contained in the body of the essay, following the same organization originally used in the body. For example, a conclusion might look like: Point 1 + Point 2 + Point 3 = Thesis, or Point 1 → Point 2 → Point 3 → Thesis Proof. Good organization makes essays easier for writers to compose and provides a guide for readers to follow. Well-organized essays hold attention better and are more likely to get readers to believe or agree with the writer.

Using Sources in Essays

Sometimes writers use information from others in their work. This is most common in expository and persuasive writing. For an expository essay, a writer may not know all of the information that he or she needs to finish the composition. The writer may use other people's work to find the missing information and complete the composition. Persuasive writers may do research to find facts or statements from others that support their own beliefs and make their writing more persuasive. In both cases, research helps the writer find information that **supports** his or her **original work**.

Outside information must be relevant, true, and helpful to be appropriate for a composition. Writers must also be careful not to use too much outside information, since this can make the composition unoriginal. If a writer does use outside information, it is extremely important that the writer mention in the composition where the information came from. If the writer forgets or chooses not to say where the information came from, he or she has stolen someone else's work and presented it as their own. Doing this is called **plagiarism**.

Informational Texts

Informational texts, also called instructional or expository texts, are compositions written to inform the reader about a specific topic. An informational essay can inform readers in a variety of ways, such as giving them instructions, telling them facts about the topic, or teaching them why something happens. Informational texts should be logical, meaning that they should present information in an order that the reader can easily understand, and they should include the right amount of information so the writer successfully informs his or her audience of new information.

Informational texts should also focus on a **central idea**. In the introduction of an informational text, there may be a sentence or two that clearly state the essay's central idea. This sentence, or sentences, is called a **thesis statement**. The central idea should be clear throughout the composition. By emphasizing the central idea in the introduction, body, and conclusion, the writer can ensure that the central idea is clear. One way to make sure that the central idea is emphasized is to think about the purpose of each part of the essay. The introduction prepares the reader by telling them what the rest of the essay is about, so the central idea should be **introduced** in this section. The body tells the reader the information the writer wants to tell the audience, so this **explains** the central idea and facts about it to the reader. The conclusion is used to **remind** the reader of how the information in the body is related and **restates** the central idea one final time.

Structures or Organizational Patterns in Informational Texts

Informational text can be **descriptive**, meaning that it gives information that can be experienced through the five senses, or it answers the questions what, who, when, where, and why. One common method of organizing informational text is to put it in a certain sequence, or order. **Chronological** texts include events in the order that they occurred, from start to finish. **How-to**, or **instructional**, texts organize information into a series of instructions in the order in which the steps should be followed. **Comparison-contrast** structures of informational text describe different ideas to their readers by pointing out how things or ideas are similar and how they are different. **Cause and effect** structures of informational text describe events that occurred and the causes or reasons for those events. **Problem and solution** structures of informational texts introduce and describe problems and offer one or more solutions for each problem described.

ARGUMENTATIVE WRITING

In argumentative writing, the writer expresses a belief or opinion that he or she wants to lead readers to agree with. When writing an argumentative composition, the writer should first identify the **topic** his or her opinion is about. The topic may be serious or fun, as long as there is one clear topic in the composition. The next step is for the writer to determine his or her opinion on the topic and determine why he or she holds that opinion. In order to persuade others to agree with their opinion, the writer must be able to give readers reasons to support the opinion. If the writer does not know why he or she has an opinion, it will be difficult to convince readers to agree. In addition to having reasons that support their opinion, writers should prepare examples that support each of these reasons in order to strengthen their composition.

Once the writer has determined his or her topic, opinion, and reasons for having the opinion, he or she is ready to begin writing an argumentative essay. In the introduction, the writer should capture the reader's interest, introduce the topic, and reveal his or her opinion about the topic. In the body of the composition, the writer should remind the reader of the opinion and give his or her reasons for holding the opinion. If the writer has any examples, facts, or other information that supports his or her opinion or reasons for believing it, these should also be included in the body. Writers may also use a body paragraph to mention opposing opinions or beliefs and explain why they disagree with them. As in other compositions, the conclusion should remind the reader of the essay's topic and purpose, as well as remind the reader how the opinion has been explained and supported. The conclusion should also invite the reader to continue thinking about the topic and writer's opinion. This can be done through questions or statements that lead readers to consider whether or not they agree with the author's opinion or what their own opinions are.

Review Video: Argumentative Writing
Visit mometrix.com/academy and enter code: 561544

INFORMATIVE VS. PERSUASIVE WRITING

Informative writing, also called explanatory or expository writing, is written to show that something is true or factual, while **persuasive** writing is written to lead the reader to agree with something that may or may not be true or factual. While persuasive text is written to **persuade** readers to agree with the author's position, informative text simply **provides information** to readers. Informative writing **informs** readers about why or how something is as it is. This can include offering new information, explaining how a process works, or describing a concept for readers.

Review Video: Informational Text
Visit mometrix.com/academy and enter code: 924964

FACTS AND OPINIONS

Writers and readers must always be aware of the difference between fact and opinion. A **fact** can be tested and proven to be true. An **opinion**, on the other hand, is someone's personal thoughts or feelings. Opinions are often not changed by information. If an author writes that a newborn elephant is about five times taller than a newborn giraffe, then he or she is stating a fact. If the author writes that giraffes are more interesting than elephants, then he or she is giving an opinion because this cannot be proven to be true or false. Opinions are often supported by facts. For instance, the author might use a comparison between the way that giraffes eat and the way elephants eat as evidence of how giraffes are more interesting. An opinion supported by facts tends to be more convincing. On the other hand, when authors support their opinions with other opinions, readers should seriously think about and read the argument carefully to see whether it is logical and trustworthy.

Review Video: Distinguishing Fact and Opinion
Visit mometrix.com/academy and enter code: 870899

Narrative Writing

Put simply, **narrative** writing tells a story. Narratives should tell stories in such a way that the readers learn something or gain understanding about a related topic or idea. Personal narratives are narratives writers create about personal experiences that were meaningful to them. Narratives should start with the story's actions or events, rather than long descriptions or introductions. However, the narrative should still include descriptions at points where they will entertain the reader or help the reader visualize or better understand the scene. To write an effective description, writers should include sensory details, asking themselves what they saw, heard, felt or touched, smelled, and tasted during the experiences they describe. In narrative writing, the details should be **concrete** rather than **abstract**. Concrete details are those that can be experienced through one of the five senses, while abstract details are not able to be experienced in this way. Using concrete details enables readers to imagine everything that the writer describes. Writers should make sure that there is a point to each story by describing what they learned from the experience they narrate.

Personal Narratives

A **personal narrative** is a story about something that happened to the writer. **Personal narrative essays** are structured the same as other types of essays, as they have an introduction, body paragraphs, and a conclusion. Like other essays, the introduction of a personal narrative should contain a hook, or an opening sentence that interests the reader and prompts them to read the rest of the narrative. The introduction may also provide context for the story told in the personal narrative. One significant difference between personal narratives and other essays is that the body paragraphs of a personal narrative should contain sensory details, or imagery. A good personal narrative will give the reader a clear picture of the events and engage their emotions, and sensory details are effective at achieving these goals. The body should describe the events in chronological order, and the story should be completed in the last body paragraph. The conclusion will summarize the main idea of the personal narrative and may include information such as the writer's brief reflection on the events, how the events taught or changed the writer, or any relevant events that have happened since the events in the narrative.

Sensory Details

Writers need to use vivid descriptions when writing descriptive essays. Narratives should also include descriptions of characters, things, and events. Writers should remember to describe not only the visual detail of what someone or something looks like, but details from other senses, as well. For example, they can contrast the feeling of a sea breeze to the feeling of a mountain breeze, describe how they think something inedible would taste, and compare sounds they hear in the same location at different times of day and night. Readers have trouble visualizing images or imagining sensory impressions and feelings from abstract descriptions, so concrete descriptions make these more real.

Informational Text Example

Below is a prompt for an informational text. There is also an example of an essay that addresses the prompt. There are multiple drafts of this essay to show what kinds of changes a writer may make during the writing process to improve his or her work.

PROMPT:

Do you ever dream of going to a new city, state, or even country? Write about one place you want to travel to on vacation. Be sure to share why you would like to visit that place.

Rough Draft

Imagine traveling into the city or the beach and being transported back in time. This is what it must be like to live in Greece. The old buildings, beautiful beaches, and Greek foods are reasons I want to visit Greece.

Several buildings from ancient Greece are still standing, and they can easily be enjoyed by visitors and the people of Greece today. Some of the most famous ones, like the Parthenon, are located throughout the capital. This means that even when you are sitting in an air-conditioned restaurant in Athens, you can still see what is left of history. There are also tours that teach visitors more about these structures and the events that happened at each one. Though seeing these structures is not the only reason I would like to visit Greece, they would be enough of a reason for me to visit.

In addition to the scenery, another reason to visit Greece is to try real Greek and Mediterranean foods. I have tried a few Greek foods, like baklava and pita bread, and I enjoyed them. While these foods are available in America, I think they are probably made a little differently in Greece. I am interested in seeing what the differences are and trying new things. I hope I can visit Greece soon, because I am getting hungry just thinking about the food there!

Greece has a variety of beaches, as some are small with rocky structures and some look like normal beaches. The water is also different from some American waters because Greece is next to the Mediterranean Sea. Also, many historical events and myths took place on some of the beaches. I would love to sit on one of those beaches and try to imagine ships or characters from myths coming to the shore! The beaches in Greece are beautiful, but I think they also sound fun and interesting!

Walking through historical structures, visiting unique beaches, and eating new foods there is my dream. If I only ever have the chance to go on one vacation, I hope it is to Greece!

Revised Draft

Imagine traveling into the city or the beach and being transported back in time. This is what it must be like to live in Greece. <u>The remaining historical sites that are still there allow visitors to see two cultures side by side.</u> The old buildings, beautiful beaches, and Greek foods are reasons I want to visit Greece.

Several buildings from ancient Greece are still standing, and they can easily be enjoyed by visitors and the people of Greece today. Some of the most famous ones, like the Parthenon, are located throughout the capital. This means that even when you are sitting in an air-conditioned restaurant in Athens, you can still see what is left of history. There are also tours that teach visitors more about these structures and the events that happened at each one. Though seeing these structures is not the only reason I would like to visit Greece, they would be enough of a reason for me to visit.

Greece has a variety of beaches, as some are small with rocky structures and some look like normal beaches. The water is also different from some American waters because Greece is next to the Mediterranean Sea. Also, many historical events and myths took place on some of the beaches. I would love to sit on one of those beaches and try to imagine ships or characters from myths coming to the shore! The beaches in Greece are beautiful, but I think they also sound fun and interesting!

In addition to the scenery, a third reason to visit Greece is to try real Greek and Mediterranean foods. I have tried a few Greek foods, like baklava and pita bread, and I enjoyed them. While these foods are available in America, I think they are probably made a little differently in Greece. I am interested in seeing what the differences are and trying new things. I hope I can visit Greece soon, because I am getting hungry just thinking about the food there!

<u>Greece is a special place where the old and the new come together.</u> Walking through historical structures, visiting unique beaches, and eating new foods there is my dream. If I only ever have the chance to go on one vacation, I hope it is to Greece!

Revised Draft Notes

Remember the purpose of the revising stage of the writing process. When revising, it is important to look at the whole composition. Do all of the paragraphs strengthen the composition? Do the introduction and conclusion help the reader understand the central idea and main points?

In this revision, nothing has been removed, but there are some additions. Look at the underlined words. In the introduction, a sentence has been added. Why? Previously, the introduction had only a hook and a thesis. The sentences were well written, but the writer did not provide a connection between the hook and the thesis. The new sentence connects the ideas in both sentences and introduces some of the main points the writer will discuss in the essay.

In the conclusion, another sentence has been added. This sentence strengthens the composition by creating a transition from the body to the conclusion. Before, the conclusion began abruptly by listing the three main points from the body of the essay. This sentence makes the essay flow better by giving the reader a transition from the body to the conclusion. This sentence reminds the reader of composition's central idea before repeating the writer's main points and sharing his or her hopes.

Finally, the third and fourth paragraphs have been switched. Why is that? Before, the writer discussed ancient buildings, then food, then the beaches. This revised draft discusses buildings, then beaches, then food. This new order puts the more closely related points, the scenery of the buildings and beaches, closer together in the essay. This helps the reader by making the organization of the essay more logical.

EDITED DRAFT

Imagine traveling into the city or the beach and being transported back in time. This is what it must be like to live in Greece, since the remaining historical sites ~~that are still there~~ allow visitors to see two cultures side by side. The ~~old~~ ancient buildings, beautiful beaches, and Greek foods are reasons I want to visit Greece.

Several buildings from ancient Greece are still standing, and they can easily be enjoyed by visitors and the people of Greece today. Some of the most famous ones, like the Parthenon, are located throughout the capital. This means that even when you are sitting in an air-conditioned restaurant in Athens, you can still see ~~what is left~~ glimpses of history. There are also tours that teach visitors more about these structures and the events that happened at each one. ~~Though seeing these structures is not the only reason I would like to visit Greece, they would be enough of a reason for me to visit.~~ Seeing these structures alone is enough of a reason for me to visit Greece!

Another reason I want to travel to Greece is to see the beaches there. There are a variety of beaches, as some are small with rocky structures and some look like ~~normal~~ typical beaches. The water is also different from some American waters because Greece is next to the Mediterranean Sea. Also, many historical events and myths took place on some of the beaches. I would love to sit on one of those beaches and try to imagine ships or characters from myths coming to the shore! The beaches in Greece are beautiful, but I think they also sound fun and interesting!

In addition to the scenery, a third reason to visit Greece is to try ~~real~~ authentic Greek and Mediterranean foods. I have tried a few Greek foods, like baklava and pita bread, and I enjoyed them. While these foods are available in America, I think they are probably made a little differently in Greece, so I am interested in seeing what the differences are and trying new things. I hope I can visit Greece soon, because I am getting hungry just thinking about the food there!

Greece is a special place where the old and the new come together. Walking through historical structures, visiting unique beaches, and eating new foods there is my dream. If I only ever have the chance to go on one vacation, I hope it is to Greece!

Edited Draft Notes

Since the writer has revised his or her work, the next step is to edit the composition. Remember that editing is very similar to revising, but editing usually includes paying attention to each paragraph, instead of the whole composition. Look at the changes that were made to each paragraph.

There are small changes throughout this draft. First, look at the introduction. Before, the introduction had four sentences that were about the same length. In this draft, the second and third sentences have been combined to make a longer sentence. This creates more sentence variety in the introduction, which makes the composition more entertaining for the writer's audience. A few words have been crossed out, as well. *That are still there* has been replaced with *remaining*. This change makes the writing more concise and formal. Also, *old* has been replaced with *ancient*. This clarifies what kind of buildings the writer is describing by using a word that more specifically describes the age of the buildings.

In the next paragraph, *what is left* has been replaced with *glimpses*. This change makes the writing more concise by using one word instead of three. Furthermore, this change makes the writing more interesting and entertaining by using a better vocabulary word. At the end of the paragraph, the last sentence has been condensed. Most of the sentences in this paragraph are long. Shortening this sentence adds sentence variety to this paragraph and makes the concluding sentence more concise. Overall, these changes make the paragraph easier to read by eliminating unnecessary words and using better vocabulary.

There are a few more changes left in the third and fourth paragraphs. A transition has been added to the beginning of the third paragraph. Now, the writer introduces the next main point before describing the beaches. This makes the essay flow better overall and making it easier for the writer's audience to read. *Normal* has been replaced with *typical*. Since there are so many different beaches in the world, there are not really any normal beaches. *Typical* is a much clearer word. Now, the reader knows that the writer is trying to distinguish the beaches in Greece from the type of beaches that he or she sees most often.

In the next paragraph, *real* has been replaced with *authentic*. The food the writer has tried in America has been real food, not fake food, so this is poor word choice. Now, *authentic* clarifies the writer's meaning that the food will be closer to its original Greek or Mediterranean style. These changes in word choice improve the clarity of the essay by using specific words that better communicate the writer's points. Finally, the third and fourth sentences have been joined together. This increases sentence variety by adding a longer sentence to this paragraph.

Final Draft

Imagine traveling into the city or the beach and being transported back in time. This is what it must be like to live in Greece, since the remaining historical sites allow visitors to see two cultures side by side. The ancient buildings, beautiful beaches, and Greek foods are reasons I want to visit Greece.

Several buildings from ancient Greece are still standing, and they can easily be enjoyed by visitors and the people of Greece today. Some of the most famous ones, like the Parthenon, are located throughout the capital. This means that even when you are sitting in an air-conditioned restaurant in Athens, you can still see glimpses of history. There are also tours that teach visitors more about these structures and the events that happened at each one. Seeing these structures alone is enough of a reason for me to visit Greece!

Another reason I want to travel to Greece is to see the beaches there. There are a variety of beaches, as some are small with rocky structures and some look like typical beaches. The water is also different from some American waters because Greece is next to the Mediterranean Sea. Also, many historical events and myths took place on some of the beaches. I would love to sit on one of those beaches and try to imagine ships or characters from myths coming to the shore! The beaches in Greece are beautiful, but I think they also sound fun and interesting!

In addition to the scenery, a third reason to visit Greece is to try authentic Greek and Mediterranean foods. I have tried a few Greek foods, like baklava and pita bread, and I enjoyed them. While these foods are available in America, I think they are probably made a little differently in Greece, so I am interested in seeing what the differences are and trying new things. I hope I can visit Greece soon, because I am getting hungry just thinking about the food there!

Greece is a special place where the old and the new come together. Walking through historical structures, visiting unique beaches, and eating new foods there is my dream. If I only ever have the chance to go on one vacation, I hope it is to Greece!

Final Draft Evaluation

The essay answers the prompt and is on topic throughout the composition. The central idea is clear and is stated in the introduction, supported in the body, and restated in the conclusion. The thesis statement restates parts of the prompt and gives the reader a preview of the rest of the essay. The body uses well-structured paragraphs to explain the supporting details and examples and connects them to the central idea. The conclusion also emphasizes the central idea and supporting details and invites the reader to consider what they have read.

The essay is also interesting and written with a variety of sentence types. It uses transitions and good paragraph structure to make the essay easy for the reader to understand. The introduction also uses a hook to get the reader's attention and help him or her relate to the information in the essay. Not only does this essay answer the prompt and have appropriate structure, but it also makes use of good, engaging, and interesting details.

Practice Test #1

Practice Questions

Questions 1-8 pertain to the following passage:

An American Hero

(1) In the year 1912, the unsinkable Titanic sank, the United States territory of Arizona became a state, and my Great Uncle Charlie was born. (2) Charlie was born in a small town in Kentucky. (3) On a farm. (4) He grew up learning about the seasons, when to plant the seeds, and when the crops were ripe for picking. (5) His mornings were spent with his hands in dirt as he tended to the growing corps.

(6) When Charlie was only 12, his father died. (7) He had to quit school to take care of his family. (8) While other children were learning and playing at school, Charlie worked in factories to help pay for his mother and sisters to eat. (9) Irregardless of how he felt about having to work, Charlie never complained.

(10) On December 7, 1941, Japan attacked the American naval base at Pearl Harbor. (11) Charlie enlisted in the army when he was 30 years old, and went to fight in the war. (12) He fought in six major battles, including landing in Normandy on D-Day. (13) While he was in the army, Charlie joined the United States horseshoe team and became the champion of the european allies. (14) After the war, Charlie returned to Kentucky married a woman named Bethany, and had three children.

(15) Today, Charlie can still be found with his hands in the dirt. (16) He loves to work in the small garden beside his front porch. (17) The bright colors of ripening strawberries, tomatoes, and ears of corn can be seen next to the house with Charlie walking though the rows of crops with his watering can. (18) He tends to them with love. (19) Charlie watches over his family like the crops in the garden, and that is why he is my hero.

1. What is the BEST way to explain the information in sentences 2 and 3?

a. Charlie was born in a small town in Kentucky. It was on a farm
b. Charlie was born in Kentucky. In a small town and on a farm
c. Charlie was born in a small town. In Kentucky, it was on a farm
d. Charlie was born in a small Kentucky town on a farm

2. What change, if any, should be made to sentence 5?

a. Change *corps* to *crops*
b. Change *were* to *was*
c. Insert a comma after *dirt*
d. Make no change

3. What change, if any, should be made to sentence 9?

a. Change *complained* to *complains*
b. Change *irregardless* to *regardless*
c. Delete the comma after *work*
d. Make no change

4. What sentence could BEST follow and support sentence 10?

a. Pearl Harbor is a naval base in Hawaii
b. The USS Arizona was one of the battleships that sank
c. This event directly led into the United States' involvement in World War II
d. Charlie had never been to Hawaii

5. What change, if any, should be made to sentence 13?

a. Change *european* to *European*
b. Change *became* to *becomes*
c. Insert a comma after *champion*
d. Make no change

6. What change, if any, should be made to sentence 14?

a. Change *returned* to *returns*
b. Insert a comma after *Kentucky*
c. Insert *and* after *Kentucky*
d. Make no change

7. What change, if any, should be made in sentence 16?

a. Change *loves* to *loved*
b. Insert a comma after *garden*
c. Change *beside* to *besides*
d. Make no change

8. What change, if any, should be made in sentence 17?

a. Change *colors* to *colours*
b. Delete the comma after *strawberries*
c. Change *though* to *through*
d. Make no change

Questions 9 – 16 pertain to the following story:

The Top Deck

(1) We walked outside through the sliding glass doors and waited in line for the large, double-decker red bus. (2) My family flew to London for a week in July to celebrate my sisters graduation. (3) She wore a blue cap and gown. (4) The sky was gray, and light puddles spotted the ground. (5) As the bus pulled up against the curb, dirty water splashed our feet.

(6) The driver's seat was on the opposite side of the bus, and the driver smiled at me when I showed him my ticket. (7) I looked out the window and realised that we were driving on the opposite side of the street. (8) All around us people who were on the wrong side of the street driving from what looked like the passenger seat. (9) The bus

was filled with people. (10) Almost every seat was taken, and people were even standing in the aisle holding onto handrails and poles. (11) Their was a spiral staircase directly behind the driver, and we walked up to it to try to find more seats. (12) There were two rows of seats upstairs and a large window that looked onto the streets. (13) For seats were open near the front of the bus and we hurried to get them.

(14) The bus stopped every few seconds, and each time I had to hold onto my seat to keep from sliding into the aisle. (15) "What street are we looking for?" my dad asked my mom. (16) "Oxford" she replied. (17) I looked out the giant window. (18) We passed a large building that was shaped like an egg, and we continued to travel. (19) The bus driver's voice came over the speakers. (20) "Now approaching Liverpool," he said

(21) My mom looked at my dad. (22) I grabbed my sister's arm, but she was busy taking pictures of the buildings out the window. (23) "Liverpool," my mom whispered with a worried look on her face. (24) "We're lost, aren't we?" my dad said.

9. What change, if any, should be made in sentence 2?

a. Change *flew* to *flied*
b. Change *week* to *weak*
c. Change *sisters* to *sister's*
d. Make no change

10. What change, if any, should be made in sentence 7?

a. Change *realised* to *realize*
b. Change *street* to *streat*
c. Change *looked* to *look*
d. Make no change

11. What change, if any, should be made in sentence 11?

a. Delete the comma after *driver*
b. Change *Their* to *There*
c. Change *staircase* to *stair case*
d. Make no change

12. What change should be made in sentence 13?

a. Change *open* to *opened*
b. Change *were* to *was*
c. Change *For* to *Four*
d. Change *hurried* to *hurried*

13. Which of the following is the BEST way to rewrite the ideas in sentence 8?

a. All around us people were driving from what looked like the passenger seat, and they were driving on the opposite side of the street
b. All around us people who were on the wrong side of the street, driving from what looked like the passenger seat
c. All around us people were driving on the wrong side of the street. Driving from what looked like the passenger seat
d. All around us people were driving from what looked like passenger seat, they were on the opposite side of the street

14. What change, if any, should be made in sentence 16?

a. Change *Oxford* to *oxford*
b. Insert a comma after *Oxford*
c. Insert a period after the quotation mark
d. Make no change

15. Which sentence does not belong in this essay?

a. Sentence 20
b. Sentence 6
c. Sentence 13
d. Sentence 3

16. What is the BEST transition word or phrase that could be added to the beginning of sentence 19?

a. However
b. Once in a while
c. Additionally
d. After a while

Questions 17 -24 pertain to the following story:

Longhorn Café

(1) Last Saturday night my dad took me to watch the Longhorns play football in Austin. (2) It was a cool evening, and the orange-painted stadium was filled with screaming fans. (3) Even though we live in San Antonio, my dad has always been a dedicated Longhorns fan, and he wears his orange proudly.

(4) We arrived in Austin early. (5) "Traffic," my dad said as his only explanation. (6) He parked the truck down a small side street and motions for me to get out and follow him. (7) "I want to take you someplace," he said. (8) "I used to come here all the time when I was in college. (9) We walked up to a small building with a large patio off to the side. (10) A large tree with low branches spread across the patio and connected with the roof. (11) The leaves were beginning to change colors, and it was like sitting under a leafy canopy.

(12) We sat at a table outside on a rusting rocking bench beside an abandoned bathtub. (13) Stands of colored lights hung across the patio. (14) Wrapped around the tree. (15) "What is this place?" I asked. (16) My dad smiled and pointed to a sign bordered with colored lights. (17) "Spider Café," he said. (18) All around us, people were drinking coffee and staring at them computer screens. (19) Our waiter was named Chris, and he had a long beard, wore a dirtied apron, and carried empty coffee mugs.

(20) The waited came up to us, and my dad ordered himself a latte and a sweet drink for me. (21) My dad looked around the patio and smiled. (22) He leaned into the bench and placed his hand on the side of the bathtub. (23) He didn't even mind when he spilled coffee onto his favorite orange shirt. (24) "You'll love it here," he said, "when you are a Longhorn football player?"

17. What change, if any, should be made in sentence 5?

a. Delete the comma after *traffic*
b. Insert a comma after *said*
c. Change *said* to *says*
d. Make no change

18. What change should be made in sentence 6?

a. Change *parked* to *park*
b. Change *street* to *Street*
c. Insert a comma after *street*
d. Change *motions* to *motioned*

19. What change, if any, should be made in sentence 8?

a. Change *come* to *came*
b. Change *to* to *too*
c. Insert a quotation mark after *college*
d. Make no change

20. What revision, if any, is needed in sentences 13 and 14?

a. Strands of colored lights hung across the patio wrapped, around the tree
b. Strands of colored lights hung across the patio and wrapped around the tree
c. Strands of colored lights hung. Across the patio, wrapped around the tree
d. No revision is needed

21. What change, if any, should be made in sentence 18?

a. Change *them* to *their*
b. Delete the comma after *us*
c. Insert a comma after *and*
d. Make no change

22. Where is the best placement for sentence 19?

a. After sentence 22
b. After sentence 20
c. Before sentence 18
d. No change is needed

Questions 23 – 25 pertain to the following story:

Strike Three

(1) As I stared down at the hitter in the batters box, I remembered what my dad had said to me. (2) "Shut everything out." (3) I focused on the glove in front of me. (4) I looked into the deep, blackened pocket, and sawed my target. (5) The batter tapped his bat against the sides of his cleats, and rested the bat on his shoulders. (6) With hard eyes, he stares back at me.

(7) I kicked the front of my cleat into the bright white rubber on the pitching mound and took a deep breath. (8) Shut everything out," he had said. (9) Slowly the noises disappeared. (10) I could no longer hear the shouts from the parents in the stands. (11) In my head, I silenced the cheers from both dugouts. (12) The umpire did not

exist. (13) There were no players, no coaches, not even a catcher. (14) There was just me. (15) The ball and the glove.

(16) I took a deep breath and brought my hands together at my chest. (17) I looked over at first base, but there was no runner. (18) In one motion, my feet left the rubber and connected with ground. (19) Dirt flew in the air as my arm rotated forward and released the ball in front of me. (20) I watched as the ball spun and landed into glove with a hard crack. (21) The umpire shot up from his crouched position and pointed his finger to the right and yelled, "Strike Three!"

(22) The noises came back. (23) The crowd cheered in the stands and I could here stomping feet. (24) My teammate clapped his hand to its glove and ran toward me. (25) My coach raised a first into the air in celebration. (26) I was surrounded by my teammates, and they were patting me on the back. (27) My dad was sitting on a bleacher behind home plate. (28) He raised his thumb to me and smiled as I ran off the field with my teammates.

23. What change, if any, should be made in sentence 1?

a. Change *stared* to *starred*
b. Change *dad* to *Dad*
c. Change *batters* to *batter's*
d. Make no change

24. What change should be made in sentence 4?

a. Change *blackened* to *blacked*
b. Change *sawed* to *saw*
c. Delete the comma after *deep*
d. Change *into* to *in to*

25. What change, if any, should be made in sentence 6?

a. Change *stares* to *stared.*
b. Change *me* to *I*
c. Delete the comma after *eyes*
d. Make no change

Questions 26 – 30 pertain to the following passage:

Imagine a Better World

(1) My favorite song is "imagine" by John Lennon. (2) It was released in 1971. (3) It is one of the few famous songs that John Lennon recorded and sang alone. (4) For the majority of his career, John Lennon was a member of an iconic rock band called the Beatles, a band that changed the music industry. (5) The Beatles accepted a lot of success in their career, with popular songs such as "I Want to Hold Your Hand," "Come Together," "Let it Be," and "Here Comes the Sun." (6) After the band decided to separate, John Lennon became a solo artist as well as an promoter for peace.

(7) "Imagine" tells the story of Lennons dream of peace in the world. He asks the listener to imagine different situations. (8) He says to imagine that there are no countries, religions, or possessions. (9) He says, "I wonder if you can." (10) This line strikes me the most I try to imagine such a world. (11) When talking about no

possessions, he continues and says, "No need for greed or hunger." (12) It is a great line. (13) Throughout the song, he says, "Imagine all the people." (14) And he gives examples. (15) At first he says, "living for today," and then moves on to say, "living life in peace," and finally, "sharing all the world."

(16) My favorite part of the song is the chorus. (17) Lennon says, "You may say I'm a dreamer, but I'm not the only one. (18) I hope someday you'll join us, and the world will be as one." (19) When I really listen to the words of this song, I realize that "Imagine" is so much more than something that sounds nicely. (20) Lennon is saying something very important and suggesting ways in which the world can live in peace. (21) Because of this song, I am a dreamer as well, and I join John Lennon in the fight for world peace.

26. What change, if any, should be made in sentence 1?

a. Change *favorite* to *favourite*
b. Change *imagine* to *Imagine*
c. Insert a comma after *song*
d. Make no change

27. What is the BEST verb to replace accepted in sentence 5?

a. Lasted
b. Liked
c. Had
d. Watched

28. What change should be made in sentence 6?

a. Change *separate* to *separated*
b. Insert a comma after *artist*
c. Change *solo* to *Solo*
d. Change *an* to *a*

29. What change, if any, should be made in sentence 7?

a. Change *Lennons* to *Lennon's*
b. Change *dream* to *dreamt*
c. Insert a comma after *peace*
d. Make no change

30. What is the BEST way to revise sentence 10?

a. This line strikes me the most as I try to imagine such a world.
b. This line strikes me the most, I try to imagine such a world.
c. This line strikes me, the most. I try to imagine such a world.
d. No revision needed.

Written Composition

"I learned that courage was not the absence of fear, but the triumph over it. The brave man is not he who does not feel afraid, but he who conquers that fear."

-Nelson Mandela

Think carefully about the difference that having courage makes.

Then, write an essay discussing the importance of exercising courage in everyday life.

Make sure you state your main idea clearly, and organize your argument logically and effectively.

Answer Key and Explanations

1. D: because this sentence is the simplest way to explain where Charlie was born. A is not correct because two sentences are not necessary. The additional subject and verb are unnecessary to express the idea. B is not correct, because *In a small town and on a farm* is a fragment. C is not correct, because the sentences contain awkward wording. The sentences need to be combined in order to express the idea in the simplest form.

2. A: because in this sentence, *crops* has been misspelled as *corps*. B is not correct, because the subject of the sentence, *mornings*, is plural. Therefore, the verb also must be plural for correct subject verb agreement. C is not correct, because this sentence does not need a comma.

3. B: because irregardless is not a word. The correct word is *regardless.* A is not correct because *complains* is in the present tense, while the rest of the paragraph is in the past tense. C is not correct, because a comma is needed after an introductory clause.

4. C: because this sentence supports both sentence 10 and sentence 11. The sentence supports the cause and effect idea that the attack on Pearl Harbor prompted the United States to become involved in the war, which caused Charlie to enlist in the army. A is not correct. Although this sentence provides new information, it does not link and support sentences 10 and 11. B is not correct. Although this sentence provides new information, it does not link and support sentences 10 and 11. D is not correct. Although this sentence provides new information, it does not link and support sentences 10 and 11.

5. A: because *European* is a proper noun and must be capitalized. B is not correct, because *becomes* is in the present tense, and the rest of the paragraph is written in the past tense. C is not correct, because a comma is not needed after *champion.*

6. B: because this sentence uses commas in a series as it lists aspects of Charlie's life after the war. Both *returned to Kentucky* and *married a woman named Bethany* are events that have happened and therefore need to be separated by a comma. A is not correct. *Returns* is in the present tense, and the rest of the paragraph is written in the past tense. C is not correct. The correct sentence uses commas in a series, and therefore only uses one *and* in the sentence.

7. D: because the sentence is correct as written. A is not correct. Although the rest of the essay is written in the past tense, the last paragraph begins with *Today* and is written in the present tense. Therefore, *loves* is correct. B is not correct, because this sentence does not need a comma. C is not correct. Both *beside* and *besides* are prepositions, but *beside* means "next to" and *besides* means "in addition to" or "other than." *Beside* is used in this sentence as "next to."

8. C: because in this sentence, *through* has been misspelled as *though.* A is not correct, because *colors* is spelled correctly. B is not correct, because this sentence needs a comma after *strawberries,* since the sentence contains a list and uses commas in a series.

9. C: In this sentence, *Sister's* is possessive and requires an apostrophe. A is not correct. *Flew* is the correct past tense of *fly*. B is not correct, because *week* is a noun and is spelled correctly.

10. A: because *realized* is misspelled in this sentence. B is not correct, because *street* is spelled correctly. C is not correct, because *look* is in the present tense, while the essay is written in past tense.

11. B: because a homonym has been misused. *There* is used to indicate a physical or abstract place, while *their* is used to indicate possession. A is not correct, because this sentence has two independent clauses joined by the conjunction *and*, and a comma is used before the conjunction. C is not correct, because *staircase* is one word.

12. C: because a homonym has been misused. *Four* is a number. A is not correct, because in this sentence *open* is used as a noun rather than a verb and does not need to be in the past tense. B is not correct. *Were* is plural, and *was* is singular. The subject of the sentence, *seats*, is plural; therefore, the verb also must be plural for correct subject verb agreement. D is not correct, because *hurried* is spelled correctly.

13. A: because this rewording of this sentence makes the meaning clear and is grammatically correct. B is not correct because this sentence is a fragment. C is not correct because the second sentence is a fragment. D is not correct because this sentence is a run-on sentence.

14. B: because a comma is needed before the closing quotation when the sentence is not completed with the quotation. A is not correct because *Oxford* is a proper noun and must be capitalized. C is not correct. The sentence does not end with the quotation; therefore, a comma, rather than a period, goes before the quotation mark.

15. D: because this sentence this sentence provides new information that is not important to the rest of the essay. Answers A, B, and C are incorrect, because all of these sentences present content that is important to the essay.

16. D: In the previous sentence, the phrase *we continued to travel*, suggests a passage of time. A proper transition into the next sentence would involve the acknowledgement that time has passed. A is not correct because *however* is not a good transition into the sentence. B is not correct. Although *once in a while* relates to time, it does not transition well into the sentence given the context of the previous sentence. C is not correct. *Additionally* is not a good transition into the sentence because it does not indicate a passage of time.

17. D: because the sentence is correct as written. A is not correct, because a comma is needed before the closing quotation when the sentence is not completed with the quotation. B is not correct because this sentence does not need a comma. C is not correct because *says* is in the present tense, and the essay is written in the past tense.

18. D: because *motions* is in the present tense, and the rest of the essay is written in the past tense. B is not correct because *street* is not used in this sentence as a proper noun and does not need to be capitalized. C is not correct. A comma is unnecessary because the second sentence is not an independent clause.

19. C: because a quotation mark is needed to end dialogue. A is incorrect because *come* is in the present tense, and the essay is written in the past tense. B is not correct. *Too* means "also" or an indication of excess.

20. B: because this sentence is grammatically correct as written. A is not correct. The comma is misplaced and disrupts the sentence. C is not correct because the second sentence is a fragment. D is not correct because sentence 14 is a fragment.

21. A: because *their* indicates possession; *them* does not. *Computer screens* belong to the subject, *people*. B is not correct. *All around us* is an introductory clause and needs a comma. C is not correct.

Staring at them computer screens is not an independent clause and therefore does not need a comma.

22. B: because the sentence provides additional information about the waiter. The sentence should be placed after the waiter has been introduced in sentence 20. A is not correct. The subject of the paragraph has shifted to the father at sentence 21, and therefore a sentence involving information about the waiter would be out of place after sentence 22. C is not correct. Sentence 18 provides setting information. A sentence involving information about the waiter before this sentence would be out of place. D is not correct. This sentence provides additional information about the waiter and should not conclude a paragraph.

23. C: In this sentence, *batter's* is possessive and needs an apostrophe. A is not correct because *stared*, the past tense of the verb, *stare*, is spelled correctly. B is not correct. In this sentence, *dad* is not a proper noun, since it is not used as a name. *My* before *dad* indicates that it is not a proper noun.

24. B: because *saw* is the correct past tense of the verb, *see*. A is not correct because *blackened* is the correct adjective. C is not correct. A comma is needed to separate adjectives when each adjective separately describes the noun. D is not correct. *Into* is spelled correctly.

25. A: because *stares* is in the present tense, and the rest of the essay is in the past tense. *Stared* is the correct past tense of *stare*. B is not correct. *Me* is the object of the sentence because it is the recipient of the action, *stares*. I is traditionally used as a subject. C is not correct. *With hard eyes* is an introductory clause, and a comma is needed after the clause.

26. B: because *imagine* is a proper noun. As the title of a song, it requires capitalization. A is not correct. *Favorite* is spelled correctly. C is not correct. *My favorite song* is not an introductory clause, so a comma is not needed.

27. C: because the missing verb in this sentence must have something to do with possession, since it discusses the band's success. *Had* indicates possession. A, B, and D are incorrect, because these verbs do not fit within the sentence.

28. D: It is correct because in the sentence, the article *an* is followed by a noun, *promoter*. *Promoter* begins with a consonant and a consonant sound and therefore must be followed by the article *a*. A is not correct. The verb in this sentence is *decided*, not *separate*, and therefore *separate* does not need to be in the past tense like the rest of the paragraph. B is not correct because the comma is unnecessary. C is not correct. *Solo* is not a proper noun and does not need to be capitalized.

29. A: because *Lennon* is possessive in this sentence; therefore, it requires an apostrophe. B is not correct. In this sentence, *dream* is a noun rather than a verb, so it does not need to be in the past tense. C is not correct, because a comma is unnecessary.

30. A: because the sentence is missing the article *as*. This is the simplest way to express the idea of the sentence. B is incorrect because this sentence is not grammatically correct. C is incorrect because the first sentence is grammatically incorrect.

Sample Composition

> Last November, I was sitting in my third period math class when my teacher told me that she needed to talk to me after class. I was worried that I had done something wrong or had forgotten to turn in a homework assignment. I thought about it, but could not remember missing any assignments. I also thought that maybe I had failed

the last test, but I felt that I had done well on it. When I finally talked to her, I was relieved to hear that she wanted to move me up into the accelerated math class. I immediately thought of my friend, Alex. He and I were in the same math class, and it was the only class we had together. I wanted to be in accelerated math, but I did not want to leave my friend.

When I came home from school, I told my parents what my teacher had said. "Wow!" my mom said, "That is great!" My dad smiled at me. "Good job," he said. "I am really proud of you." It made me happy to know that my parents were proud and excited for me. I was excited too, but I was also scared. I decided to talk to my mom about it. I told her that I did not want to leave class with Alex because we had no other classes together and that I was afraid. "What are you afraid of?" she asked. I told her that I was already behind in the accelerated math class, and that I was afraid I would not be able to catch up. I was also afraid that the class would be too hard for me.

"Well, that's a lot to think about," my mom said. She told me to look at everything I was afraid of and think about each thing. She said I needed a plan. She told me that if my teacher thought I could do well in the accelerated class, I should listen to her and believe in myself. I told her I thought that I could spend extra time with the new teacher learning the material that I had missed. "But what about Alex?" I said. I still did not want to leave my friend. "You always have recess," she said.

I decided to join the accelerated math class and am very happy. It was hard at first to keep up with the work that I had missed, but I like learning new things. I have made a lot of new friends, but I also see Alex at recess. We all have fun. The accelerated math class was better for me, and I am happy I made this hard decision.

Practice Test #2

Practice Questions

Questions 1 – 6 pertain to the following story:

The Greek Festival

(1) Every October my family attends the Greek Festival at the Greek Orthodox Church close to our house. (2) We were first invited four years ago by one of my friends, Amelia. (3) Her family attends the Greek Orthodox Church and works several booths at the festival each year. (4) They telled us that everyone was welcome.

(5) When we first arrived at the festival, we could hear the music from the parking lot? (6) It was music that I had never heard before, and some of it was in another language. (7) Amelia told me later that it was traditional Greek music. (8) We also noticed the smells that seemed to come from all over the festival grounds. (9) All around us, there were signs for meat, pastry, coffee drinks, and other side dishes. (10) My mom's favorite were the grape leaves, and my dad loved the Baklava. (11) It is a dessert is made up baked thin sheets of pastry dough covered in a sweet sauce like honey. (12) Amelia suggested us eat it with ice cream and chocolate sauce. (13) As much as I liked the baklava, my favorite was the gyro pita. (14) Gyro is lamb meat in a warm pita with tomato, lettuce, onion, and a Greek sauce. (15) I ate two pitas and it was deliciously!

(16) After we had eaten, everyone gathered around the dance floor and watched as people from all different age groups danced traditional Greek dances. (17) The dancers were dressed in special clothing and black dress shoes.

(18) Amelia danced in the second group of dancers, and her mom tossed money toward her. (19) Soon, the dance floor was covered in dollar bills from all of the dancers families. (20) The food was great, the music was fun, and the dancing was even better. (21) We had a great time at the greek Festival, and now I look forward to it every year!

1. What change, if any, should be made in sentence 4?

a. Change everyone to every one
b. Change telled to told
c. Change welcome to welcomed
d. Make no change

2. What change should be made in sentence 5?

a. Change arrived to arrive
b. Change festival to Festival
c. Delete the comma after festival
d. Change the question mark to a period

3. What change, if any, should be made in sentence 10?

a. Change were to was
b. Change mom's to moms
c. Change loved to loves
d. Make no change

4. What revision, if any, is needed in sentence 11?

a. It is a dessert that is made up of baked thin sheets of pastry dough covered in a sweet sauce like honey.
b. It is a dessert, is made up baked thin sheets of pastry dough covered in a sweet sauce like honey.
c. It is a dessert. Made up baked thin sheets of pastry dough covered in a sweet sauce like honey.
d. No revision needed.

5. What is the BEST way to revise sentence 12?

a. Amelia suggested, us eat it with ice cream and chocolate sauce.
b. Amelia suggested to us eat it with ice cream and chocolate sauce.
c. Amelia suggested us eat it, with ice cream and chocolate sauce.
d. Amelia suggested that we eat it with ice cream and chocolate sauce.

6. What change, if any, should be made in sentence 15?

a. Change ate to eat
b. Change deliciously to delicious
c. Change two to too
d. Make no change

Questions 7 – 12 pertain to the following passage:

Dogs in the Park

(1) On Saturday, my mom took me to a dog show at a park by our house. (2) The sun was out, and it was a really warm day. (3) I ride my bike to the park almost every day in the summer. (4) The dogs were all lying in the grass when we arrived, and they looked warm in the sun. (5) One of my mom's friends Mary, is a dog trainer, and she invited us to watch the dog show after my mom told her how much I love dogs.

(6) Their were all kinds of dogs at the show. (7) Some were really little, some were big, and some had really long hair. (8) My favorite were the dogs in the toy category and the sporting category. (9) The dogs that were waiting to be shown were with their trainers at different areas of the park getting ready. (10) Some trainers brushed its dog's hair, and some gave treats.

(11) We sat on the grass and watched the show. (12) The trainers were all dressed up. (13) The men wore suit pants and jackets, and the women wore dress skirts, stockings, and blazers. (14) All of the dogs were lined up and stood still wile the judges walked down and looked closely at all the dogs. (15) The judges looked at the dogs' hair, paws, and teeth. (16) Then it was time for each dog to show off. (17) Each trainer ran with their dog and held the leash high in the air. (18) The judges watched as the dogs ran, and judged how good they turned corners and listened to their trainers.

(19) At the end of the show, the judges awarded prizes. (20) The dogs and their trainers gathered in a line, and the judges presented the winners with large ribbons. (21) Mary's dog won first place, and she was given a purple ribbon that was bigger than most of the small dogs in the toy category. (22) We left the park, and I told my mom that I want to learn how to train dogs.

7. What change should be made in sentence 5?

a. Change is to was
b. Delete the comma after Mary
c. Change invited to invites
d. Insert a comma after friends

8. What change, if any, should be made in sentence 6?

a. Change Their to There
b. Change dogs to dog's
c. Change were to was
d. Make no change

9. What change, if any, should be made in sentence 8?

a. Change were to was
b. Insert a comma after category
c. Change favorite to favorites
d. Make no change

10. What change should be made in sentence 10?

a. Change its to their
b. Change its to it's
c. Change brushed to brush
d. Change dog's to dogs

11. Which sentence does not belong in this essay?

a. Sentence 18
b. Sentence 11
c. Sentence 7
d. Sentence 3

12. What is the BEST transition word that could be added to the beginning of sentence 22?

a. However
b. Later
c. Otherwise
d. Consequentially

Questions 13 – 18 pertain to the following story:

First Party

(1) Today my brother turned one year old. (2) We had a big party to celebrate, and a lot of people came. (3) My ant came to the house early to help my mom hang streamers. (4) My cousin helped me make party favors for both the big kids and the babies. (5) We packed the little bags with candy, pencils, whistles, and noisemakers.

(6) My parents invited a lot of people. (7) Soon the house was filled with family, friends, and even some babies for my brother to play with.

(8) My grandparents on my dad's side flew even flew in from California the day before to help. (9) My dad lighted the barbeque in the back yard and took orders from the guests. (10) He made hamburgers, turkey burgers, hot dogs, chicken wings, and sausages. (11) My aunt sliced strips of onion, tomato, pickles, and lettuce. (12) She also cuts up an avocado because she knows that it is my favorite topping on my hamburger. (13) My cousins, friends, and I all played in the backyard after we ate.

(14) My brother slept through most of the party, he was awake by the time he had cake. (15) He don't know he was missing his party by napping. (16) My mom put him in his high chair, and we all sang "Happy birthday," to him. (17) There was one candle in the center of the large cake, and my mom blew it out since he was two little.

(18) My brother sat in his chair and ate cake. (19) Soon there was cake everywhere. (20) It was all over his hands, his face, his tabletop and chair. (21) There was blue icing everywhere. (22) He even lifted up his arms and grabbed pieces of his hair. (23) His big, blue eyes looked at everyone as they smiled and laughed. (24) He stuffed some more cake into his mouth and smiled. (25) I think he knew he had a good first birthday.

13. What change should be made in sentence 3?

a. Change hang to hanged
b. Change ant to aunt
c. Change help to helped
d. Change came to comes

14. Where is the best placement for sentence 8?

a. After sentence 2
b. After sentence 4
c. After sentence 5
d. No change is needed

15. What change, if any, should be made in sentence 9?

a. Change took to takes
b. Change barbeque to BBQ
c. Change lighted to lit
d. Make no change

16. What change, if any, should be made in sentence 12?

a. Change know to knew
b. Change cuts to cut
c. Change an to a
d. Make no change

17. What is the BEST transition word that could be added to the beginning of sentence 14?

a. Later
b. Therefore
c. Although
d. However

18. What change, if any, should be made in sentence 15?

a. Change don't to didn't
b. Change was to is
c. Change napping to nap
d. Make no change

Questions 19 – 24 pertain to the passage:

Dinner is Served

(1) Every year my friend and I celebrate each other's birthdays by going out to dinner because our birthdays are three weeks apart. (2) On my birthday, my family took us to Aribba, my favorite mexican food restaurant. (3) For Annmae's birthday, she chose a Japanese restaurant called Tomo where the food is cooked at the table.

(4) I had never eaten Japanese food before and didn't know what to expect? (5) When the hostess brought us to our table, I was surprised to see that there were four extra seats. (6) That was not the only thing that was strange. (7) The table was not a regular restaurant dinner table. (8) It was a half circle and there was a giant sheet of metal in the center. (9) The hostess came back with other people and sat them with us at our table.

(10) We filled out cards that said what kind of food we wanted. (11) We had to pick between chicken, beef, shrimp, and pork. (12) A man then came to our table and lit the metal sheet. (13) He laid out rice and vegetables, and started cutting and cooking. (14) He worked very fast it was almost hard for me to see his hands. (15) After the rice, he cooked each of the different meats and started serving plates. (16) While things were cooking he would take his spatula and fling a piece of bell pepper or carrot at someone at the table. (17) He toss the most at Annmae since it was her birthday, but they all hit her chin and slid down onto her shirt.

(18) It was really exciting watching our food cooked right in front of us. (19) The chef was nice and the food is delicious. (20) I even liked having other people sit at our table because it was like being at a party at dinner. (21) I am really glad that my friend chose Tomo and I can't wait to see where we try next year!

19. What change, if any, should be made in sentence 2?

a. Change birthday to birth day
b. Delete the comma after birthday
c. Change mexican to Mexican
d. Make no change

20. What change should be made in sentence 4?

a. Change had to have
b. Change Japanese to japanese
c. Change didn't to don't
d. Change the question mark to a period

21. What sentence could BEST follow and support sentence 9?

a. Now I understood why there were extra seats
b. The hostess smiled at us as she left
c. The woman wore a blue dress and her hair was tied back
d. I wondered how many times she was going to come back

22. What change, if any, should be made in sentence 16?

a. Change were to are
b. Insert a comma after cooking
c. Change take to took
d. Make no change

23. What change, if any, should be made in sentence 17?

a. Delete the comma after birthday
b. Change hit to hitted
c. Change toss to tossed
d. Make no change

24. What change should be made in sentence 19?

a. Change is to was
b. Change was to is
c. Change delicious to deliciously
d. Change chef to Chef

Questions 25 – 30 pertain to the following passage:

History's Unsinkable Lessons

(1) In Ruth Campbell's book Exploring the Titanic, the events of the famous ship's only journey and sinking are brought to life. (2) In 1912, Titanic was built and was the largest passenger steamship at the time. (3) On what would be its first and only journey, the ship departed from Southampton in England and was supposed to arrive in New York City. (4) The ship hit an iceberg late at night on April 14, 1912, and sunked less than three hours later.

(5) Titanic was designed by some of the best engineers and had the latest technology of the time. (6) The ship was made to carry over three and a half thousand passengers and crew members, but had only twenty lifeboats. (7) There was not enough lifeboats for all of the people onboard, and as a result, only seven hundred six people survived.

(8) One interesting thing about Titanic, is that the ship was divided into classes. (9) The most expensive tickets were first class, and first class passengers had the biggest and much luxurious rooms. (10) The first class rooms were the closest to the ship's deck. (11) Because this the majority of survivors came from first class. (12) They were able to reach the deck fastest to get a seat on a lifeboat. (13) The third class rooms

were located the farthest below deck, and the majority of the third class passengers did not survive.

(14) Ruth Campbell's book was very interesting but also sad because the story of Titanic is true. (15) However, Campbell ended the book by talking about the positive things that have happened because of this tragedy. (16) Most importantly, experts now recommend that ships' carry enough lifeboats for all passengers onboard. (17) This would have saved a lot of lifes. (18) It was a good book, and it displayed a good message in history that lessons should be learned from mistakes.

25. What change should be made in sentence 1?

a. Change ship's to ships
b. Insert a comma after book
c. Change are to is
d. Change brought to bring

26. What change, if any, should be made in sentence 4?

a. Change sunked to sank
b. Delete the comma after 14
c. Change hours to hour's
d. Make no change

27. What change should be made in sentence 7?

a. Change There to They're
b. Delete the comma after onboard
c. Change lifeboats to lifeboats'
d. Change was to were

28. What change, if any, should be made in sentence 8?

a. Change was to were
b. Delete the comma after Titanic
c. Change divided into divide
d. Make no change

29. What is the BEST way to revise and combine sentence 11 and sentence 12?

a. Because, the majority of survivors came from first class as they were able to reach the deck fastest to get a seat on a lifeboat
b. Because of this, the majority of survivors came from first class, as they were able to reach the deck fastest to get a seat on a lifeboat
c. Because this, the majority of survivors came from first class, they were able to reach the deck fastest to get a seat on a lifeboat
d. Because of this, the majority of survivors came from first class as they were able to reach the deck fastest to get a seat on a lifeboat

30. What is the BEST transition that could be added to the beginning of sentence 13?

a. Lastly
b. For example
c. On the other hand
d. Therefore

WRITTEN COMPOSITION

> "Never throughout history has a man who lived a life of ease left a name worth remembering."
>
> -Theodore Roosevelt

Think carefully about some of the great things you have seen accomplished in your lifetime.

Then, write an essay discussing the importance of working hard to accomplish great things.

Make sure you state your main idea clearly, and organize your argument logically and effectively.

Answer Key and Explanations

1. B: because told is the correct past tense of the verb tell. Telled is not a word. A is not correct. When used as a noun, everyone is one word. C is not correct. Welcome is not a verb in this sentence and therefore does not need to be in the past tense like the rest of the essay.

2. D: because this sentence is a statement rather than a question. As a result, it should be punctuated with a period and not a question mark. A is not correct. Arrive is in the present tense, and the rest of the paragraph is in the past tense. B is not correct. Festival is not used in this sentence as a proper noun and therefore does not need to be capitalized. C is not correct. When we first arrived at the festival is an introductory clause, and a comma is needed after the introductory clause.

3. A: because the subject of this sentence is favorite. Favorite is singular; therefore, the verb also must be singular in order for the subject and verb to agree. Were is plural. Was is singular. B is not correct. Mom's in this sentence is possessive and an apostrophe is needed. C is not correct. Loves is in the present tense, and the rest of the essay is in the past tense.

4. A: because this is the simplest way to express the idea in a grammatically correct sentence. B is not correct, because this sentence is not grammatically correct. C is not correct, because the second sentence is a fragment.

5. D: because it is the simplest way to express the idea in a grammatically correct sentence. A, B, and C are incorrect because these sentences are not grammatically correct. This sentence is not grammatically correct.

6. B: because deliciously is an adverb rather than an adjective. It describes the noun, pitas, not the verb. A is not correct. Eat is in the present tense, and the rest of the essay is in the past tense. C is not correct. Two is spelled correctly and indicates the number. Too means "as well" or an indication of excess.

7. D: It is correct because a comma is needed to separate the interjection of the name. A is not correct. Even though is is in the present tense and the rest of the essay is in the past tense, the sentence is describing a current person and should be in the present tense. B is not correct. A comma is needed to separate the interjection of the name. C is not correct. Invites is in the present tense and the rest of the essay, as a past event, is in the past tense.

8. A: It is correct because a homonym has been misused. There is used to indicate a physical or abstract place. Their is used to indicate possession. B is not correct. In this sentence, dogs does not indicate possession and does not need an apostrophe. C is not correct. Was is in the present tense, and the rest of the essay is in the past tense.

9. C: It is correct because the verb in the sentence, were, is plural, and the subject must be plural for subject-verb agreement. A is not correct. Was is in the present tense, and the rest of the essay is in the past tense. B is not correct. A comma is not needed because and the sporting category is not an independent clause.

10. A: It is correct because there is plural and displays possession. Its is singular. The subject, trainers, is plural; therefore, the possession is plural as well. B is not correct. It's is only used as a contraction for it is, not for possession. C is not correct. Brush is in the present tense, and the rest of the essay is in the past tense. D is not correct. Dog's is possessive and needs an apostrophe.

11. D: It is correct because although this sentence provides new information, the content is not important to the rest of the essay. A, B, and C are because these sentences are important to the essay.

12. B: It is correct because the opening phrase, We left the park, indicates a time lapse from the earlier events of the essay. An appropriate transition word would indicate time. A is not correct. However is not a good transition because sentence 22 is not contradicting anything in the previous sentence. C is not correct. Otherwise is not a good transition because sentence 22 does not suggest an alternate to something that occurred previously. D is not correct. Consequentially is not a good transition because the content of the sentence is not cause and effect from the previous sentence.

13. B: It is correct because a homonym has been misused. Ant refers to an insect, and aunt refers to the sister of one's mother. A is not correct. Hang is not the verb of this sentence and does not need to be in the past tense. C is not correct. Help is not the verb of this sentence and does not need to be in the past tense. D is not correct. Came is the verb of this sentence. Comes is in the present tense and the rest of the essay is in the past tense.

14. A: It is correct because the sentence discusses the grandparents traveling from California to help with the part. Therefore, this sentence should be placed after the description of the party and that a lot of people came. B is not correct. Sentence 4 discusses the cousin helping with party favors, and therefore a sentence about the grandparents' travel would not follow well.

C is not correct. Sentence 5 discusses the party favors, and therefore a sentence about the grandparents' travel would not follow well.

15. C: It is correct because lit is the correct past tense for the verb light. A is not correct. Takes is in the present tense and the rest of the essay is in the past tense. B is not correct. Barbeque is spelled correctly. BBQ is an abbreviation, not a word.

16. B: It is correct because cuts is in the present tense, and the rest of the essay is in the past tense. Cut is in the past tense. A is not correct. Even though the essay is in the past tense, the act of the aunt knowing is a present and ongoing action and should be in the present tense. C is not correct. In this sentence, the article an is followed by a noun, avocado. Avocado begins with a vowel and a vowel sound; therefore, it needs to be introduced with the article an.

17. C: It is correct because although means "in spite of" and is appropriate within the sentence. A is not correct. Later is not an appropriate transition word because it contradicts the beginning of the sentence. B is not correct. Therefore is not an appropriate transition word because there is no cause an effect from the previous sentence. D is not correct. However is not an appropriate transition word because sentence 14 does not contradict anything from the previous sentence.

18. A: It is correct because don't is the conjunction of do not. Do not is in the present tense, and the rest of the essay is in the past tense. The past tense of do is did. B is not correct. Is is in the present tense, and the rest of the essay is in the past tense. C is not correct. Napping is a verb in this sentence, not a noun.

19. C: It is correct because Mexican is a proper noun, and proper nouns need to be capitalized. A is not correct. Birthday is one word. B is not correct. A comma is needed after an introductory clause.

20. D: It is correct because the sentence is a statement, not a question, and needs a period as punctuation. A is not correct. Have is in the present tense, and the rest of the essay is in the past tense. B is not correct. Japanese is a proper noun and needs to be capitalized. C is not correct. Didn't is a contraction of did not and is in the past tense, like the rest of the essay. Don't is a contraction of do not and is in the present tense.

21. A: It is correct because the sentence both supports the previous sentences and provides additional information. Sentence 5 states that extra seats were available at the table. This sentence provides additional information that supports sentence 5 as well as sentence 9. B, C, and D are incorrect. Although these sentences provide new information, they do not link and support the previous sentences.

22. B: It is correct because While things were cooking is an introductory clause, and a comma is needed after the clause. A is not correct. Are is in the present tense and the rest of the essay is in the past tense. C is not correct. Take is part of would take and is in the past participle, not the present tense.

23. C: It is correct because tossed is in the past tense, like the rest of the essay. Toss is in the present tense. A is not correct. A comma is needed before the conjunction when two independent clauses are joined by a conjunction. B is not correct. Hit is the correct past tense of hit. Hitted is not a word.

24. A: It is correct because was is in the past tense, like the rest of the essay. Is is in the present tense. B is not correct. Is is in the present tense and the rest of the essay is in the past tense. C is not correct. Delicious is an adjective, not an adverb. It is used in this sentence to describe the noun, not the verb. D is not correct. Chef is not a proper noun and does not need to be capitalized.

25. B: It is correct because a comma is needed to separate the interjection of the book title. A is not correct. Ship in the sentence is possessive and requires the apostrophe. C is not correct. Are is the plural of is. The subject, events, is plural and therefore the verb needs to be plural in subject-verb agreement. D is not correct. Are brought is in the past participle, and bring is in the present tense.

26. A: It is correct because sank is the correct past tense of the verb sink. Sunked is not a word. B is not correct. A comma is needed to separate dates of the month from the year. H is not correct. Hours is not possessive and does not require the apostrophe.

27. D: It is correct because were is the plural past tense of is. The subject of the sentence, lifeboats, is plural, and the verb also must be plural in subject-verb agreement. A is not correct. There is used correctly. They're is a contraction of they are. B is not correct. A comma is needed to separate the interjection, and as a result. C is not correct. Lifeboats is not possessive and does not require the apostrophe.

28. B: It is correct because there is no need for a comma. As it stands, the comma disrupts the normal flow of thought in the sentence. A is not correct. The subject, ship, is singular, and the verb also must be singular in subject-verb agreement. C is not correct. Was divided is in the past participle. Divide is in the present tense, and the rest of the essay is in the past.

29. B: It is correct because it is the simplest way to express the idea in a grammatically correct sentence. Because of this refers to the content of the previous sentence. A is not correct. This sentence is not grammatically correct. C is not correct. This sentence is not grammatically correct. D is not correct. This sentence is not grammatically correct and needs a comma after class.

30. C: Choice C shows the contrast between first-class and third-class passengers. The previous sentences explained why majority of the survivors were a part of the first class passengers. Sentence 13 shifts to explain explains why most of the third class passengers did not survive. "On the other hand" clearly signals this contrast. "Lastly" is not an appropriate transition word, as there was not a series of listed facts. "For example" is not an appropriate transition to use since it is not giving an example. "Therefore" is not an appropriate transition word because the new information does not involve cause and effect with the previous sentences.

Sample Composition

It is a tradition in my family that we all go shopping for Thanksgiving together. Every year we buy two of everything. We buy two turkeys, two bags of potatoes, two pies, and lots of canned foods. My mom says it is important for us to go shopping as a family and really think about what we are buying. At the end of the shopping trip, we take half of the food, put it away in the house, and leave the other half in the car. Then we all get back into the car and Dad drives us to the homeless shelter. We give the shelter the rest of the food.

I did not want to go to the homeless shelter when I was younger. I wanted to stay at home and watch cartoons. I did not even want to go shopping for the food. I thought it was boring and that I had better things to do. My mom told me that I had to go and that it was very important. I remember my mom looking at the turkeys. She bought two of them. One was medium sized, and one was so big that she needed help putting it into the cart. “Go pick out some potatoes,” she said to me. “And some green beans.” I looked for a really long time to get the best green beans and potatoes for the shelter. It was fun to try to find the best.

When we got to the homeless shelter, people were lined up for over a block. They were all standing and wrapped in old blankets. I didn’t understand. I asked my mom why they were lined up and why they were standing in the cold. She said that they did not live in a house like me and that they were lined up to get dinner for the night. She said that the shelter cooked dinner every night and gave it to the people who did not have any food or a place to live. My dad said that was why we were giving them food and why we had gone shopping. We were there so other people would have food to eat.

I now really look forward to going shopping for Thanksgiving. I try to pick the biggest turkey and the best potatoes. A few times a year my family cleans out our closets and gives old clothes, shoes, and blankets to the shelter. It still makes me sad to go to the shelter and see people standing in the cold and waiting for food, but I learned to be thankful for what I have and that it is really important to give to others.

How to Overcome Test Anxiety

Just the thought of taking a test is enough to make most people a little nervous. A test is an important event that can have a long-term impact on your future, so it's important to take it seriously and it's natural to feel anxious about performing well. But just because anxiety is normal, that doesn't mean that it's helpful in test taking, or that you should simply accept it as part of your life. Anxiety can have a variety of effects. These effects can be mild, like making you feel slightly nervous, or severe, like blocking your ability to focus or remember even a simple detail.

If you experience test anxiety—whether severe or mild—it's important to know how to beat it. To discover this, first you need to understand what causes test anxiety.

Causes of Test Anxiety

While we often think of anxiety as an uncontrollable emotional state, it can actually be caused by simple, practical things. One of the most common causes of test anxiety is that a person does not feel adequately prepared for their test. This feeling can be the result of many different issues such as poor study habits or lack of organization, but the most common culprit is time management. Starting to study too late, failing to organize your study time to cover all of the material, or being distracted while you study will mean that you're not well prepared for the test. This may lead to cramming the night before, which will cause you to be physically and mentally exhausted for the test. Poor time management also contributes to feelings of stress, fear, and hopelessness as you realize you are not well prepared but don't know what to do about it.

Other times, test anxiety is not related to your preparation for the test but comes from unresolved fear. This may be a past failure on a test, or poor performance on tests in general. It may come from comparing yourself to others who seem to be performing better or from the stress of living up to expectations. Anxiety may be driven by fears of the future—how failure on this test would affect your educational and career goals. These fears are often completely irrational, but they can still negatively impact your test performance.

Elements of Test Anxiety

As mentioned earlier, test anxiety is considered to be an emotional state, but it has physical and mental components as well. Sometimes you may not even realize that you are suffering from test anxiety until you notice the physical symptoms. These can include trembling hands, rapid heartbeat, sweating, nausea, and tense muscles. Extreme anxiety may lead to fainting or vomiting. Obviously, any of these symptoms can have a negative impact on testing. It is important to recognize them as soon as they begin to occur so that you can address the problem before it damages your performance.

The mental components of test anxiety include trouble focusing and inability to remember learned information. During a test, your mind is on high alert, which can help you recall information and stay focused for an extended period of time. However, anxiety interferes with your mind's natural processes, causing you to blank out, even on the questions you know well. The strain of testing during anxiety makes it difficult to stay focused, especially on a test that may take several hours. Extreme anxiety can take a huge mental toll, making it difficult not only to recall test information but even to understand the test questions or pull your thoughts together.

Effects of Test Anxiety

Test anxiety is like a disease—if left untreated, it will get progressively worse. Anxiety leads to poor performance, and this reinforces the feelings of fear and failure, which in turn lead to poor performances on subsequent tests. It can grow from a mild nervousness to a crippling condition. If allowed to progress, test anxiety can have a big impact on your schooling, and consequently on your future.

Test anxiety can spread to other parts of your life. Anxiety on tests can become anxiety in any stressful situation, and blanking on a test can turn into panicking in a job situation. But fortunately, you don't have to let anxiety rule your testing and determine your grades. There are a number of relatively simple steps you can take to move past anxiety and function normally on a test and in the rest of life.

Physical Steps for Beating Test Anxiety

While test anxiety is a serious problem, the good news is that it can be overcome. It doesn't have to control your ability to think and remember information. While it may take time, you can begin taking steps today to beat anxiety.

Just as your first hint that you may be struggling with anxiety comes from the physical symptoms, the first step to treating it is also physical. Rest is crucial for having a clear, strong mind. If you are tired, it is much easier to give in to anxiety. But if you establish good sleep habits, your body and mind will be ready to perform optimally, without the strain of exhaustion. Additionally, sleeping well helps you to retain information better, so you're more likely to recall the answers when you see the test questions.

Getting good sleep means more than going to bed on time. It's important to allow your brain time to relax. Take study breaks from time to time so it doesn't get overworked, and don't study right before bed. Take time to rest your mind before trying to rest your body, or you may find it difficult to fall asleep.

Along with sleep, other aspects of physical health are important in preparing for a test. Good nutrition is vital for good brain function. Sugary foods and drinks may give a burst of energy but this burst is followed by a crash, both physically and emotionally. Instead, fuel your body with protein and vitamin-rich foods.

Also, drink plenty of water. Dehydration can lead to headaches and exhaustion, especially if your brain is already under stress from the rigors of the test. Particularly if your test is a long one, drink water during the breaks. And if possible, take an energy-boosting snack to eat between sections.

Along with sleep and diet, a third important part of physical health is exercise. Maintaining a steady workout schedule is helpful, but even taking 5-minute study breaks to walk can help get your blood pumping faster and clear your head. Exercise also releases endorphins, which contribute to a positive feeling and can help combat test anxiety.

When you nurture your physical health, you are also contributing to your mental health. If your body is healthy, your mind is much more likely to be healthy as well. So take time to rest, nourish your body with healthy food and water, and get moving as much as possible. Taking these physical steps will make you stronger and more able to take the mental steps necessary to overcome test anxiety.

Mental Steps for Beating Test Anxiety

Working on the mental side of test anxiety can be more challenging, but as with the physical side, there are clear steps you can take to overcome it. As mentioned earlier, test anxiety often stems from lack of preparation, so the obvious solution is to prepare for the test. Effective studying may be the most important weapon you have for beating test anxiety, but you can and should employ several other mental tools to combat fear.

First, boost your confidence by reminding yourself of past success—tests or projects that you aced. If you're putting as much effort into preparing for this test as you did for those, there's no reason you should expect to fail here. Work hard to prepare; then trust your preparation.

Second, surround yourself with encouraging people. It can be helpful to find a study group, but be sure that the people you're around will encourage a positive attitude. If you spend time with others who are anxious or cynical, this will only contribute to your own anxiety. Look for others who are motivated to study hard from a desire to succeed, not from a fear of failure.

Third, reward yourself. A test is physically and mentally tiring, even without anxiety, and it can be helpful to have something to look forward to. Plan an activity following the test, regardless of the outcome, such as going to a movie or getting ice cream.

When you are taking the test, if you find yourself beginning to feel anxious, remind yourself that you know the material. Visualize successfully completing the test. Then take a few deep, relaxing breaths and return to it. Work through the questions carefully but with confidence, knowing that you are capable of succeeding.

Developing a healthy mental approach to test taking will also aid in other areas of life. Test anxiety affects more than just the actual test—it can be damaging to your mental health and even contribute to depression. It's important to beat test anxiety before it becomes a problem for more than testing.

Study Strategy

Being prepared for the test is necessary to combat anxiety, but what does being prepared look like? You may study for hours on end and still not feel prepared. What you need is a strategy for test prep. The next few pages outline our recommended steps to help you plan out and conquer the challenge of preparation.

Step 1: Scope Out the Test

Learn everything you can about the format (multiple choice, essay, etc.) and what will be on the test. Gather any study materials, course outlines, or sample exams that may be available. Not only will this help you to prepare, but knowing what to expect can help to alleviate test anxiety.

Step 2: Map Out the Material

Look through the textbook or study guide and make note of how many chapters or sections it has. Then divide these over the time you have. For example, if a book has 15 chapters and you have five days to study, you need to cover three chapters each day. Even better, if you have the time, leave an extra day at the end for overall review after you have gone through the material in depth.

If time is limited, you may need to prioritize the material. Look through it and make note of which sections you think you already have a good grasp on, and which need review. While you are studying, skim quickly through the familiar sections and take more time on the challenging parts.

Write out your plan so you don't get lost as you go. Having a written plan also helps you feel more in control of the study, so anxiety is less likely to arise from feeling overwhelmed at the amount to cover.

STEP 3: GATHER YOUR TOOLS

Decide what study method works best for you. Do you prefer to highlight in the book as you study and then go back over the highlighted portions? Or do you type out notes of the important information? Or is it helpful to make flashcards that you can carry with you? Assemble the pens, index cards, highlighters, post-it notes, and any other materials you may need so you won't be distracted by getting up to find things while you study.

If you're having a hard time retaining the information or organizing your notes, experiment with different methods. For example, try color-coding by subject with colored pens, highlighters, or post-it notes. If you learn better by hearing, try recording yourself reading your notes so you can listen while in the car, working out, or simply sitting at your desk. Ask a friend to quiz you from your flashcards, or try teaching someone the material to solidify it in your mind.

STEP 4: CREATE YOUR ENVIRONMENT

It's important to avoid distractions while you study. This includes both the obvious distractions like visitors and the subtle distractions like an uncomfortable chair (or a too-comfortable couch that makes you want to fall asleep). Set up the best study environment possible: good lighting and a comfortable work area. If background music helps you focus, you may want to turn it on, but otherwise keep the room quiet. If you are using a computer to take notes, be sure you don't have any other windows open, especially applications like social media, games, or anything else that could distract you. Silence your phone and turn off notifications. Be sure to keep water close by so you stay hydrated while you study (but avoid unhealthy drinks and snacks).

Also, take into account the best time of day to study. Are you freshest first thing in the morning? Try to set aside some time then to work through the material. Is your mind clearer in the afternoon or evening? Schedule your study session then. Another method is to study at the same time of day that you will take the test, so that your brain gets used to working on the material at that time and will be ready to focus at test time.

STEP 5: STUDY!

Once you have done all the study preparation, it's time to settle into the actual studying. Sit down, take a few moments to settle your mind so you can focus, and begin to follow your study plan. Don't give in to distractions or let yourself procrastinate. This is your time to prepare so you'll be ready to fearlessly approach the test. Make the most of the time and stay focused.

Of course, you don't want to burn out. If you study too long you may find that you're not retaining the information very well. Take regular study breaks. For example, taking five minutes out of every hour to walk briskly, breathing deeply and swinging your arms, can help your mind stay fresh.

As you get to the end of each chapter or section, it's a good idea to do a quick review. Remind yourself of what you learned and work on any difficult parts. When you feel that you've mastered the material, move on to the next part. At the end of your study session, briefly skim through your notes again.

But while review is helpful, cramming last minute is NOT. If at all possible, work ahead so that you won't need to fit all your study into the last day. Cramming overloads your brain with more information than it can process and retain, and your tired mind may struggle to recall even previously learned information when it is overwhelmed with last-minute study. Also, the urgent nature of cramming and the stress placed on your brain contribute to anxiety. You'll be more likely to go to the test feeling unprepared and having trouble thinking clearly.

So don't cram, and don't stay up late before the test, even just to review your notes at a leisurely pace. Your brain needs rest more than it needs to go over the information again. In fact, plan to finish your studies by noon or early afternoon the day before the test. Give your brain the rest of the day to relax or focus on other things, and get a good night's sleep. Then you will be fresh for the test and better able to recall what you've studied.

Step 6: Take a Practice Test

Many courses offer sample tests, either online or in the study materials. This is an excellent resource to check whether you have mastered the material, as well as to prepare for the test format and environment.

Check the test format ahead of time: the number of questions, the type (multiple choice, free response, etc.), and the time limit. Then create a plan for working through them. For example, if you have 30 minutes to take a 60-question test, your limit is 30 seconds per question. Spend less time on the questions you know well so that you can take more time on the difficult ones.

If you have time to take several practice tests, take the first one open book, with no time limit. Work through the questions at your own pace and make sure you fully understand them. Gradually work up to taking a test under test conditions: sit at a desk with all study materials put away and set a timer. Pace yourself to make sure you finish the test with time to spare and go back to check your answers if you have time.

After each test, check your answers. On the questions you missed, be sure you understand why you missed them. Did you misread the question (tests can use tricky wording)? Did you forget the information? Or was it something you hadn't learned? Go back and study any shaky areas that the practice tests reveal.

Taking these tests not only helps with your grade, but also aids in combating test anxiety. If you're already used to the test conditions, you're less likely to worry about it, and working through tests until you're scoring well gives you a confidence boost. Go through the practice tests until you feel comfortable, and then you can go into the test knowing that you're ready for it.

Test Tips

On test day, you should be confident, knowing that you've prepared well and are ready to answer the questions. But aside from preparation, there are several test day strategies you can employ to maximize your performance.

First, as stated before, get a good night's sleep the night before the test (and for several nights before that, if possible). Go into the test with a fresh, alert mind rather than staying up late to study.

Try not to change too much about your normal routine on the day of the test. It's important to eat a nutritious breakfast, but if you normally don't eat breakfast at all, consider eating just a protein bar. If you're a coffee drinker, go ahead and have your normal coffee. Just make sure you time it so that the caffeine doesn't wear off right in the middle of your test. Avoid sugary beverages, and drink enough water to stay hydrated but not so much that you need a restroom break 10 minutes into the test. If your test isn't first thing in the morning, consider going for a walk or doing a light workout before the test to get your blood flowing.

Allow yourself enough time to get ready, and leave for the test with plenty of time to spare so you won't have the anxiety of scrambling to arrive in time. Another reason to be early is to select a good seat. It's helpful to sit away from doors and windows, which can be distracting. Find a good seat, get out your supplies, and settle your mind before the test begins.

When the test begins, start by going over the instructions carefully, even if you already know what to expect. Make sure you avoid any careless mistakes by following the directions.

Then begin working through the questions, pacing yourself as you've practiced. If you're not sure on an answer, don't spend too much time on it, and don't let it shake your confidence. Either skip it and come back later, or eliminate as many wrong answers as possible and guess among the remaining ones. Don't dwell on these questions as you continue—put them out of your mind and focus on what lies ahead.

Be sure to read all of the answer choices, even if you're sure the first one is the right answer. Sometimes you'll find a better one if you keep reading. But don't second-guess yourself if you do immediately know the answer. Your gut instinct is usually right. Don't let test anxiety rob you of the information you know.

If you have time at the end of the test (and if the test format allows), go back and review your answers. Be cautious about changing any, since your first instinct tends to be correct, but make sure you didn't misread any of the questions or accidentally mark the wrong answer choice. Look over any you skipped and make an educated guess.

At the end, leave the test feeling confident. You've done your best, so don't waste time worrying about your performance or wishing you could change anything. Instead, celebrate the successful completion of this test. And finally, use this test to learn how to deal with anxiety even better next time.

Review Video: Test Anxiety
Visit mometrix.com/academy and enter code: 100340

Important Qualification

Not all anxiety is created equal. If your test anxiety is causing major issues in your life beyond the classroom or testing center, or if you are experiencing troubling physical symptoms related to your anxiety, it may be a sign of a serious physiological or psychological condition. If this sounds like your situation, we strongly encourage you to seek professional help.

Online Resources

Due to our efforts to try to keep this book to a manageable length, we've created a link that will give you access to all of your online resources:

mometrix.com/resources719/ssgmg7ela

It's Your Moment, Let's Celebrate It!

Share your story @mometrixtestpreparation